REPOSITIONING
RACE

SUNY series in African American Studies
_____
John R. Howard and Robert C. Smith, editors

REPOSITIONING
RACE

PROPHETIC RESEARCH IN A
POSTRACIAL OBAMA AGE

Edited by

SANDRA L. BARNES
ZANDRIA F. ROBINSON
EARL WRIGHT II

SUNY
PRESS

Published by State University of New York Press, Albany

For information, contact State University of New York Press, Albany, NY
www.sunypress.edu

Production by Eileen Nizer
Marketing by Anne M. Valentine

Library of Congress Cataloging-in-Publication Data

Repositioning race : prophetic research in a postracial Obama age / edited by
  Sandra L. Barnes, Zandria F. Robinson, and Earl Wright II.
      pages cm. — (SUNY series in African American studies)
  Includes bibliographical references and index.
  ISBN 978-1-4384-5085-8 (hc : alk. paper) 978-1-4384-5086-5 (pb : alk. paper)
    1. United States—Race relations.   2. African Americans—Social conditions—
21st century.   3. Race relations.   I. Barnes, Sandra L.   II. Robinson, Zandria F.
III. Wright II, Earl.

  E184.A1R446 2014
  305.800973—dc23   2013019604

10 9 8 7 6 5 4 3 2 1

This volume is dedicated to those scholars who, 40 years ago, affirmed the prophetic tradition in Black sociology. Moreover, it is dedicated to the many scholars, teachers, students, and community activists of color who serve tirelessly and sacrificed on behalf of disenfranchised people worldwide. With the continued help of other prophetic thinkers and doers, your labor will not be in vain.

~

Contents

Acknowledgments

In 1973 sociologist Joyce Ladner edited *The Death of White Sociology: Essays on Race and Culture*, a collection of works that affirmed the epistemological and scientific rigor of the Black sociological tradition. Published in the wake of the establishment of the Association of Black Sociologists, *The Death of White Sociology* signified a critical moment in the reclamation of the Black sociological tradition established by W. E. B. Du Bois, Ida B. Wells, Oliver Cromwell Cox, E. Franklin Frazier, and a host of other twentieth-century scholars of race. This volume emerged from a similar critical moment: the historic election of Barack Obama and the 40th anniversary of the Association of Black Sociologists. We endeavored to answer two primary questions: (1) what is the meaning of race in the twenty-first century, and (2) what role should the black sociological tradition play in advancing racial justice in the twenty-first century? This volume is a result of members' grappling with these and other questions at the 40th annual conference in August 2010 in Atlanta, Georgia.

This volume is indebted to the Black sociological tradition, which informs our scholarly and activist contributions to ameliorating the condition of marginalized peoples globally. We are grateful to the volume's contributors, who herein highlight key issues in sociological research on race that will shape research inquiry in the twenty-first century. We are most appreciative to the members of the Association of Black Sociologists, past and present, whose commitment to social change is reflected in these pages.

Introduction

~

Repositioning Race

Prophetic Research in a Postracial Obama Age

On Tuesday, January 20, 2009, 75-year-old Mildred Pierce sat mesmerized during the televised inauguration of Barack Obama as the 44th
president of the United States. Her experiences as a Black child living in
the Jim Crow South and later as an adult resident of several northern cities all confirmed that such an event would never take place—at least not
in her lifetime. Yet she silently shed a tear as the seemingly impossible
episode unfolded. This scenario took place in homes around the country
as U.S. citizens witnessed the historic inauguration. Some people were
overjoyed, others were dismayed, and still others were ambivalent. Yet
no one could deny the reality that the United States had elected its
first Black president. Our collective understandings of race and national
politics would forever be altered. That the majority of Blacks voted for
Obama is not surprising (note: Black and African American are used
interchangeably throughout this volume). Furthermore, that members
of other minority groups also provided strong support may not be surprising. Racial and ethnic minorities have for several decades formed an
important part of the Democratic base (Lincoln and Mamiya 1990). Yet
many scholars, political pundits, and skeptics were astonished by the substantial number of Whites—most reports show about 40%—who helped
elect Obama. Younger as well as more formally educated Whites were

particularly supportive as they moved across racial lines, and some across party lines, to support the Black candidate (Cohen 2008; Kuhn 2008). Similar voting patterns were evident for the now President Obama during the 2012 election (Sherman 2012; Sherwood 2012). What do these seminal turns of events mean for racial identity, race relations, and racial reconciliation, as well as international, national, regional, and local views about race in the twenty-first century? Of equal importance, what do the 2008 and 2012 presidential elections mean for people, particularly racial minorities, on a day-to-day basis? While in some ways discussions, research, and even our ideas and beliefs about race have been irrevocably turned on end, in other ways a tradition of *prophetic* research and scholarship that dates back to Alexander Crummell, Ida B. Wells, and W. E. B. Du Bois, has prepared us to proactively examine these relatively unchartered intellectual and emotional spaces.

We formally borrow this term from scholar, theologian, cleric, and social democrat Cornel West in *Race Matters* (1993) calls for *prophetic* Black thinkers and leaders to turn the tide of nihilism in Black America and apathy toward race matters in the larger society. A prophetic mode of inquiry is inherently inquisitive, proactive, culturally sensitive, introspective, collaborative, and creative. It is not necessarily religious, but it is invariably radical. In our volume, prophetic research is framed by sound sociological approaches and draws on other disciplines and thought processes where productive to comprehensively consider subjects of inquiry. Most importantly, repositioning race based on a prophetic stance means recognizing that rigorous academic research is impotent without applied efforts and social policy that empower the Black community and other disenfranchised people worldwide. One is not required to be Black or a sociologist to participate in the prophetic repositioning of race for the twenty-first century, but one must be willing to center her or his research within the experiences of the historically oppressed—and willing to accept the challenge to grapple with the exciting but often-troubling complexities inherent in such an undertaking. In this context, prophetic research is a metaphor for the cutting-edge approaches and academic lenses required to study the nuances of race and racial matters in society today as well as to *move* academic disciplines, researchers, students, grassroots activists, and everyday folks beyond our current views and responses on the subject.

Crummell, Wells, and Du Bois were engaged in prophetic work that not only highlighted and challenged the social construction of race but also inspired activist interventions on local, national, and international levels. Yet, in a "postracial" era, is the kind of prophetic research in which Crummell, Wells, Du Bois, and others engaged still necessary?

The election of a Black man to the highest office of the most powerful country in the world signifies, for some, the end of the "race problem" and constitutes the ultimate reparations for slavery and Jim Crow. This volume recognizes the postracial discourses that have emerged in the wake of President Obama's election and reelection, but systematically rejects the notion that his election moves us "beyond race." Moreover, this volume continues in the prophetic tradition of making the workings of race visible—even when they are obscured by powerful discourses—by drawing on varied theories, analytical approaches, and data sources. The writers contextualize President Obama's historic election and reelection, examining the features and consequences of the "postracial" era his elections have ushered in.

The chapters herein include research on race and race-related subjects from a cross-section of scholars in the humanities and social sciences. Writers take on a prophetic examination of the multidimensionality of race by using unexpected lenses, critiquing prevailing sentiments, or providing contradictory findings using traditional research methods. This mosaic of intellectual engagement means that subject matter is addressed from a variety of methods beyond anecdotal assessments. The comparative nature of the chapters will help readers better understand: (1) how race and race matters currently manifest in a postracial Obama age; (2) how laypersons, scholars, and policymakers attempt to "make sense" of race and race matters; (3) social policy implications of the twenty-first century racial moment; and (4) the changing contours of contemporary race relations. To our knowledge, no existing edited volume specifically examines these topics from the perspective of top scholars in the discipline, burgeoning researchers, and community activists.

'Good News' and 'Bad News': Repositioning Race Prophetically

Many opine that we now live in a *postracial society*: one in which race no longer matters or influences individual opportunities and life chances. Therefore, in this postracial society, the success of Blacks and other racial minorities is limited only by their initiative, work ethic, and dedication (Bonilla-Silva 2001, 2010; Feagin 2006, 2010). Statistics show that Blacks are graduating from college in record numbers (*Journal of Blacks in Higher Education* 2005, 2010). The relatively resilient Black middle class (Kalil and Wightman 2010; Pattillo-McCoy 1999) and its more elite upper-class counterpart (Graham 1999) represent other postracial markers. Moreover, family income among Blacks has risen over the past few decades (Isaacs 2008). Black and brown folks are negotiating international and national spaces and marketplaces in unprecedented ways. Oprah Winfrey continues to make *Forbes*'s list of wealthiest Americans (*Forbes* 2013); other Blacks such as Tiger Woods, Robert Johnson, Michael Jordan, Artron Brown, William Cosby, and Sheila Johnson have experienced notable success as athletes, media moguls, entertainers, and entrepreneurs (Blount 2012; *Forbes* 2009).

Yet, for most people who espouse a postracial perspective, the 2008 election of Barack Obama, the first Black president of the United States is the clearest indication that we are now in a definitively postracial moment. President Obama's subsequent *reelection* in 2012 only reinforced this belief. True, in light of the legacy of chattel slavery and subsequent racial oppression and segregation (Billingsley 1992; Cox 1948; Drake and Cayton [1942] 1962; Frazier 1964; Hannerz 1969; Massey and Denton 1993; Morris 1984; Omi and Winant 1994), few people, particularly people like Mildred Pierce, could have possibly imagined that a Black man would be elected and reelected leader of the most powerful country in the world. These dramatic changes are resulting in new norms, values, beliefs, and behavior about race for Blacks and non-Blacks alike. Yet, despite the ascendancy of the Black middle class, the election and reelection of Barack Obama, and other oft-cited indicators of a postracial society, segments of the Black populace continue to experience challenges on multiple levels.

For example, according to 2009 Census statistics, almost 26% of Blacks are impoverished—at least twice the rate of both Whites and Asians. Additionally, more than 50% of Black children are growing up in poverty. Whites are more likely than their Black counterparts to complete high school (89.4% and 80.0%, respectively) and to earn a four-year college degree (30.0% versus 17.3%, respectively) (Kalil and Wightman 2010). Furthermore, perhaps most challenging to the notion of a postracial society is the fact that even middle-class African Americans experience negative health, employment, and housing disparities compared to their White counterparts (Isaacs 2008; Kalil and Wightman 2010; Oliver and Shapiro 1997). Isaacs finds that middle-class Blacks are significantly less likely to maintain a middle-class status across generations: 45% of Black children who grew up in middle-class homes are in the bottom quintile of the earnings distribution as adults, whereas only 16% of their White peers experienced similar levels of downward mobility. Black men continue to be incarcerated at substantially higher rates than White men (*Bureau of Justice Statistics* 2005) and Blacks tend to be without health insurance at higher rates than Whites (U.S. Bureau of Census 2002). According to statistics from the Centers for Disease Control and Prevention (2008), about 50% of infected men, 63% of all new cases among females, and 66% of pediatric AIDS cases are Black.

These reports provide a sobering reminder that a disproportionate percentage of Blacks continue to lag beyond their White counterparts on most of the major indices associated with economic stability and positive quality of life (Oliver and Shapiro 1997; U.S. Bureau of Census 2009). The good news associated with Black progress cannot supplant these significant challenges. The chasm between the haves and have-nots grows (Isaacs 2008; Kalil and Wightman 2010; Massey and Denton 1993; Oliver and Shapiro 1997; Wilson 1987), and racism continues (Bonilla-Silva 2001, 2010; Feagin 2006, 2010; Gallagher 2003). Because of the paradox of unprecedented successes and suffering in the Black community, scholars are challenged to consider how race, racism, and race-related dynamics are manifesting in the Obama age. They are compelled to examine what race means anew, as well as how it is framed in academic discourses and in the lives of everyday citizens. We contend that responding to this challenge requires researchers to think in prophetic ways. This symbolism is more than a buzzword; it is a call to radical, transformative research that informs readers and challenges them to individually and collectively engage in community action and social justice work. This prophetic research is a continuation of long-established sociological, Black intellectual, and activist trends that engages modern configurations of race with the long view of racial histories squarely in sight.

This edited volume examines questions such as: Does race as we have known it *still matter*? How is race being reconstructed at both institutional and individual levels? How must sociologists, other researchers, community leaders, and laypersons reposition race prophetically to do justice to the triumphs and trials in the Black community? What are some of the international and national implications of race for people of African descent in the Diaspora? Theories and empirical work herein suggest that although contemporary forms of racism are often less visible than previous instantiations of racism, they are no less pernicious in their outcomes for marginalized groups. Modern forms of racism are embedded in individual attitudes and actions as well as in structural forces and shrouded in a "color-blind" posture that is more difficult to detect.

The impetus for this volume was the 40th annual meeting of the Association of Black Sociologists (ABS) in August 2010. Scholars, grassroots leaders, and students grappled with the concept of race in light of the recent presidential elections. Most attendees have been directly or indirectly studying race or race-related subjects for years. But the energy and excitement of the presidential election and its broader implications engendered a plethora of discussions, discourses, and on several occasions, heated debates as attendees considered how issues and interactions tied to race should now be assessed. Clearly, additional information was needed, and rigorous academic inquiry would have to undergird such efforts. But race and race matters are complicated, nuanced subjects; they cannot be effectively studied in isolation. For this same reason, diverse analytical approaches, theories, methodologies, and models are incorporated to systematically consider contemporary emergent themes, issues, and implications of race in the twenty-first century. This volume therefore includes theoretical and empirical work from multiple disciplines and interdisciplinary areas of inquiry, including sociology, cultural studies, and Afro-Hispanic studies. Findings are intriguing and sometimes controversial, yet each chapter engages and challenges readers to move beyond myopic, dichotomous, and often entrenched definitions and views about race and racism. These forward-thinking analyses position the volume for academics, undergraduate and graduate students, community leaders, as well as mainstream readers interested in tackling contemporary issues related to race.

Scholarship on Race, Racism, and Race Matters

In the nineteenth century, biologists developed three broad categories of race—Caucasoid, Mongoloid, and Negroid—to identify groups phenotypically associated with Whites, Asians, and Blacks, respectively. This conceptualization of race ascribed racial inequality to naturally occurring biological differences, evident, these scientists argued, in phenotypical differences such as eye shape, hair texture, and head shape (Cox 1948; Graves 2001). Throughout the first half of the twentieth century, social scientists from W. E. B. Du Bois to Franz Boas challenged the assumed causal link between phenotype and ability. As biological notions of race became increasingly untenable, they were replaced with cultural notions of race. Popularized during the latter half of the twentieth century, cultural notions of race asserted that biological difference or inferiority did not necessarily lead to racial inequalities, but rather cultural differences did (Ladner 1973; Moynihan 1965; Myrdal 1975; Omi and Winant 1994; Wilson 1987). In general, sociologists reject both biological and cultural conceptualizations of race. Instead, in sociology, *race* is commonly considered a socially constructed concept used to broadly categorize groups of people and disproportionately allocate resources based on those categorizations (Blackwell and Janowitz 1974a, 1974b; Ladner 1973). Sociologists work to uncover how the concept of race is deployed to engender, maintain, and justify inequality. Understanding the concept of race has important implications for analyzing topics related to ethnicity, the minority experience, prejudices, stereotypes, and discrimination. Furthermore, beyond its academic implications, race and racial matters are inextricably linked to life chances and quality of life (Blackwell and Janowitz 1974a, 1974b; Cox 1948; Ladner 1973; West 1993; Wilson 1987). To contextualize the chapters in this volume, this section provides an overview of some of the seminal theories and research associated with race, especially by Black scholars. Although not exhaustive, this summary provides a segue into an examination of how race is repositioned prophetically in this volume.

Beyond definitional debates, many existing studies about race focus on its history, institutionalized nature, and the deleterious consequences associated with racism and racial discrimination. Early U.S. studies tended to focus on relationships and comparisons between Blacks and Whites, examining topics from lynching, chattel slavery, and segregation to interpersonal prejudice, economic disenfranchisement, and structural inequality. Sociologist and prolific intellectual W. E. B. Du Bois is credited with performing the first comprehensive studies on the subject, beginning with the seminal 1899 text, *The Philadelphia Negro*, and continuing this tradition with the many studies accomplished during his tenure as director of the Atlanta University Studies on the Negro Problems. As a trailblazer, scholar, and community activist, Du Bois is an exemplar of prophetic leadership. Among numerous works Du Bois produced, *The Negro Church* ([1903] 2003) and *Souls of Black Folk* ([1903] 1996) shine a sociological light on the Black experience. The former's empirical analysis of Black religious life in a racist society provides both documentation of a key dimension of the Black community and a societal critique. The latter "slender book" helps both academic and mainstream readers understand the trials of racial identity and race prejudice in the United States as well as the triumphant spirit of a people fraught by such difficulties.

The comprehensive manner in which early African American sociologists, including Du Bois, Ida B. Wells, and Charles S. Johnson, examined race and its legacy provided the context for the development of subsequent theories and studies. In the post–World War II period, scholars across disciplines continued the work of interrogating race, expanding their analyses to broader, global systems of power that perpetuated racial inequality in the United States and abroad. Groundbreaking tomes such as Oliver Cox's *Class, Caste, and Race* (1948) illustrate the ideological underpinnings of race and racism, its benefits to Whites at the expense of non-Whites, and the historical use of race to pit majority against minority groups in a capitalistic society. In addition to examining the workings of race on structural levels in global contexts, Black intellectuals, particularly those working in the academy, turned a critical eye to the systems of power at work in the academic hierarchy that silenced the perspectives of racial and ethnic minorities. Working in tandem with the momentum of the Civil Rights and Black Power movements, Black intellectuals in the 1960s and 1970s carved out spaces to address myriad issues unique to Black people because of their structural positioning. Out of this period came key structural analyses of race such as Stokely Carmichael and Charles V. Hamilton's *Black Power* (1967); articulations of the transformative and radical nature of culture and religion such as James Cone's ([1969] 1999) *Black Theology and Black Power* and *God of the Oppressed* (1997); and, increased attention to the role of women in liberation struggles from slavery to freedom through the writings and activism of scholars such as Angela Davis, Francis Beale, and Michele Wallace.

The work of Black feminist scholars built the foundation for an expanded exploration of the combined effects of race, class, and gender as interlocking systems of power beginning in the 1980s. In *Black Feminist Thought* (2000), Patricia Hill Collins combined conflict theory and symbolic interactionism in an analysis of the nexus of race, class, and gender, contending that centering the poor Black female experience illuminated how Black women and other excluded groups negotiate a society characterized by inequities. Concepts Collins developed, such as *outsider-within, controlling images,* and *self-definition,* provided new and exciting language for the study of race, its interconnectedness with class and gender oppression, and the adaptive, resilient nature of the Black community. These analyses emerged alongside new theoretical appraisals of the history and structural functioning of the concept of race. Omi and Winant (1994) described the systemic nature of racial inequality embedded in racial projects. Still other scholars examined how residential segregation, economic inequality, and poverty evidenced the cumulative effects of racism (West 1993; Wilson 1980, 1987).

Recent social science studies report a decline in more overt forms of racism and an increase in more covert manifestations of racial slights. "Old fashioned" or dominative racism appears to be largely supplanted by an aversive racism that manifests in the form of discomfort, uneasiness, disgust, and fear of Blacks; avoidance of Blacks; and rejection of social policy and programs intended to address historic racism and discrimination (Gaertner and Dovidio 1986). Ground-breaking work on color-blind racism by Gallagher (2003), Bonilla-Silva (2001, 2010), and Feagin (2006, 2010) provides startling results about what many

Whites in the United States believe about race, racism, and minority group interactions. The latter two scholars continue their expositions on the subject in this book.

This summary, though not exhaustive, endeavors to remind readers about existing research on race as a social system, racial inequality, and the effects of racism on marginalized groups. Just as these noted studies are seminal, many other scholars not mentioned are also engaged in this important work. Beyond their academic import, these types of endeavors remind us about the microlevel implications of race matters in terms of personal identity and interracial interactions, as well as macrolevel correlates to social problems such as poverty, health-care inequities, and environmental racism. Continued efforts such as those in this book help ensure that we remain abreast about ever-changing dynamics associated with race.

Black Sociologists and the Critical Tradition

This is not the first volume to bring together the theory and research of Black sociologists at a key and collaborative political and intellectual moment. Shortly after the inception of ABS 40 years ago, a group of Black sociologists contributed to three key edited volumes that took stock of the work of Black sociologists over the course of the twentieth century and asserted a critical Black epistemological position that provided comprehensive structural analyses of conditions in the Black community by Black scholars. In the context of the monumental changes of the Civil Rights and Black Power movements, these volumes represent a pivotal moment in the discipline. Joyce Ladner's 1973 volume *The Death of White Sociology*, along with James E. Blackwell and Morris Janowitz's 1974 volumes *Black Sociologists: The First Half Century* and *Black Sociologists: Historical and Contemporary Perspectives*, challenged "White sociology" and encouraged Black scholars to engage in research that augmented understandings of the social processes affecting Black communities. Ladner's volume exposed the epistemological pitfalls and detrimental policy consequences of White sociology's interpretation of Black issues, presenting Black reevaluations of subjects from the Black family to Black identity. Blackwell and Janowitz's works presented a previously obscured history of radical Black sociology that situated Black intellectuals as astute and prophetic analysts who could anticipate racial outcomes through thorough, empirically and theoretically sound research. In *Sociology and the Race Problem: Failure of a Perspective* (1993), author James McKee argues that because most White sociologists ignored the contributions of Blacks to the discipline, and by extension Black theoretical and epistemological perspectives, the discipline was unable to fully assess and comprehend race as both a concept and system of power. Essentially, White sociology underestimated the prophetic nature of Black sociology.

While significant changes have occurred in the discipline and scholarship on race since the publication of Ladner's and Blackwell and Janowitz's volumes during the early years of ABS, the need for the critical tradition in sociology endures. This volume continues that tradition with attention to the ways in which race matters in everyday interactions and social institutions; in classrooms and communities; and in domestic and global contexts. We hope in this moment of intellectual and activist energy—one not unlike the moment in which ABS was formed—that this volume embodies a prophetic assessment of race that will inform the positioning of the concept across disciplines and inspire intellectuals and communities to work to address the continuing challenges of the future.

Volume's Format: Race Matters Past, Present, and Future

In addition to its introduction and conclusion, the eight chapters herein are grouped into three broad themes: (1) theories and new frameworks; (2) implications and responses; and (3) international issues. We focus on these three broad themes because considering the influence of structural forces such as capitalism, culture, and politics on contemporary understandings of racial dynamics is important. Key aspects of theories presented in part I are tested in national and international contexts in parts II and III, respectively. This strategy facilitates the volume's examination of common themes and dynamics relative to race and racism today as well as the conceptual multifacetedness of race across contexts.

In part I, "The Pitfalls and Possibilities of Prophetic Race Theory: Cultivating Leadership," the first three chapters theoretically illuminate race as a concept and its implications for Black leadership, beginning with a provocative appraisal of the contemporary moment and the foreseeable racial future. In Chapter 1, "Race Matters in 'Postracial' *OBAMERICA* and How to Climb Out of the Rabbit Hole," Eduardo Bonilla-Silva (with Trenita Brookshire Childers) engages in an examination of Barack Obama's presidential election as the backdrop for understanding contemporary racial politics. Bonilla-Silva challenges prevailing sentiments that the election represents an example of strides toward eliminating racism, deconstructing the accompanying prevailing notion of a bourgeoning color-blind nation. Contrary to the dominant postracial logics outlined above, he posits that President Obama's success is the product neither of social movement politics nor of Whites' racial altruism, but a direct expression of the fundamental racial transformation that transpired in the United States in the 1960s and 1970s. The new racial order that has emerged—the "new racism"—reproduces racial domination through subtle and covert discrimination that is often institutionalized, defended with coded language, and bonded by the racial ideology of color-blind racism. Bonilla-Silva challenges readers to be reflective and to become leaders and activists inside and outside academe.

Next, chapter 2, "Am I My Brother's and My Sister's Keeper? W. E. B. Du Bois's New Talented Tenth," is a novel reconsideration of Du Bois's theory of the talented tenth as a prophetic directive for Black leadership—leadership Bonilla-Silva asserts is absent in contemporary Black politics and academia. In chapter 2, author Earl Wright II addresses misinterpretations of Du Bois's talented tenth as members of the Black community with the social capital to lead, but who, in turn capitulated to the allure and trappings of upper-class status. Wright uses Du Bois's notion of the talented tenth as an "ideal type" to examine inaccuracies and position this thesis for consideration by contemporary Black leaders. Based on Du Bois's role as one of the premier race scholars in the United States, this chapter provides another theoretical catapult for this volume by challenging readers to reassess a commonly believed premise about an historic scholar. In chapter 3, "Blackening Up Critical Whiteness: Dave Chappelle as Critical Race Theorist," author Robert Reece uses the performances of this often controversial comedian to develop contemporary race theory. His analysis of Chappelle's use of whiteface and sketches about Black-White interactions illustrates the comedian's attempts to describe and critique racism and race relations in the United States. Reece contends that by using nontraditional teaching and learning moments, Chappelle reaches younger audiences in ways academics have not and that this constitutes prophetic work.

Part II, "Daily Experiences and Implications of a Postracial Obama Age," includes chapters 4 and 5 that are empirical studies about more contemporary socioeconomic and cultural implications of race. These writers illustrate the troubling truth that, despite the postracial sentiments that have emerged, the presidential election of Barack Obama did not significantly improve the economic problems and negative racial experiences segments of the Black community continue to face. The quantitative analysis Cedric Herring, Loren Henderson, and Hayward Derrick Horton performed, "Race, the Great Recession, and the Foreclosure Crisis: From American Dream to Nightmare," illustrates how the consequences of the recent U.S. recession were not evenly distributed, but disproportionately affected Blacks in unemployment, health care, foreclosures, and the ability to complete the daily round. The authors also provide policy recommendations to help stimulate economic growth and reduce racial and ethnic disparities resulting from the recession. Chapter 5 presents another analytical consideration. "Black Experiences, White Experiences: Why We Need a Theory of Systemic Racism" by Louwanda Evans and imminent race scholar Joe Feagin, makes the case for more nuanced theoretical concepts about race that reflects both the systemic and foundational nature of racism and oppression. Based on open-ended surveys and candid, often troubling, interviews with White and Black students, the writers suggest that concepts such as "White racial frame" and "systemic racism" most appropriately convey the impetus, extent, and nature of structural and interpersonal racism in society today. These two chapters are prophetic in the manner in which they provide direct evidence to challenge postracial perspectives as well as strategies and best practices to stem the tide of economic and race-based social problems in the Black community.

In part III, "Diasporic Black Identities in International Contexts," the final three chapters consider the implications of race in international contexts, as well as the function of global notions of blackness in highlighting the nuances of racism. In chapter 6, "Contextualizing 'Race' in the Dominican Republic: Discourses on Whitening, Nationalism, and Anti-Haitianism," Antonio D. Tillis, one of the leading scholars on the Afro-Hispanic experience, investigates the ideology of race as presented within the nationalistic framework of Dominicanness. His analysis considers how Dominicans view themselves as global citizens as well as how they view themselves vis-à-vis their relationship with their conjoined neighbor, the Republic of Haiti. Tillis argues that Dominicans' construction of themselves as a Spanish-origin community is predicated on anti-Black, and specifically anti-Haitian, sentiment. Analyzing the neoslave sugar cane community or *batey* as a geopolitical space, Tillis demonstrates the universality of the effect of anti-Black sentiment on spatial arrangements, economic outcomes, and everyday interactions for groups racialized as Black. Drawing on a sociohistorical analysis of the concept of race in Haiti and the Dominican Republic as well as modern conceptualizations of race in Dominican popular culture, chapter 6 is not only a global prophetic reflection of race relations, but also a prophetic consideration of important differences in racialization in specific place contexts.

In Chapter 7, " 'U.S. Blacks are beautiful but Brazilian Blacks are not racist': Brazilian Return Migrants' Perceptions of U.S. and Brazilian Blacks," Tiffany D. Joseph's study shines a lens on Brazilian immigrants and U.S. Blacks' relations. The chapter chronicles the experiences of Brazilian return migrants to examine how residing in the United States influences their perceptions of racial stratification in this country and Brazil. The author's novel comparative study illustrates how Black Brazilians understand race and racism through reflections on their experiences in the United States once they have returned to Brazil. Her results show that Brazilian immigrants consider U.S. Blacks more beautiful, upwardly mobile, and politically engaged and powerful than Brazilian Blacks. However, she finds that these return migrants also see U.S. Blacks as "racist" because many American Blacks do not interact with or live near Whites. Conversely, her respondents argue that Brazilian Blacks, who they consider generally more impoverished, are engaged in more positive interactions with non-Black Brazilians. Still, these respondents argue that unlike U.S. Blacks, Brazilian Blacks are politically apathetic. Her findings are prophetic because they reveal the ways in which global naiveté about racialization processes for Blacks in the United States, coupled with perceptions of U.S. Blacks' affluence, may complicate global Black solidarity against anti-Black oppression. Joseph's findings also suggest how we might increase understandings of race and racism across national contexts to address this complication.

Lastly, in chapter 8, "Africa Speaks: The 'Place' of Africa in Constructing African American Identity in Museum Exhibits," Derrick R. Brooms uses Africa as a point of departure to investigate issues of cultural consumption and cultural authenticity in Black-centered museums. Moreover, he explores how Africa is presented within institutions specifically designed to narrate the Black experience and chronicle its historical and cultural vitality. Brooms focuses on an underresearched social and representational space—the museum—to examine the representation of the relationship between African and Black culture. This research is prophetic in its examination of an understudied space where race is strategically presented and framed to educate and empower visitors.

Finally, the volume's conclusion provides commentary to frame the overall endeavor and challenges readers to continue to navigate the exciting, potentially arduous, often uncharted scholarly terrain this edited volume has traversed. We ask them to reflect on the varied ways a prophetic discourse is presented in the volume, their own thoughts on prophetic research praxis, as well as next steps as leaders and community servants. Through constant engagement with the prophetic tradition in Black sociological scholarship, the production of new prophetic scholarship, cross-disciplinary conversations, and collaborations between community members, scholars, and policymakers, we can strive toward a more equitable, *postracism* future.

References

Billingsley, Andrew. 1992. *Climbing Jacob's Ladder: The Enduring Legacy of African-American Families.* New York: Touchstone.
Blackwell, James E. and Morris Janowitz. 1974a. *Black Sociologists: The First Half-Century.* Chicago: University of Chicago Press.
———. 1974b. *Black Sociologists: Historical and Contemporary Perspectives.* Chicago: University of Chicago Press.
Blount, Terry. 2012. "Antron Brown Makes History." Retrieved November 12, 2012 (http://espn.go.com/racing/nhra/story/_/id/8620468/antron-brown-becomes-first-african-american-driver-win-major-racing-title).
Bonilla-Silva, Eduardo. 2001. *White Supremacy and Racism in the Post-Civil Rights Era.* Boulder, CO: Lynne Rienner Publishers.
———. 2010. *Racism without Racists: Color-Blind Racism and the Persistence of Racial Inequality in the United States.* Lanham, MD: Rowman and Littlefield.
Carmichael, Stokely and Charles V. Hamilton. 1967. *Black Power: The Politics of Liberation.* New York: Random House.
Centers for Disease Control and Prevention. 2008. *Behavioral Risk Factor Surveillance System Data.* Retrieved July 13, 2009 (http://www.statehealthfacts.org/comparebar.jsp?ind=91&cat=2).
Cohen, Claire. 2008. "Breakdown of Demographics Reveals How Black Voters Swept Obama into White House." *Daily Mail,* November 5. Retrieved January 10, 2013. (http://www.dailymail.co.uk/news/article-1083335/Breakdown-demographics-reveals-black-voters-swept-Obama-White-House.html#ixzz2Cz61YfTO).
Collins, Patricia Hill. 2000. *Black Feminist Thought: Knowledge, Consciousness, and the Politics of Empowerment.* New York: Routledge.
Cone, James. 1997. *God of the Oppressed.* Maryknoll, NY: Orbis Books.
———. [1969] 1999. *Black Theology and Black Power.* Maryknoll, NY: Orbis Books.
Cox, Oliver Cromwell. 1948. *Caste, Class, and Race: A Study in Social Dynamics.* New York: Monthly Review Press.
Drake, St. Clair and Horace R. Cayton. [1942] 1962. *Black Metropolis: A Study of Negro Life in a Northern City.* Vol. I and II. New York: Harper and Row.
Du Bois, W. E. B. [1903] 1996. *The Souls of Black Folk.* New York: Modern Library.
———. [1903] 2003. *The Negro Church.* Walnut Creek, CA: AltaMira Press.
Feagin, Joe R. 2006. *Systemic Racism: A Theory of Oppression.* New York: Routledge.
———. 2010. *The White Racial Frame: Centuries of Racial Framing and Counter- Framing.* New York: Routledge.
Forbes. 2009. "The Wealthiest Black Americans." Retrieved January 10, 2013 (http://www.forbes.com/2009/05/06/richest-black-americans-busienss-billionaires-richest-black-americans_slide_8.html).

———. 2013. "The Richest People in America." Retrieved January 10, 2013 (http://www.forbes.com/forbes-400/).

Frazier, E. Franklin. 1964. *The Negro Church in America*. New York: Schocken Books.

Gallagher, Charles A. 2003. "Color-Blind Privilege: The Social and Political Functions of Erasing the Color Line in Post-Race America." *Race, Gender and Class* 10(4): 1–17.

Gaertner, John and Samuel Dovidio. 1986. *Prejudice, Racism, and Discrimination*. Orlando, FL: Academic Press.

Graham, Lawrence. 1999. *Our Kind of People: Inside America's Black Upper Class*. New York: Harper Perennial.

Graves, Joseph L. 2001. *The Emperor's New Clothes: Biological Theories of Race at the Millennium*. New Brunswick, NJ: Rutgers University Press.

Hannerz, Ulf. 1969. *Soulside: Inquiries into Ghetto Culture and Community*. New York: Columbia University Press

Isaacs, Julia. 2008. "Economic Mobility of Black and White Families." Pp. 1–10 in *Getting Ahead or Losing Ground: Economic Mobility in America*, edited by J. Isaacs, I. Sawhill, and R. Haskins. Washington, DC: Brookings Institute. Retrieved January 10, 2013 (http://www.economicmobility.org/assets/pdfs/EMP_BlackandWhite_ChapterVI.pdf).

Journal of Blacks in Higher Education. 2010. "College Graduation Rates: Where Black Students Do the Best and Where They Fare Poorly Compared to Their White Peers." Retrieved October 13, 2013 (http://www.jbhe.com/features/65_gradrates.html).

———. 2005. "The Persisting Racial Gap in College Student Graduation Rates." Retrieved October 11, 2006 (http://www.jbhe.com/features/45_student_grad_rates.html).

Kalil, Ariel and Patrick Wightman. 2010. "Parental Job Loss and Children's Educational Attainment in Black and White Middle-Class Families." National Poverty Center Working Paper Series. Retrieved January 10, 2013 (http://www.npc.umich.edu/publications/working_papers/).

Kuhn, David P. 2008. "Exit Polls: How Obama Won." *Politico*, November 5. Retrieved June 2, 2009 (http://www.politico.com/news/stories/1108/15297.html).

Ladner, Joyce A. 1973. *The Death of White Sociology: Essays on Race and Culture*. New York: Random House.

Lincoln, C. Eric and Lawrence H. Mamiya. 1990. *The Black Church in the African-American Experience*. Durham, NC: Duke University Press.

McKee, James. 1993. *Sociology and the Race Problem: The Failure of a Perspective*. Champaign: University of Illinois Press.

Massey, Douglas S. and Nancy A. Denton. 1993. *American Apartheid: Segregation and the Making of the Underclass*. Cambridge, MA: Harvard University Press.

Morris, Aldon D. 1984. *The Origins of the Civil Rights Movement: Black Communities Organizing for Change*. New York: Free Press.

Moynihan, Daniel. 1965. *The Negro Family: The Case for National Action*. Washington, DC: Dept. of Labor, Office of Policy Planning and Research.

Myrdal, Gunner. 1975. *An American Dilemma: The Negro Problem and Modern Democracy*. New York: Pantheon.

Oliver, M. and Shapiro, T. 1997. *Black Wealth, White Wealth: A New Perspective on Racial Inequality*. New York: Routledge.

Omi, Michael and Howard Winant. 1994. *Racial Formation in the United States: From the 1960s to the 1990s*. New York: Routledge.

Pattillo-McCoy, M. 1999. *Black Picket Fences*. Chicago: University of Chicago Press.

Sherman, Ted. 2012. "Obama Wins 2012 Presidential Election, Defeats Romney in Tight Race." *Star-Ledger* (November 06. Retrieved January 10, 2013 (http://www.nj.com/politics/index.ssf/2012/11/obama_wins_2012_presidential_e.html).

Sherwood, I-Hsien. 2012. "Popular Vote 2012: Results Breakdown of Presidential Election by Religion, Race, Education and Income." *Latinos Post*, November 17. Retrieved January 10, 2013 (http://www.latinospost.com/articles/6980/20121117/popular-vote-2012–results-breakdown-presidential-election.htm#MPp1qmsbPFbdjm5D.99).

U.S. Bureau of the Census. 2009. "Census Current Population Survey Annual Social and Economic Supplement." Washington, DC: U.S. Government Printing Office. Retrieved June 23, 2012 (http://www.census.gov).

———. 2002. "Health Insurance in America: Number of Americans with and without Health Insurance Rise" (press release). Sept. 30. Washington, DC: Center on Budget and Policy Priorities. Retrieved January 10, 2013 (http://www.cbpp.org/cms/?fa=view&id=699).

U.S. Bureau of Justice Statistics, 2005. U.S. Department of Justice. Retrieved January 9, 2013 (http://www.bls.gov/).

U.S. Bureau of Labor Statistics. 2008. *Current Population Survey*. Washington, DC: U.S. Bureau of Labor Statistics. Retrieved June 23, 2012 (http://www.bls.gov/).

West, Cornel. 1993. *Race Matters*. Boston: Beacon Press.

Wilson, William Julius. 1980. *The Declining Significance of Race: Blacks and Changing American Institutions*. 2nd ed. Chicago: University of Chicago Press.

———. 1987. *The Truly Disadvantaged: The Inner City, the Underclass, and Public Policy*. Chicago: University of Chicago Press.

Part I

~

The Pitfalls and Possibilities of Prophetic Race Theory

Cultivating Leadership

Since Africans were initially brought to North America as indentured servants and forced into slavery shortly thereafter, myriad theories have emerged about Black Americans' experiences as racial minorities, adaptive strategies and resilience, and the process of cultivating individual and collective racial identity. For nearly 400 years, macro- and microlevel theories on race and leadership have emanated in diversity and intensity from pulpit preachers, academicians in ivory towers, politicians at city halls, everyday people, and grassroots activists. Whether anecdotal, empirical, situational, or experiential, each paradigm provides a glimpse of the complex legacy of people of African descent in the Americas and the rise and fall of their various leaders. Since the historic election of the first African American President of the United States, Barack Obama, in 2008, and his reelection in 2012, additional theories about race and leadership have been created. Furthermore, existing theories have been reexamined and reimagined. Two imperatives have been central to these theories of the relationship between race and leadership: (1) people of African descent must provide authentic, culturally relevant descriptive and proscriptive leadership models, and (2) they must craft counternarratives against controlling images and negative structural forces. To achieve these imperatives, numerous Black leaders have engaged in a prophetic process of thinking, writing, teaching, and living that challenged the status quo; pushed back against inequality in its many forms; fostered critical dialogue and community engagement; and unabashedly reflected a lifelong process of informing society about what it means to be of African descent. However, these leaders also confronted the recurring pitfalls and possibilities of Black leadership, which frequently had consequences for Black communities.

This part examines three notions of prophetic race theory and leadership. Each theory emphasizes the significance of being dedicated, proactive, and uncompromising in confronting the challenges of a racialized society. Each chapter considers what constitutes a Black leader; how critical race theory can inform the relationship between race and leadership; and ultimately how laypersons can become equipped, educated, and empowered to take on leadership roles in the fight against racism. Through a critical lens, the chapters in this part provide clarity on multiple theoretical models that can be used in this postracial era (which some scholars refer to as neoracism): that is, an era where traditional forms of racism (i.e., lynching, mob rule, and race riots) have given way to more subtle and nuanced forms of race-based inequality linked to color-blind racism, ambivalence, psychic violence, microaggressions, ethnocentrism, and class-based intraracial disagreements over the continuing significance of race. These postracial manifestations of racial animus exclude *undesirables* from White and "honorary White" spaces, as well as from positions of power and privilege.

The race paradigms presented in these chapters undergird and inform the empirical studies in parts II and III of this volume. In the face of both traditional and postracial sentiments, and buttressed by an African American male's ascension to the most powerful seat of leadership in the Western world, Eduardo Bonilla-Silva, Earl Wright II, and Robert L. Reece argue for new understandings of the possibilities and pitfalls of prophetic race theory and how it can translate into self-reflection, self-efficacy, self-empowerment, collective racial uplift, and minority leadership.

Eduardo Bonilla-Silva offers a critical assessment of contemporary minority leadership in political and academic arenas that, consistent with W. E. B. Du Bois's call for collective reflection and social engagement, emphasizes self-sacrifice and the recognition that injustice must be challenged by every person of good will regardless of their station in life. The prophetic vision of Bonilla-Silva's theory on leadership amidst the new racial terrain in the United States mandates an uncompromising challenge to existing racial and cultural barriers in the

seemingly postracial world he refers to as "Obamerica." Far from simply applauding the political, economic, and social advancements of a
cadre of Blacks and minority leaders, Bonilla-Silva argues that many of
these accomplishments are superficial and have come at the expense of
Black and brown persons whose concerns are not seriously engaged by
Black elites. Instead, many Black and brown political and professional
leaders, according to Bonilla-Silva, take the masses for granted, often
actively engaging in efforts antithetical to the best interests of their base
racial or ethnic group(s). Using President Barack Obama as an exemplar,
Bonilla-Silva outlines how leaders and members of the Black community
who emerged in the post–Civil Rights and Obamerica eras remain silent
on important issues concerning race, thus allowing Whites to absolve
themselves of any responsibility for or obligation to confront and rectify
issues of race and racism. This position, he argues, is a betrayal of the
very people on whose shoulders they were afforded the opportunities
they now hold. Moreover, Bonilla-Silva argues that the silence of Black
leaders such as Obama on issues of racial inequality is arguably an affront
to the spirit of the ancestors who led the fight for Black empowerment.

In 1903, W. E. B. Du Bois articulated the most well-known, and
perhaps oldest, theory on minority group empowerment and leadership
in the United States: the talented tenth. Emerging from, among other
factors, a fusion of Henry L. Morehouse's theory on leadership and his
experiences at Fisk University as an undergraduate student, Du Bois's
theory of Black leadership is grounded in the idea that the most effective leadership model is void of self-interest, infused with self-sacrifice,
and girded with an overt and unbending desire to engage in one's best
works for the benefit of the masses. We cannot know whether Du Bois
believed the nation that ended slavery three years before his birth and
was in the throes of the Civil Rights movement while on his death
bed at age 95 would ever elect one of its sons from within the veil to
its highest position of power. However, what one can discern from his
theory on Black empowerment and leadership is a prophetic vision that
renders the scenario possible.

Earl Wright II's chapter challenges some of the misperceptions
concerning Du Bois's theory. Principally, it reframes the notion of Black
leadership within Du Bois's own clarification of the theory of the talented tenth, debunking the notion that Black leadership is based singularly on one's academic accomplishments. While most are aware of
his original 1903 articulation, Du Bois's 1948 clarification of his theory
is rarely mentioned, let alone examined in the same critical manner as
the original. Grounded in self-sacrifice and the exclusion of self-interest,
Du Bois's restated theory serves as a foundation for those committed

to confronting the challenges of Black and brown people in the United States. Wright ultimately argues that admission into this fraternity should be based on one prerequisite—one's affirmative answer to the question, "Am I my brother's and my sister's keeper?" Although Bonilla-Silva and Wright examine prophetic race theory and the formal and informal leaders who should emerge through traditional channels, the final analysis in this part examines contemporary leadership and theorizing that has emerged from popular culture.

From hip hop to the latest upscale fashion trends, the influence of popular culture as a change agent has become more pronounced over the past few decades. In 2003, Dave Chappelle's "Chappelle's Show," a 30-minute comedy show, debuted to a record audience. With an array of sketches often directly or indirectly grounded in issues of race, "Chappelle's Show" provided a weekly entrée into the world of race from a comedic perspective. In this analysis, Robert L. Reece suggests that comedy can be an effective tool in educating and challenging society members on issues of race. Reece posits Chappelle as a nontraditional example of Black leadership who emerged via popular culture and used his comedic talents to analyze, understand, and respond to problems of race and racism in ways that represent an unexpected model of critical race theory. Given the manner in which comedic and popular culture icons such as Chris Rock, Michael Baisden, Steve Joyner, Whoopi Goldberg, Dick Gregory, and Wanda Sykes are influencing the Black masses in ways previously possible only by Black clergy, comedy as a mode of social critique and commentary may be becoming as impactful as the traditional types discussed earlier. Reece's argument concerning the comedic brilliance and societal impact of Chappelle and others on issues of race creates a space for nontraditional leaders and community activists to emerge and contribute to the debunking and challenging of stereotypes and racism in creative, informative, and thought-provoking ways. Thus, prophetic race theory becomes a more inclusive, diverse, and potentially empowering space where allies in the struggle for racial equality access information from varied sources and potential leaders are able to emerge from spaces that may afford them more, and easier, access into public and private arenas. In these spaces, these new likely and unlikely leaders can grapple with the issues confronting Black and brown people.

The prophetic potential of Bonilla-Silva's racial critique of Black leaders, Wright's reevaluation of Du Bois's leadership theory, and Reece's application of critical race theory for a nontraditional Black leader are presented as models to encourage individual and collective action. Results from the three chapters are designed to energize formal and informal leaders among Africans in the Diaspora. The prophetic vision of each chapter is designed to promote righteous indignation about all forms of racism by citizens unafraid to put America's most pernicious stain under the critical microscope while potentially risking personal and professional loss. Moreover, each work offers a stern challenge to readers to look into the window of their soul, ask what they are willing to stand for and against, and how they will do it. The question remains: Who is prepared to stand in opposition to racism and ethnic slights even if it may come at a personal and professional cost?

1

~

Race Matters in "Postracial" OBAMERICA and How to Climb Out of the Rabbit Hole[1]

Eduardo Bonilla-Silva
with Trenita Brookshire Childers

Duke University

In this curious moment when many believe the election and reelection of a Black man as the 44th president of the nation are clear and convincing evidence of racial progress, race matters have in truth become more complex and problematic for most of us. The new racial order that has emerged—the "new racism"—unlike Jim Crow, reproduces racial domination mostly through subtle and covert discriminatory practices that are often institutionalized, defended with coded language, and bonded by the racial ideology of color-blind racism. Compared to Jim Crow, this new system seems genteel, but it is nonetheless extremely effective in preserving systemic advantages for most Whites and keeping most people of color at bay. This chapter examines how contemporary racial trends in Obamerica are affecting Amerikan sociology. (I spell America with a "k" to denote some racial progress—we used to be "Amerikkka.") After all, sociology and sociologists are embedded in social relations and thus reflect in many ways, despite our method-ological objections to the contrary, social forces. More significantly, it is fundamental that we correctly understand how this curious moment is affecting sociologists of color, their organizations, as well as how it may shape our future in sociology.

The "Postracial" Obamerica Moment

We live in peculiar times that resemble the upside-down world Alice entered when she fell down the rabbit hole. In the wonderland I have called "Obamerica,"[2] most Whites, and some people of color, believe Barack Obama's presidential election in 2008 and his subsequent reelection in 2012 confirmed that ours is now indeed a color-blind nation. In the tradition of prophetic research, I am on record[3] criticizing not only this problematic view, but also more controversially, the "hopey-changey"[4] politics that allowed someone such as Obama to become president. Obama's success is neither the product of social movement politics nor of Whites' racial altruism, but a direct expression of the fun-damental racial transformation that transpired in America in the 1960s and 1970s. This racial transformation continues a political history of encoding white supremacy into social institutions through discriminatory practices, including in healthcare delivery, the criminal justice system, housing, the labor market, and the family. These practices of "the new racism" draw on the coded lexicon of color-blind racism ("*those* urban people" or "*those* people on welfare") to both preserve white privilege and deflect charges of racial discrimination.

It is crucial that we take a moment to trace the origins of this new racial regime. This order came about as the result of various social forces and events that converged in the post–World War II era: (1) the civil rights struggles of the 1950s and 1960s; (2) the contradiction between an America selling democracy abroad and disenfranchising and discriminating against minorities at home that forced the government to engage more seriously in the business of racial fairness; (3) Black migration from the South that made Jim Crow less effective as a strategy of social control; and (4) the change of heart of so-called enlightened representatives of capital who realized they had to retool the racial aspects of the social order to maintain an adequate "business climate." The most visible positive consequences of this process are well-known: the slow and incomplete school desegregation that followed the 1954 *Brown v. Board of Education* Supreme Court decision; the enactment of the Civil Rights Act of 1964, the Voting Rights Act of 1965, and the

Housing Rights Act of 1968; and, the haphazard political process that brought affirmative action to life.

Unfortunately, alongside these meaningful changes, many Whites developed very negative interpretations of what was transpiring in the nation.[6] The concerns they expressed in the late 1960s and early 1970s about these changes gelled into a two-headed beast in the 1980s (Caditz 1976). The first head of the monster was Whites' belief that the changes the tumultuous 1960s brought represented the end of racism in America. Therefore, because they believed racism had ended, they began regarding complaints about discrimination by people of color as both baseless and a product of their "hypersensitivity" on racial affairs. The second head of the beast meant that a substantial segment of the White population understood the changes not just as evidence of the end of racism, but also as the beginning of a period of "reverse discrimination."[7] Hence, this was the ideological context that helped cement what is referred to as the "new racism."

The new regime in the political arena is evident in three major factors that limit the advancement of people of color. First, multiple structural barriers, such as racial gerrymandering and multimember legislative district members, prevent the election of Black and minority politicians. Second, despite some progress in the 1970s, people of color are still severely underrepresented among elected (Whites still show a preference to vote for White candidates) and appointed officials—the proportion of elected and appointed Black officials still lags well behind their proportion in the population. Third, because most minority politicians must either "compromise" to get elected or are dependent on local White elites, their capacity to enact policies that benefit the minority masses is quite limited.[8]

More significantly, since my early analysis of these matters, I described the emergence of a new type of minority politician (Bonilla-Silva 2001). By the early 1990s both major political parties, and the Democratic Party in particular, clearly had learned from the perils of trying to incorporate veteran civil rights leaders such as Jesse Jackson. Regardless of the limitations of Jackson as a leader and of his 1980s "rainbow coalition" strategy, he and his coalition proved to be too much of a challenge to those in authority.[9] Hence, both parties and their corporate masters developed a new process for selecting and vetting minority politicians. Consequently, today's electorally oriented minority politician (1) is not the product of social movements, (2) usually joins the party of choice while in college, (3) moves up quickly through the party ranks, and, most importantly, (4) is not a race rebel.[10]

The new breed of minority politicians, unlike their predecessors, are not radicals talking about "the revolution" and "uprooting systemic racism." If Republican, they are antiminority conservatives such as Michael Steele (immediate past chairman of the Republican National Committee), Bobby Jindal (governor of Louisiana since 2008), Alan Keyes (conservative commentator and perennial candidate for any office), and J. C. Watts (former congressman from Oklahoma and still a very influential leader in the Republican Party). If Democrat, they are postracial leaders with center to center-right politics such as Harold Ford Jr. (former congressman from Tennessee, current head of the conservative Democratic Leadership Council, and an MSNBC commentator), Cory Booker (former Newark, New Jersey mayor and U.S. senator since 2013), Deval Patrick (governor of Massachusetts since 2006), Adrian Fenty (mayor of Washington, D.C., 2006–2010), and, of course, President Barack Obama. Not surprisingly, plutocrats love these kinds of minority politicians because whether Republican or Democrat, none represents a threat to the power structure of America.[11]

Accordingly, before Barack Obama was elected president, I predicted he would exhibit center-right politics and would do almost nothing on the race front—and the facts so far have proven this.[12] I have done a formal review elsewhere (chapter 10 in Bonilla-Silva 2010a), but provide some highlights as well as updates here. I contend that President Obama:

- Passed mediocre health-care reform that did not address cost containment, the monopolistic practices of the pharmaceutical industries, the health maintenance organizations' preeminent standing in the system, and the growth of hospitals-for-profit.

- Increased the U.S. military presence in Afghanistan to 100,000 troops, escalated the drone attacks in countries such as Afghanistan, Pakistan, and Yemen; continued Bush-era covert Central Intelligence Agency and U.S. Army intervention in Pakistan; and has outlined a Korean-like deal for Iraq whereby a large number of American troops and contractors will remain in place for an undetermined amount of time (Scahill 2013).

- Helped Wall Street bankers and investors by passing a bailout bill of $858 billion as well as a tax break for the wealthy in December 2010 for $400 billion (Sahadi 2010). In addition, he has revamped his already center-right Cabinet to make it even more Wall Street–friendly by adding Jeff Immelt, the former CEO of General Electric, and William Daley, a Wall Street insider.

- Helped weaken labor unions by endorsing conservative educational plans (Race to the Top) and undermining teachers' unions. In 2010, Obama and his Secretary of Education, Arnie Duncan, endorsed the actions of a Rhode Island school superintendent, who fired nearly 90 teachers at a high school.[13] In 2011 he spoke at a Miami high school and shared the stage with former Florida Governor Jeb Bush, "the king of corporate-driven standardized tests-obsessed school reform that devalues teachers and their unions" (Strauss 2011). Recently he has made comments in defense of union workers in Wisconsin, but he has done so in a limited way while still expecting them to make concessions—this despite the fact that Governor Walker's first office task was to pass a corporate tax break for the super wealthy at a time of a so-called budget crisis (Flanders 2011).

- Passed financial reform that did not deal with "too big to fail," which according to observers was key. Analysts predict that this inadequate reform will not help the nation in the near future with similar financial crises.

- Has not delivered an immigration reform and has actually increased the annual deportations to about 400,000—10% more than President Bush (Slevin 2010).

- Has made a timid stand on race matters (refer to my elaborate discussion on the Obama phenomenon in *Racism without Racists* [2010a]). Noteworthy events in his administration are his rapid change from an initially strong stand on the "Gates controversy" to his "beer summit" in the White House as well as the astonishingly ineffective way he handled the Shirley Sherrod incident. In the latter story, after his Secretary of Agriculture demanded Sherrod's resignation following a one-day news cycle of negative news based on the work of a conservative blogger, Obama refused to use his position to talk about the continuing significance of race in America and said those conversations should happen "around kitchen tables across America, and not necessarily from a presidential podium."[14]

The following reviews how the Obama moment, which has deepened trends already present in the racial polity, is manifested at the
national level. However, my main goal in this chapter is to examine
how these national racial trends are affecting Ameri*k*an[15] sociology. As
I intimated at the outset of this chapter, sociologists are not immune
to overarching power of social forces. Despite our contentions otherwise, we are not Comtean objective and positivist priests of humankind
unaffected by social relations.[16] Thus, I begin with an examination of
the broader racial context of Obamerica and then turn to an evaluation
of how the sets of social relations in this moment affect the future of
scholars of color, and our organizations in particular, in the discipline.

Race Matters in 'Postracial' Obamerica

Outlining some national trends will provide a context for a commentary
on the standing of Blacks in American society today, scholars of color,
and society in general. First, at this historical juncture, Whites have
the discursive upper hand. They have racial and ethnic minorities in a
political corner because they can now say things such as, "You have a
Black president, so, . . . ?" "I voted for Obama, so, . . ." or more prob-
lematically, "Obama and Michelle worked hard and look at where they
are. So what's wrong with the rest of you people?" People such as Bill
Cosby, Will Smith, Bill Bennett, John Lewis, and the Thernstroms have
also uttered such sentiments. The conclusion is—"No more excuses!"[17]
Michelle and Barack have accommodated this view by pushing the "You
Can Do It!" line in their visits to schools and comments to the media
(White House Press Office 2009). While encouragement and role models are necessary, they must first insist that the structures, practices, and
institutions that maintain race-based inequality be removed.

Second, a few years ago I suggested that racial stratification in
the United States was becoming similar to Latin American with three
large racial groups or spaces: Whites, "honorary Whites," and "the
collective Black" group (Bonilla Silva 2009). The "us" versus "them"
racial dynamic will lessen as "honorary Whites" grow in size and social
importance. This new racial stratification system will be more effective
in maintaining White supremacy. Whites will still be at the top of the
social structure, but will face fewer race-based challenges. As a Latin
American–like country, the United States will become a society with
more rather than less racial inequality but with a reduced forum for racial
contestation (Bonilla-Silva 2010a). This prediction may be crystallizing
faster than I had anticipated, and Barack Obama's election fits many

of the elements of my thesis.[18] Furthermore, because Obama does not have an anti-imperialist stance, the "we" in foreign affairs is becoming seemingly inclusive. More troubling is that given the nationalist spell the Black community has been under since at least 2008 (i.e., "Obama is one of us, so . . ."), most of us have remained silent while President Obama has escalated the imperialist intervention in Afghanistan and Pakistan, reneged or slowed down on ending Bush-era controversial policies such as "renditions" or closing the Guantanamo Bay detention camp, retooled his promise of getting us out of Iraq (50,000 troops as military advisers), and done little to force Israel to negotiate in good faith with the Palestinians. The claim by some that this is a matter of "governance" or of supporting a historic president[19] facing severe attacks from the right[20] makes us accomplices of Ameri*k*an foreign policy. I contend that we will pay dearly for this mistake. We will no longer be able to say that American wars are the "White man's wars." From now on we are symbolically and perhaps even practically part of the American Empire.

Third, and related to my Latin Americanization thesis, we are witnessing the rapid rise of "neomulattoes" (Horton 2002)—or "honorary Whites." Although most Blacks are going through a nationalist moment and support President Obama regardless, we need to separate the class and race dynamics of the Black community.[21] At this juncture, many assimilated, light-skinned, aristocratic Blacks seem to be on a path to develop their own space and place in the American racial order. This segment, which has always maintained social distance from "regular" Black folks, may be in a process of separation from the Black community altogether. Whether in government, media, business, or academia, neomulattoes are on the move and will become vital for maintaining White power because they will help Whites discipline the rest of us. Tyrone A. Forman (forthcoming), a sociologist at Emory University, is examining the specific attitudes and politics of the "Black Elite" and suggests that in addition to the new mulattoes, two other segments may be equally problematic: the cultural Blacks who do not care about the Black masses and are happy making money in a mal-integrated America and the middle-class Blacks who have had such limited political experience that they are blind to how race matters "for real" in contemporary America. Fourth, broadly speaking, the White community is divided in three groups: a very small "racially progressive" segment (less than 10%), a dominant segment of color-blind or racially apathetic Whites (70–80%), and an amorphous segment of old-fashioned racists (10–20%).[22] Survey data on racial attitudes tends to overrepresent people on the progressive side because most work is focused on old-fashioned views that were considered racist (Bonilla-Silva 2010a).[23] Although we must be vigilant of old- and new-fashioned bigots, in post–Civil Rights America I contend that the "regular White folks" are most problematic. Accordingly, they should be the focus of our racial politics and, if you will, of our animus. The more we concentrate on the "racists" (i.e., old-fashioned, Archie Bunker–like folks) the less attention we dedicate to average color-blind Whites who are, in my view, the central cogs of America's new racial regime.

Fifth, a "multicultural White supremacy" regime (Rodriguez 2010)—or the highest stage of what I have called in my work the "new racism"—seems to be crystallizing, which has hegemonically incorporated some minority members to the extent that they can now be in leadership positions in the economy, academia, civil society, and politics without affecting the "normal" operations of the American race, class, and gender order. In this new political order, the mere presence of "minorities" and women in leadership positions is not enough to yield progressive outcomes. In fact, increasingly the minorities and women themselves will maintain the race, class, and gender order as they experience limited privilege. Sixth, culturally the new order has reinstated as "legitimate" things we had all but banned from public interactions such as using blackface or making racist jokes on television shows such as *30 Rock* and *The Office*; reframing "racist" occurrences including the Tea Party movement and the birther movement as nonracial; or bringing back biological readings of race in the social and natural sciences as well as in popular discussions (Duster 2003). Although these types of racial matters may be difficult, even painful for many people to acknowledge, we are challenged to prudently and critically consider them and their implications. Those of us in academia are all the more required to identify, describe, and both write and speak about these issues.

Racial Trends in the Postracial (White) Academy

This section considers some of the implications of Obamerica on the realities of existing and burgeoning sociologists of color as we strive to engage in relevant teaching, research, and service. What are the expressions of the "Obama moment" in academia? First, "people of color" are still regarded as "the problem people." All the long-ago arguments— biology, cultural deficiencies, underclass or ghetto-specific behavior— coexist alongside critical perspectives, but the latter perspectives garner little support from the media, the public, foundations, and, predictably, from most sociologists. (How many White sociologists talk about institutional or structural racism and are working to address racial inequality?)

One example of this is Oscar Lewis's "culture of poverty" argument that we thought was dead but that keeps coming back, often with greater intensity (Lewis 1963). For instance, several well-known sociologists and political analysts published in the last few years two special issues in the *Annals of the American Academy of Political and Social Science* trying to reestablish the validity of this perspective. A 2009 issue, edited by Douglas Massey and Ralph Sampson entitled, "The Moynihan Report Revisited: Lessons and Reflections after Four Decades," includes chapters by both authors (and a few others) reinstating Moynihan as a "liberal" thinker whose ideas and accurate comments on the Black family were censored by "extremists" (Massey and Sampson 2009). Their perspective was widely cited in an article that appeared in a 2010 *New York Times* article, " 'Culture of Poverty' Makes a Comeback" (Cohen 2010). Of interest here is a quote from Professor Massey: "We've finally reached the stage where people aren't afraid of being politically incorrect." In the same piece Professor Sampson revisited his own problematic "broken windows" culturist thesis (Sampson, Morenoff, and Gannon Rowley 2002; Sampson and Raudenbush 2004), saying that "the reason a neighborhood turns into a 'poverty trap' is also related to a common perception of the way people in a community act and think. When people see graffiti and garbage, do they find it acceptable or see serious disorder? Do they respect the legal system or have a high level of 'moral cynicism,' believing that 'laws were made to be broken'?" (Cohen 2010).

In a 2010 issue of the *Annals of the American Academy of Political and Social Science*, edited by David J. Harding, Michélle Lamont, and Mario L. Small, "Reconsidering Culture and Poverty," some of the scholars attempt a balancing act on this perspective, but most were willing to embrace the revitalization of culturist interpretations for poverty particularly among minority people (Small, Harding, and Lamont 2010). The editors seemed truly excited that "culture" was back in the policy circles as an explanation for poverty. In their words, "Culture is back on the poverty research agenda. Over the past decade, sociologists, demographers, and even economists have begun asking questions about the role of culture in many aspects of poverty and even explicitly explaining the behavior of the low-income population in reference to cultural factors" (Harding et al. 2010:2).

Parties interested in a critique of the resurgence of culturist interpretations of poverty and the folly of the authors in this tradition should read, "Poor Reason: Culture Still Doesn't Explain Poverty," in the *Boston Review* (Steinberg 2011). In a telling paragraph, Steinberg undresses the nonsense of Professors Massey, Sampson, and others by correctly pointing out that the issue has never been the denial of troubles in

Black America or even in Black families, but assessing what the weight of "culture" is in Blacks' plight and whether "culture" is an independent factor. In his words:

> Yet even Moynihan's harshest critics did not deny the manifest troubles in Black families. Nor did they deny that the culture of poor people is often markedly at variance with the cultural norms and practices in more privileged sectors of society. How could it be otherwise? The key point of contention was whether, under conditions of prolonged poverty, those cultural adaptations "assume a life of their own" and are passed down from parents to children through normal processes of cultural transmission. In other words, the imbroglio over the Moynihan Report was never about whether culture matters, but about whether culture is or ever could be an independent and self-sustaining factor in the production and reproduction of poverty. (Steinberg 2011)

Worse than the revival of culturist explanations for Black and minority poverty, however, is the slow but consistent turn to genetic and biological explanations to explain the plight of people of color. In my 20 years or so as a professional sociologist I have witnessed four versions of this dynamic, namely, sociobiology, evolutionary psychology, evolutionary sociology, and bio-demography. All these perspectives share a common agenda: explaining social outcomes from a biological perspective—and funding agencies and universities seem quite eager to endorse and sponsor this kind of work (Fujimura, Duster, and Rajagopalan 2008; Guo 2008).

Second, sociology, which was very slow in incorporating a few of us into its midst in the late 1960s and 1970s (Simpson and Simpson 1994), has now developed a process of systemic token inclusion. Almost all departments make sure they have "one of us" and that's about it! "Diversity" has become an ideology (Embrick forthcoming) and, thus, for White sociologists it is a thing to consider but definitely not a matter of restructuring the sociological apparatus (i.e., its traditions, theory, methods, and structure). Without this restructuring, very few of us will ever filter into top historically White colleges and universities (HWCUs)[24] as we seldom are in a position to amass the records, networks, and standing needed to land jobs in those places. Thus, integrated academia in postracial Obamerica still has mostly White sociology departments.[25] In 1999, Cedric Herring and I wrote a stinging critique of sociology in an article that appeared in *Footnotes* titled, " 'We'd Love to Hire Them But' . . . : The Underrepresentation of Sociologists of Color and Its Implications" (Bonilla-Silva and Herring 1999). There we documented the limited representation of sociologists of color at the top, critiqued the rationales used to justify this situation (i.e., "We do not find qualified minorities."), and provided a plan of action to address this underrepresentation. Twelve years later, the situation has not changed dramatically.

Two talented undergraduate students helped me replicate the examination of sociology departments that we did in the past, but in addition to examining the racial profile of the top 30 sociology departments according to the *U.S. News and World Report*, we examined a sample of departments in Tiers III and IV. The findings are sobering. The average proportion of minority faculty in the top 30 departments is 7.3% for Blacks and 5.0% for Latinos—well below their national proportion of 12.4% and 15.8% for Blacks and Latinos, respectively. Given that the average department in this list has 31.2 professors, this ratio means it has 2.28 Black and 1.56 Latino professors. This miniscule representation becomes even more problematic if we realize that in post–Civil Rights America one can have "minority representation" that is not expressive of the best interests of minority people (i.e., one can have a Black man in the Supreme Court behaving in ways that hurt the interests of the Black majority or a Latino professor in a sociology department who is not at all connected to the Latino experience in America). Hence, one can have "the chocolate look without the flavor," meaning that sociology departments can have three or more Black or Latino professors who do not necessarily represent the best interest of their communities. This abysmal situation in so-called top departments is actually slightly worse in lower tiers in the academic hierarchy. In our sample of departments in Tiers III and IV, the proportion of Black and Latino professors was 6.4% and 3.3% and 10.3% and 6.1% (Tier IVs were slightly better), respectively. But these proportions, given that the average size of units in these lower tiers is smaller (15 or fewer), translates to one or fewer Black or Latino professor in each of these departments, which means that the minority status and minority experience at an HWCU is no different than elsewhere.

Third, the token inclusion we experience in sociology is exhausting. We struggle for recognition, understanding, and appreciation and seldom get any because we lack the most vital qualification needed to be successful in HWCUs: we're not White and never will be. And if anyone wonders how this can be when we have been elected to an American Sociological Association (ASA) Council, received ASA awards, and work at a top university, I say wonder no more. No minority scholar is ever safe. Most of us experience this second-class academic experience at some point in our careers. No matter the awards, the salary,[26] the niceties of working at top universities, in the eyes of White sociologists, minority scholars are part of the problem people or affirmative action hires—mere subjective analysts trying to keep race alive to keep our jobs.

A few of the major racial practices[27] that help reproduce sociology departments as White organizations thus maintaining White rule include:

1. *Race as fictive kinship:* Race works as quasi-kinship, which explains why Whites form a "family" in sociology departments. This White family provides protection, information, resources, support, and other things to its members, which makes for an on average better experience for family members than for those not in the family.[28] Of course, sociologists of color form a kinship group with other folks of color, too, but because of their small size in departments, diversity (not all are from the same racial background), and limited power, the minority family usually provides limited protection and, more significantly, can do little to provide a solid opportunity structure for its members.

2. *Informal and emotional exclusion:* Sociologists of color are formally part of departments, but like in the polity at large, are not "emotionally embedded" (Aranda 2007). We may be members of these departments, but in a deep human way, we do not belong and are quite often made to feel that exclusion. Although we may say we do not care if we are not invited to go drinking, to parties, and the like, these informal events are important because many departmental decisions and networks are developed there.

3. *Labeling:* Almost every sociologist of color I know has heard from a White colleague something like, "You make me uncomfortable . . ." or "You are always talking about race . . . and, come on, we have a Black president, so . . ." We hear comments like these as students and as faculty. Whites, who rule this business and the environments where we labor, project onto us by labeling us "controversial," "difficult," "one-sided," and "political."

4. *Microaggressions:* I travel across the nation and consult with many minorities on a variety of race-related matters.

Many tell me about the "microaggressions" they endure—small slights that "kill us softly" (Feagin and Sikes 1994). Their stories include instances of being berated in their offices by a White colleague, being told in their face they are "overpaid" or not "qualified," being threatened (i.e., "If you don't do this, you will not get tenure here."), and being told their success (i.e., publishing an article in a top journal or receiving an award) is just another illustration of affirmative action gone awry. I have personally experienced each of the examples.

5. *White promotion*: In terms of race, if one's area of expertise is Europe, one is deemed a genius. If, however, one's area of expertise is Africa or the Caribbean, one is not. In the curious White imagery, people of color choose to work on areas of personal concern, whereas Whites choose their areas based on objective research interests. But even if one is White and writes on race, one is usually[29] deemed objective and has a shot at greatness. White sociologists can even pontificate about racial matters they know little about, such as when Bourdieu and Wacquant (1999) dared make some uninformed statements about race in Latin America and, in the process, attack the work of many minority scholars doing informed work on the subject. And given that Whites deem themselves objective and frame us as subjective (Bonilla-Silva and Zuberi 2008), few dare suggest White sociologists are pro-White or anti-Black. These are but a few of the racial practices that reproduce the "(racial) order of things" (Foucault 1970) in contemporary sociology and the emotional toll they produce among sociologists of color is astounding. People of color in academia are, as Will Smith has argued, in a permanent state of "fight or flight" (Smith, Allen, and Danley 2007). Dealing with racial injuries is very hard indeed, but it is even harder when one has neither the space nor the language to fight back largely because many of the techniques of racial domination in post–Civil Rights America are seemingly nonracial or institutionalized.

Fourth, most minority graduate students and junior faculty of color struggle for survival almost literally. White colleagues and students regard our insistence that race matters as "political." Hence, we suffer in courses where race is not appreciated as a central factor; we struggle to get published in journals controlled by color-blind Whites; and we may feel forced to behave in a manner to make White students and colleagues feel "comfortable" and avoid being labeled anti-White. This trend of denying the salience of race started a long time ago but has intensified in this "postracial" moment because many White sociologists can now tell us, "Come on, I voted for Obama, so . . ." preempting or at least seriously circumscribing the possibility of challenging racial stratification as something relevant for analysis, discussion, and debate.

Fifth, the postracial turn—and the turn began not in 2008 but in the 1970s—has produced, as I mentioned, a new kind of minority politician as well as a new kind of minority scholar: the conservative or neoliberal minority scholar. In contrast to the trailblazers who "integrated" sociology in the late 1960s and 1970s, these minority scholars lack a connection to social activism and movements and believe their standing in life is purely meritocratic. This new kind of scholar, whether Black, brown, or Asian, tends to be well-regarded and well-compensated. As long as these scholars preach postracialism and blame minority folks for their standing in society, they are embraced. Their ilk, I predict, will grow in size and significance because they fit the postracial moment and provide sociology departments with the "chocolate look without the flavor."

Another segment of the postracial minority sociological community is the apolitical and apathetic minority student or faculty. Because so few of the post-1990 minorities who earned doctorates in sociology have experienced any major social movement, many are apolitical. The best of them are book-smart on race matters, but do not have sharp political instincts on how to deal with racial issues and situations. The worst are truly unaware and in desperate need of a wake-up call. This is making our collective situation increasingly worse because mobilizing people who for various reasons have internalized the racial logic and practices of the moment—in Gramsci's conceptualization, they are *consenting* to their domination (Gramsci 1992)—is difficult. What are some prophetic responses to these opportunities and challenges?

What Is to Be Done in the Nation as Well as in Sociological Obamerica?

In this curious moment when many believe the election and reelection of a Black man[30] as the 44th president of the nation are clear and convincing evidence of racial progress, race matters have in truth become more complex and problematic for most of us. The Black majority, the working class that has been under attack since the 1970s,[31] is facing today perhaps its deepest crisis. Maligned and forgotten, today they are all but invisible because very few people are talking about their specific predicament because as skewed and ethnocentric as the debates often were about female-headed households, the underclass, and other disenfranchised people, we were at least talking about such groups. Instead we are all still mesmerized by having our first Black president. Neither Whites nor Blacks seem to want to talk about race seriously. Most Whites have all but absolved themselves from the "sin of racism" and many Blacks, in their understandable but problematic nationalistic joy ("We have a Black president."), do not want to push any discussion[32] on this front because that would alienate most Whites and threaten black political progress. The silence on race produced by this peculiar pact between Whites and Blacks[33] is hurting all of us because it is quickly cementing the color-blind ideology that has been at play in the nation for a while, thus further reducing the space for racial engagements in the public square. Although we are not yet like Latin American countries—polities where there is limited discursive space to discuss race—this moment is pivotal in determining whether we will become like them or refocus our attention on the centrality of race in America. And President Obama's reelection in 2012 has reinforced postracial beliefs among Whites and many Blacks. As a Black man who grew up in Puerto Rico where one can hardly talk about race,[34] I fear this possibility and, accordingly, propose here some things we might consider doing in our effort to derail the fast-moving postracial train.

In the nation at large we need nothing short of a "revolution" of mind, practice, and perhaps even spirit to get out of the rabbit hole in which we find ourselves. We need to revitalize and retool our race-based organizations inside and outside of academia to deal effectively with the new racial regime we face and the seemingly "nonracial" racial practices that reproduce White privilege. The civil rights organizations—although I think they should be called "racial equality organizations"—need to be either restructured or replaced altogether as they have become too professional, too legalistic, too clubby, and are they still fighting the monsters of the past rather than the seemingly gentile enemy of the present.[35] But more pressing than anything we can do organizationally is the fierce urgency of a radical transformation of our politics now. We must get busy once again and challenge the powers that be, even if they are Black. Otherwise we are condemned to remain in this wonderland where nothing is what it seems to be. The ostensible beauty of having a Black man "in charge" is becoming a curse for people of color because the racial-class order seems as firm as ever. We need to recognize what should be obvious: leaders should be judged not by the color of their skin but by the content of their politics. By this criterion, Obama's politics have not been pro-minority, and we, as any of the other members of his base,[36] have the right to demand change in which we can truly believe. Furthermore, in academia, given the censorship and affronts we endure, we now must strive to create our own journals, networks, and alternative centers of power. Although we must continue working within organizations such as ASA and challenge the "powers that be" there, we must remember that the fundamental changes we have forced in sociology and in academia have been the product of struggles that usually began on the outside and were translated inside.[37] For Black sociologists, ABS has traditionally been an important organization for learning, networking, developing, and finding support. Unfortunately our organization has been declining in significance for some time and must return to its radical, prophetic origins to remain the watchdog defending Black and minority interests in sociology.

In terms of our research, we must continue performing critical analyses of how race matters nowadays in schools, the criminal justice system, and in other domains (Pager and Shepherd 2008; Smith 1995). But we must do something else. We must work harder to address the White side of so-called race relations. We must move from racial defense to racial offense. Although we must continue doing "defensive work" to show we are not the problem, we need to show how those who rule society accomplish their domination. We must, for instance, perform ethnographic studies of whiteness and show how Whites think, behave, and live. This "offensive work" should also be done in our own discipline and departments. We must examine how racial kinship explains Whites' collective standing and guarantees a higher likelihood of success for them in sociology—even those with limited talents. We must speak out about racial practices and racial situations and the people involved in them such as "open searches" that usually only yield White candidates as well as the racist labeling most minority scholars endure regardless of their theoretical and political stand.

Doing all these things will not be easy, but nothing we have attained in America has ever been easy. I realize that some of the specific things I have outlined (e.g., outing the racial practices and naming the practitioners) are dangerous, particularly for young and untenured Black sociologists and readers unaccustomed to activism. But this is what being prophetic is all about. The road to equality must begin with us behaving as true equal and free members of society and that means not only expecting respect from Whites, but also demanding it. We must disrupt, once again, the happy image of the sociological family and the color-blind society, particularly when we know problems exist. Therefore, the way we get out of our rabbit hole is by fighting our way out Old Testament style—an eye for an eye, a tooth for a tooth—combining a little bit of Martin Luther King with a lot of Malcolm X in our repertoire of collective action as prophetic leaders. On this the sage words of Frederick Douglass written more than 100 years ago still ring true today: "Power concedes nothing without a demand. It never did and it never will" (Douglass 1857:22).

Notes

1. This is an adaptation of a presentation by Bonilla-Silva for the Opening Plenary Panel at the ABS meeting in Atlanta, Georgia, August 11, 2010.

2. I refer to President Obama's administration as "Obamerica" by which I mean that he was not elected under normal political circumstances, but rather was the product of traditional electoral politics mixed with Black nationalism and rock star–like adulation for Obama from many Whites. He was not, as some liberal and progressive commentators have suggested, the product of a social movement. Instead, he raised more money than any other politician, through the same channels and from the same people, and worked his campaign no different than Presidents Bush or Clinton did in their time.

3. I started my left-oriented criticism of President Obama in early 2008. I have written articles and chapters on the matter and given speeches in multiple venues. For an extended discussion, see chap. 10 in the third edition of my book *Racism without Racists*, "Will Racism Disappear in *Obamerica*? The Sweet (but Deadly) Enchantment of Color Blindness in Black Face" (2010a).

4. Although some may be offended by my use of this phrase from Sarah Palin, we must at least admit that the phrase is funny and I think accurate if recalibrated.

5. For a full discussion of "the new racism," see chap. 4 in Bonilla-Silva, *White Supremacy and Racism in the Post–Civil Rights Era* (2001). See also Robert Smith's *Racism in the Post–Civil Rights Era: Now You See It, Now You Don't* (1995).

6. For books with interview data on this period that show this change see Judith Caditz, *White Liberals in Transition* (1976), and Bob Blauner, *Black Lives, White Lives* (1989).

7. Two books on this broad subject are Jennifer L. Hochschild, *Facing Up to the American Dream* (1995), and Martin Gilens, *Why Americans Hate Welfare* (1999).

8. For a detailed discussion of these three aspects, see chap. 4 in Bonilla-Silva (2001).

9. See Manning Marable, "Jackson and the Rise of the Rainbow Coalition" (1989).

10. Political scientists have been exploring this trend, which they call "deracialization," for a while. See, for example, Georgia Persons, ed., *Dilemmas of Black Politics: Issues of Leadership and Strategy* (2009).

11. Still one of the best books on the "power structure" of America and how the system works is the classic yet magnificently updated book by William G. Domhoff, *Who Rules America? Power, Politics, and Social Change* (2006).

12. For a full elaboration of my arguments, see chap. 9 in the third edition of my book *Racism without Racists* (2010a).

13. Their claim was that the school was failing the students. Obama said, "If a school continues to fail its students year after year after year, if it doesn't show signs of improvement, then there's got to be a sense of accountability." He failed to mention that 96% of the students in this school are eligible for free or reduced lunches and that 65% of students are Latino. More important, the firing coincided with a labor dispute based on the district demanding teachers work and extra twenty-five minutes per day without compensation.

14. See Sunlen Miller and Yunji de Nies, "Obama: Sherrod 'Deserves Better' for 'Bogus Controversy'" (2010).

15. I spell America with a "k" to denote both racial progress (we used to be "Amerikkka") as well as the continuing significance of racism. See *Racism without Racists* (2010a) for my comments on this.

16. Sociologists have tried since the late 1920s to mimic economics by quantifying our discipline, severing ties with anthropology, and upholding value neutrality. Sporadically we have seen outbursts in the discipline and calls for doing sociology "for the people" or, in its most recent version, for a "public sociology." Every time we have had these rebellions within, the mainstream (represented by the sociological elite—the top 100 or so sociologists in mostly "top" academic departments who rule the discipline) has fought back and reestablished "sociological order." Please see the debates for and against public sociology in the pages of the ASA newsletter, *Footnotes* (O'Neill 2008), in books by Nichols (2007), and Clawson (2007), and in Burawoy's (2005) ASA presidential address.

17. See Lisa Wade's 2008 article; Bill Cosby and Alvin F. Poussaint, *Come On People: On the Path from Victims to Victors* (2007); Abigail and Stephan Thernstrom, *No Excuses: Closing the Racial Gap in Learning* (2003).

18. For instance, the nationalist ideology typical of Latin American regimes has deepened and is now upheld and promulgated by our first Black president (comments such as "There's not a Black America, a White America . . ." and "I am my brother's keeper . . ."). In his 2004 Democratic National Convention speech delivered in Boston we see how he uses this language of nationalism to minimize racial separation (Transcript 2004).

19. In Afghanistan and Pakistan, the President talked tough to Iran, Venezuela, and Cuba while doing and saying little about Israel's aggressions in the Middle East, and left many of Bush's terror policies in place—from Guantanamo, to extractions, to fascist policies at home against presumed "terrorists."

20. How bad is our memory? Have we forgotten how much backlash President Clinton got from *Fox News* and other people and organizations of the same ilk?

21. Political scientists have assumed Black unity (that is, racial unity) across class based on the notion of common or "linked fate" (see Dawson 1994). But agreeing on a number of items in a survey is not the same as truly sharing a class or race interest. The "Black elite" has always had its own class and race interests often against those of the "Black majority." See books by Manning Marable such as *How Capitalism Underdeveloped Black America: Problems in Race, Political Economy and Society* (1983), and Michael Katz, *The "Underclass" Debate: Views from History* (1993*)*, especially the chapter dealing with the Black elite.

22. See chap. 6, "Are All Whites Refined Archie Bunkers? An Examination of White Progressives" in Bonilla-Silva, *Racism without Racists* (2010a). See also Tyrone Forman, "Conceptual and Methodological Challenges to Studying Racism and Prejudice in the Post–Civil Rights Era" (forthcoming).

23. Professors Vincent Hutchings and Tom Pettigrew delivered papers at the conference "Still Two Nations?" at Duke University in March 2009 on their survey work on Barack Obama and the 2008 election. Whites who supported Obama were not "beyond race." They used questions that have been used over the last 30 years to assess racial attitudes. Interestingly, Whites who voted for Obama were just slightly less "prejudiced" than other Whites. A similar proportion of Whites agreed with typical stereotypes of Blacks, but Whites who voted for Obama were more likely to hide this fact. (The survey Professor Hutchings used included an experiment where the mode of administration was varied randomly—face-to-face or self-administered—which allowed the examination of whether respondents report their beliefs consistently.)

24. I have argued that most colleges and universities in the United States that present themselves as universal, neutral sites of knowledge production and transmission are in fact HWCUs. As such, these colleges have a history, demography, curriculum, traditions, climate, and visual and aesthetic ecology that reflect and reproduce whiteness.

25. If a neighborhood or a school is 90% White, we correctly label it a White or mostly White neighborhood or school. However, we still avoid extending the courtesy and clarity of this analysis to sociology departments. It is time we honestly call White departments "White" and move on.

26. Many White sociologists believe that sociologists of color are overpaid. I have been told this on two occasions by people with very different politics and motivations. In truth, the average minority sociologist receives less compensation than the average White sociologist. And if the "exceptional" minority sociologist makes a lot of money, it is because Whites rule the business and decide how few of us are "qualified." They in fact create a classical market situation of a great demand and a limited supply making these "commodities" highly valuable and desirable. But in the end, we must always remember that for every highly paid sociologist, there are hundreds of others making very little money, enduring poor working conditions, and framed as "undeserving" and "unqualified" minorities.

27. For a more elaborate discussion of these practices, see my "The Real 'Race Problem' in American Sociology: The Power of White Rule in Our Discipline," a keynote presentation at the Southern Sociological Society meeting in April 2011.

28. I am aware that class and gender divide the White family and that, therefore, not all members receive the "wages of whiteness" (Roediger 2007). The point here, however, is sociological and one has to look at the average experience and the likelihood of White and non-White sociologists receiving protection from the clan.

29. This may not be the case for White scholars such as Joe R. Feagin, Howard Winant, and Stephen Steinberg who are viewed by many members of the sociological elite as biased, not objective, and "political" sociologists.

30. We always have to keep in mind that Whites do not view Obama as a "typical" Black man, but as an "exceptional" Black man. And Obama and his team did not do much to challenge this perception. In fact, they cherished it because it made him more palatable for Whites.

31. After the Moynihan Report in the mid-1960s, Moynihan joined the Nixon administration and articulated a policy of "benign neglect" that has been in place since.

32. The only discussion on racism occurring today is about the Tea Party and the birther movement. But as I mentioned above, these are not the main engines moving the racial apparatus of America. Hence, the more we focus our attention on these people, the more we leave the real masters of the game untouched.

33. I have not included in this discussion Latinos and Asians, but would like to say a few things about these two segments of the population in this note. Some Latino leaders and the Congressional Hispanic Caucus have been pushing the Obama administration concertedly to deliver on its promise of immigration reform. Some even threatened not to support his health-care bill if he did not put an immigration reform bill in Congress (see Rivlin 2010). The Latino support for Obama was strong in both 2008 and 2012 (about 70%) (Marrero 2011). Asian Americans have been trending Democratic since 1992, when George H. Bush won 55% of their vote (Lee and Ramakrishnan 2012). Obama received about 62% of their vote in 2008 (and similarly in 2012), and based on comments by members of the Congressional Asian Pacific American Caucus after Obama's State of the Union address in 2011, it seems he has their strong support. See the news release by the chair of their caucus (Honda 2011).

34. Interested parties on some of my thoughts on race in Puerto Rico may check, "Reflections about Race by a *Negrito Acomplejao*" (2010b).

35. On this point, I urge you to read chap. 6, "The Fire This Time," in Alexander (2010).

36. Labor unions and representatives of the lesbian, gay, bisexual, and transgender (LGBT) community have been challenging President Obama for some time demanding that he take a stronger stance on their behalf. The LGBT community has been able to extract the repeal of the Don't Ask, Don't Tell policy in the military and, more recently, instructed his Department of Justice not to defend the constitutionality of the Defense of Marriage Act in Courts. Labor unions have been quite vocal about Obama's limited response to the Republican attempt to stymie unions legislatively in states. Obama's response to the Republican attempt to crush unions legislatively in states was timid and, as

I finish this chapter, I believe Obama will be forced to be more proactive and follow-up on the promise he made to unions in a 2007 campaign speech from Spartanburg, S.C. With regard to demands of the LGBT community, Obama has since responded by openly supporting same-sex marriage. (In the 2007 campaign speech, President Obama said the following: "And understand this: If American workers are being denied their right to organize and collectively bargain when I'm in the White House, I'll put on a comfortable pair of shoes myself. I'll walk on that picket line with you as president of the United States." See article by Amanda Terkel in the *Huffington Post*, "Wisconsin Protests: Labor Protesters Call on Obama to Join Them in Madison," posted on February 18, 2011, at http://www.huffingtonpost.com/2011/02/18/wisconsin-protesters-call-on-obama_n_825361.htm.)

37. On the history of ABS see Blackwell (1974); see also Conyers (1992).

References

Alexander, Michelle. 2010. *The New Jim Crow: Mass Incarceration in the Age of Colorblindness.* New York: New Press.

Aranda, Elizabeth M. 2007. *Emotional Bridges to Puerto Rico: Migration, Return Migration, and the Struggles of Incorporation.* Lanham, MD: Rowman and Littlefield.

Blackwell, James E. 1974. "Role Behavior in a Corporate Structure: Black Sociologists in ASA." Pp. 341–67 in *Black Sociologists: Historical and Contemporary Perspectives,* edited by J. E. Blackwell and M. Janowitz. Chicago: University of Chicago Press.

Blauner, Bob. 1989. *Black Lives, White Lives: Three Decades of Race Relations in America.* Berkeley: University of California Press.

Bonilla-Silva, Eduardo. 2001. *White Supremacy and Racism in the Post-Civil Rights Era.* Boulder, CO: Lynne Rienner Publishers.

———. 2009. "Are the Americas 'Sick with Racism' or Is It a Problem at the Poles? A Reply to Christina A. Sue." *Ethnic and Racial Studies* 32(6):1071–82.

———. 2010a. *Racism without Racists: Color-Blind Racism and the Persistence of Racial Inequality in the United States.* Lanham, MD: Rowman and Littlefield.

———. 2010b. "Reflections about Race by a *Negrito Acomplejao.*" Pp. 445–52 in *The Afro-Latin@ Reader: History and Culture in the United States,* edited by M. J. Román and J. Flores. Durham, NC: Duke University Press.

———. 2011. "The Real 'Race Problem' in American Sociology: The Power of White Rule in Our Discipline." Keynote speech at Southern Sociological Society meeting, Jacksonville, FL, April 6–9.

Bonilla-Silva, Eduardo and Cedric Herring. 1999. " 'We'd Love to Hire Them, But . . .': The Underrepresentation of Sociologists of Color and Its Implications." *Footnotes* 27(3):1.

Bonilla-Silva, Eduardo and Tukufu Zuberi. 2008. *White Logic, White Methods: Racism and Methodology.* Lanham, MD: Rowman and Littlefield.

Bourdieu, Pierre and Loci Wacquant. 1999. "On the Cunning of Imperialist Reason." *Theory, Culture and Society* 16 (1):41.

Burawoy, M. 2005. "For Public Sociology." *American Sociological Review,* 70(1):4–28.

Caditz, Judith. 1976. *White Liberals in Transition: Current Dilemmas of Ethnic Integration.* New York: Spectrum.

Clawson, D. 2007. *Public Sociology: Fifteen Eminent Sociologists Debate Politics and the Profession in the Twenty-First Century.* Berkeley: University of California Press.

Cohen, Patricia. 2010. "'Culture of Poverty Makes a Comeback." *New York Times,* October 18, p. A1.

Conyers, James E. 1992. "The Association of Black Sociologists: A Descriptive Account from an 'Insider.'" *American Sociologist* 23(1):49.

Cosby, Bill and Alvin F. Poussaint. 2007. *Come On People: On the Path from Victims to Victors.* Nashville, TN: Thomas Nelson.

Dawson, Michael C. 1994. *Behind the Mule: Race and Class in African American Politics.* Princeton, NJ: Princeton University Press.

Domhoff, William G. 2006. *Who Rules America? Power, Politics, and Social Change.* 5th ed. New York: McGraw-Hill.

Douglass, Frederick. 1857. *Two Speeches by Frederick Douglass.* Rochester, NY: C. P. Dewey Manuscript Division.

Duster, Troy. 2003. "Buried Alive: The Concept of Race in Science." Pp. 258–77 in *Genetic Nature/Culture: Anthropology and Science beyond the Two-Culture Divide,* edited by A. H. Goodman, D. Heath, and M. S. Lindee. Berkeley: University of California Press.

Embrick, David G. Forthcoming. "Corporate Diversity in the Post–Civil Rights Era: Colorblindness and the Diversity Ideology." *Critical Sociology.*

Feagin, J. R. and M. P. Sikes. 1994. *Living with Racism: The Black Middle-Class Experience.* Boston: Beacon Press.

Flanders, Laura. 2011. "The F Word: Capital or Community in Wisconsin." *Nation,* March 1. Retrieved March 3, 2011 (http://www.thenation.com/blog/158942/f-word-capital-or-community-wisconsin).

Forman, Tyrone. Forthcoming. "Conceptual and Methodological Challenges to Studying Racism and Prejudice in the Post-Civil Rights Era." In *Racism and Methodology,* edited by E. Bonilla-Silva and T. Zuberi.

Foucault, Michel. 1970. *The Order of Things: An Archaeology of the Human Sciences.* New York: Pantheon Books.

Fujimura, Joan, Troy Duster, and Ramya Rajagopalan. 2008. "Race, Genetics, and Disease: Questions of Evidence, Matters of Consequence." *Social Studies of Science* 38(5):643–56.

Gilens, Martin. 1999. *Why Americans Hate Welfare: Race, Media, and the Politics of Antipoverty Policy.* Chicago: University of Chicago Press.

Gramsci, Antonio. 1992. *Prison Notebooks.* New York: Columbia University Press.

Guo, Guang. 2008. "Introduction to the Special Issue on Society and Genetics." *Sociological Methods and Research* 37:159–63.

Hochschild, Jennifer L. 1995. Fac*ing Up to the American Dream: Race, Class, and the Soul of the Nation.* Princeton, NJ: Princeton University Press.

Honda, Mike. 2011. "CAPAC Response to President Obama's State of the Union Address." Retrieved February 28, 2011 (http://www.cga.ct.gov/asianamerican/Press%20Releases/CAPAC%20response%20to%20President%20Obama's%20State%20of%20the%20Union%20Address.pdf).

Horton, Hayward Derrick. 2002. "Rethinking American Diversity: Conceptual and Theoretical Challenges for Racial and Ethnic Demography." Pp. 261–78 in *American Diversity: A Demographic Challenge for the Twenty-First Century*, edited by N. A. Denton and S. E. Tolnay. Albany, NY: SUNY Press.

Hutchings, Vincent. 2009. Paper presented at the conference "Still Two Nations?" March 20–21, Duke University, Durham, NC.

Katz, Michael B. 1993. *The "Underclass" Debate: Views from History.* Princeton, NJ: Princeton University Press.

Lee, Taeku and Karthick Ramakrishnan. 2012. "Asian Americans Turn Democratic." *Los Angeles Times*, November 23. Retrieved November 7, 2013 (http://articles.latimes.com/2012/nov/23/opinion/la-oe-lee-asian-american-voters-20121123).

Lewis, Oscar. 1963. "The Culture of Poverty." *Society* 1(1):17–19.

Marable, Manning. 1983. *How Capitalism Underdeveloped Black America: Problems in Race, Political Economy and Society.* Boston: South End Press.

Marable, Manning. 1989. "Jackson and the Rise of the Rainbow Coalition." *New Left Review* (149):3–44.

Marrero, Pilar. 2011. "Latino Voters Continue Supporting Obama." *Impre Media.* Retrieved February 28, 2011 (http://www.impre.com/noticias/2011/2/14/latino-voters-continue-support-239269-1.html#commentsBlock).

Massey, Douglas S. and Robert J. Sampson. 2009. "The Moynihan Report Revisited: Lessons and Reflections after Four Decades." In *Annals of the American Academy of Political and Social Science*, vol. 621, edited by D. S. Massey and R. J. Sampson. Thousand Oaks, CA: Sage.

Miller, Sunlen and Yunji de Nies. 2010. "Obama: Sherrod 'Deserves Better' for 'Bogus Controversy.'" *z*, July 29. Retrieved March 3, 2011 (http://blogs.abcnews.com/politicalpunch/2010/07/obama-sherrod-deserves-better-for-bogus-controversy.html).

Nichols, L. T. 2007. *Public Sociology: The Contemporary Debate.* New Brunswick, NJ: Transaction.

O'Neill, Karen M. 2008. "Public Sociology and Participatory Action Research in Rural Sociology." *Footnotes. American Sociological Association.* 36(9):1.

Pager, Devah and Hana Shepherd. 2008. "The Sociology of Discrimination: Racial Discrimination in Employment, Housing, Credit, and Consumer Markets." *Annual Review of Sociology* 34:181–209.

Paulson, Amanda. 2010. "Rhode Island School to Rehire Fired Teachers, Shelving Drastic Plan," May 17. Retrieved November 7, 2013 (http://www.csmonitor.com/USA/Education/2010/0517/Rhode-Island-school-to-rehire-fired-teachers-shelving-drastic-plan)

Persons, Georgia, ed. 2009. *Dilemmas of Black Politics: Issues of Leadership and Strategy.* New York: HarperCollins.

Pettigrew, Thomas F. 2009. Paper presented at the conference "Still Two Nations?" March 20–21, Duke University, Durham, NC.

Rivlin, Douglas. 2010. "Stakes Getting Higher for Obama, Latino Voters, and Immigration." *News Junkie Post*, March 12. Retrieved March 3, 2011 (http://newsjunkiepost.com/2010/03/12/stakes-getting-higher-for-obama-latino-voters-and-immigration/).

Rodriguez, Dylan. 2010. *Suspended Apocalypse: White Supremacy, Genocide, and the Filipino Condition.* Minneapolis: University of Minnesota Press.

Roediger, David R. 2007. *The Wages of Whiteness: Race and the Making of the American Working Class.* London: Verso.

Sahadi, Jeanne. 2010. "Tax Cut Deal: How It Affects You." *CNN.* Retrieved March 3, 2011 (http://money.cnn.com/2010/12/15/news/economy/tax_deal_what_is_in_bill/index.htm).

Sampson, R. J., J. D. Morenoff and T. Gannon-Rowley. 2002. "Assessing 'Neighborhood Effects': Social Processes and New Directions in Research." *Annual Review of Sociology* 28:443–78.

Sampson, Robert J. and Stephen W. Raudenbush. 2004. "Seeing Disorder: Neighborhood Stigma and the Social Construction of 'Broken Windows.'" *Social Psychology Quarterly* 67(4):319–42.

Scahill, J. (2013). *Dirty Wars: The World Is a Battlefield.* New York: Nation Books.

Simpson, Ida Harper and Richard L. Simpson. 1994. "The Transformation of the American Sociological Association." *Sociological Forum* 9(2):259.

Slevin, Peter. 2010. "Deportation of Illegal Immigrants Increases under Obama Administration." *Washington Post*, July 26. Retrieved March 1, 2011 (http://www.washingtonpost.com/wp-dyn/content/article/2010/07/25/AR2010072501790.html).

Small, M. L., D. Harding and M. Lamont. 2010. "Reconsidering Culture and Poverty." In *Annals of the Academy of Political and Social Science*, vol. 629, edited by Harding, David J., Michèle Lamont, and Mario Luis Small. Thousand Oaks, CA: Sage.

Smith, Robert Charles. 1995. *Racism in the Post–Civil Rights Era: Now You See It, Now You Don't.* Albany, NY: SUNY Press.

Smith, William A., Walter R. Allen and Lynette L. Danley. 2007. "'Assume the Position . . . You Fit the Description': Psychosocial Experiences and Racial Battle Fatigue among African American Male College Students." *American Behavioral Scientist* 51(4):551–78.

Steinberg, Stephen. 2011. "Poor Reason: Culture Still Doesn't Explain Poverty." *Boston Review*, January 13. Retrieved March 3, 2011 (http://www.bostonreview.net/BR36.1/steinberg.php).

Strauss, Valerie. 2011. "Obama's Mistimed Miami School Visit—with Jeb Bush." *Washington Post*, March 2. Retrieved November 7, 2013 (http://voices. washingtonpost.com/answer-sheet/school-turnaroundsreform/obamas-questionable-trip-to-mi.html)

Terkel, Amanda. 2011. "Wisconsin Protests: Labor Protesters Call on Obama to Join Them in Madison." *Huffington Post*, February 18. Retrieved February 27, 2011 (http://www.huffingtonpost.com/2011/02/18/wisconsin-protesters-call-on-obama_n_825361.html).

Thernstrom, Abigail M. and Stephan Thernstrom. 2003. *No Excuses: Closing the Racial Gap in Learning*. New York: Simon and Schuster.

"Transcript: Illinois Senate Candidate Barack Obama." 2004. *Washington Post*, July 27. Retrieved March 8, 2011 (http://www.washingtonpost.com/wp-dyn/articles/A19751–2004Jul27.html).

Wade, Lisa. 2008. "CNN Pundit: Obama Won, Therefore Racism Is no Longer a Problem." November 7. Retrieved March 4, 2011 (http://thesocietypages. org/socimages/2008/11/07/cnn-pundit-obama-won-therefore-racism-is-no-longer-a-problem/).

White House Press Office. 2009. "President Obama's Message for Students." Retrieved March 3, 2011 (http://www.Whitehouse.gov/the_press_office/Remarks-by-the-President-in-a-National-Address-to-Americas-School children/).

2

~

Am I My Brother's and My Sister's Keeper?

W. E. B. Du Bois's New Talented Tenth

EARL WRIGHT II

University of Cincinnati

In 1903 William Edward Burghardt Du Bois penned a seminal statement on Black American leadership. Du Bois's theory of the talented tenth champions the development of a cadre of Black Americans willing to engage in ethical leadership while sacrificing their personal ambitions to improve the social, economic, and physical condition of the members of their race. While the theory mandates members of this fraternity to be ethical and self-sacrificing, historically, the talented tenth have been misconstrued as college-educated persons who, after obtaining their degrees, become elitist, self-serving, and largely unconcerned with the plight of ordinary Black Americans and leery of involving themselves in situations that threaten their economic stability. This misinterpretation of Du Bois's challenge to his fraternity members is the impetus for this endeavor. This inquiry (1) highlights the discrepancies between the ideal type talented tenth member and the many historical misinterpretations; (2) highlights Du Bois's revised 1948 talented tenth theory; and

(3) extends his theory on leadership beyond its present state. While previous explorations into this area highlight the influence of Alexander Crummell, Frederick Douglass, and Henry L. Morehouse on the development of Du Bois's philosophy of leadership, this investigation departs from the existing literature with its emphasis on misperceptions of Du Bois's theory on Negro leadership (Dennis 1977; Gates and West 1996). By reconstructing Du Bois's talented tenth theory, I draw on the prophetic tradition in Black sociology of systematically uncovering truths and correcting enduring misconceptions. What follows is an examination of the origin of Du Bois's theory of the talented tenth.

Henry L. Morehouse's *Tenth Man*

In 1896 Henry L. Morehouse, the man for whom Morehouse College in Atlanta, Georgia, is named, wrote the article "The Talented Tenth." Morehouse's article, albeit written years prior to their public sparring, can be viewed as an attempt by someone situated in the midst of the ideological debate between Booker T. Washington and Du Bois to forge common ground between the giant figures of Black American economic and intellectual life. While Morehouse expresses no preference for either vocational or liberal arts education in his essay, he suggests that the exceptional persons within a society should serve as its leaders. Morehouse (1896), articulating his ideas on leadership seven years prior to Du Bois's similarly titled essay, states, "Industrial education is good for the nine; the common English branches are good for the nine; that tenth man ought to have the best opportunities for making the most of himself for humanity and God" (p. 1). The lynchpin of Morehouse's talented tenth is the development of a cadre of leaders, regardless of educational dogma, who will embrace the challenge of bettering the social, economic, and physical condition of humankind while guided by a spiritual base. Morehouse's vision of leadership is captured in his proclamation that the tenth man should be the one to whom "the many look [to] for suggestion and advice in important matters" (p. 1). Clearly, for Morehouse, his idea of the tenth man rests on the belief that there must be a critical mass of persons who are prepared and willing to serve in positions of leadership while dedicated to improving the social condition of their compatriots. This idea is reflective of the social gospel movement of the era. "The Social Gospel . . . emphasized the human aspects of Christianity . . . [and was guided by the idea that] the salvation of society replaced the salvation of an individual soul as the principal religious goal" (Chudacoff and Smith 181). For Morehouse, and later Du Bois, the salvation of society should be led by exceptional persons whom they label the talented tenth. While it is common knowledge that Du Bois borrows the title of his cadre of race leaders from Morehouse, the 1896 essay by the former corresponding secretary of Northern Baptist Home Missions Society is also useful because it clarifies various misconceptions concerning Du Bois's theory.

First, historically, many had criticized Du Bois's theory on leadership as elitist because some have literally interpreted his phrase "talented tenth" to refer to leadership of the race by an actual 10% of the Black population. Nowhere in Du Bois's writings on the talented tenth does he refer to leadership of the race being shepherded by an actual 10% of the Black population. As the passages above evidences, Du Bois clearly borrows Morehouse's phrase of "the tenth man" as the label for his cadre of leaders. Du Bois not only borrows the notion of the tenth man from Morehouse, but he also does so without regard to establishing a specific number of members eligible for admission into his fraternity. Second, despite historical suggestions to the contrary, Du Bois, similar to the position Morehouse took, does not completely oppose Booker T. Washington's educational philosophy. Instead, he desires a balance between liberal arts and vocational education programs. Du Bois ([1903] 1994) refutes the notion that he completely opposes vocational education in *The Souls of Black Folk*:

> The bright ideals of the past,—physical freedom, political power, the training of brains and hands,—all these in turn have waxed and waned, until even the last grows dim and overcast. Are they all wrong,—all false? No, not that, but each alone was over-simple and incomplete. (P. 6)

Du Bois, an ardent promoter of the liberal arts, did not support the exclusive development of either education program. As indicated above, he championed a balanced approach to education that awarded equal respect to both philosophies. While Du Bois does not oppose the notion of vocational education for the Negro, he contends that a pragmatic system of developing a lineage of holistically trained teachers and scholars grounded in the liberal arts must be established before advancing to a more comprehensive focus on vocational education. Toward this end, Du Bois ([1903] 1970) states in his talented tenth article:

> I would not deny . . . the paramount necessity of teaching the Negro to work . . . or seem to deprecate in the slightest

degree the important part industrial schools must play in the accomplishment of these ends, but I do say, and insist upon it, that it is industrialism drunk with its vision of success, to imagine that its own work can be accomplished without providing for the training of broadly cultured men and women to teach its own teachers, and to teach the teachers of the public schools. (P. 61)

With liberal arts education as the model, Du Bois suggests that the desired outcome of his educational paradigm is students of ethical character who will voluntarily engage in self-sacrificing leadership activities for the benefit of their race. After receiving this specific training, then, members of the talented tenth will be prepared to identify, confront, and ameliorate the social, economic, and physical challenges facing Blacks in America. Although Du Bois is open to the idea of forging more than one educational path to progress for Black Americans, we can surmise that he does not believe Washington shares this notion. Instead, Du Bois believes that he actively propagandizes against liberal arts education programs since, according to Washington ([1903] 1970), "It seems to me that too often mere book education leaves the Negro young man or woman in a weak position" (p. 22). The weak position that Washington may be alluding to is the employability of liberal arts–trained Blacks. While Washington wrestles with the question of whether employment opportunities are available for educated Negroes in the early 1900s, he is resolute in the belief that his vocational education program is ideal since its benefits are immediate employment opportunities and economic security.

Last, the lynchpin of Du Bois's theory on Negro leadership hinges on the willingness of the exceptional members of the race to engage in ethical and self-sacrificing leadership activities for the betterment of the race and society. This idea is also borrowed from Morehouse. Although Morehouse suggests the tenth man should engage in leadership activities to make life better for themselves and humanity in general, Du Bois's theory rests on a similar foundation but with specific regard to Blacks in America. This last point is addressed in detail later, but is essential in understanding the ideal type talented tenth member as proposed by Du Bois and the historical misinterpretations of his theory by subsequent scholars. In order to understand how some misinterpretations of Du Bois's theory evolved, we must review his stated objectives in the original talented tenth essay before outlining how his revised theory clarifies some misinterpretations.

'The Negro race, like all races,
is going to be saved by its exceptional men'

Du Bois's ([1903] 1970) objectives in his seminal essay on Negro leadership are "first to show from the past that the Talented Tenth as they have risen among American Negroes have been worthy of leadership; secondly, to show how these men may be educated and developed; and thirdly, to show their relation to the Negro problem" (p. 34). Du Bois, in fulfilling his first objective, identifies several men and women who, by virtue of their self-sacrificing and ethical leadership activities in defense of the human rights of Black Americans during the years of overt and pernicious American racism, prove themselves worthy of admittance into his fraternity. Notable first generation members of the talented tenth Du Bois lists include Alexander Crummell, Paul Cuffe, James Derham, Frederick Douglass, Lemuel Haynes, Sojourner Truth, David Walker, Phillis Wheatley, and Eli Whitney.

Historically, Du Bois's theory has been criticized as being exclusionary, elitist, and a society reserved for college-educated persons. Although Du Bois's second objective aggressively promotes a college education as the desired prerequisite for membership into the talented tenth, he does make allowances for those of exceptional ability to become members of this group despite not possessing postsecondary credentials, and in some cases, no formal education at all. Speaking directly to the talented tenth status bestowed on non–college-educated Black Americans such as Paul Cuffe, Frederick Douglass, Sojourner Truth, David Walker, and Phillis Wheatley, Du Bois ([1903] 1970) states:

> Too little notice has been taken of the work which the Talented Tenth among Negroes took in the great abolition crusade. . . . There was Purvis and Remond, Pennington and Highland Garnett, Sojourner Truth and Alexander Crummell, and above all, Frederick Douglass—what would the abolition movement have been without them? . . . Where were these [B]lack abolitionists trained? Some, like Frederick Douglass, were self-trained, but trained liberally; others . . . graduated from famous foreign universities. (P. 42)

This passage indicates that Du Bois knowingly admits into his fraternity men and women who lack college training, thus effectively debunking the long-held belief that membership into this group is based singularly on one's higher education credentials. Du Bois ardently believes the ideal member of the talented tenth should be college educated, however, more important than one's educational background is the inclusion of persons who have demonstrated exceptional ability and the willingness to be self-sacrificing and ethical leaders for their race. Support for this notion is gleaned from the first sentence of his classic text that reads, "The Negro race, like all races, is going to be saved by its exceptional men [and women]" (Du Bois [1903] 1970: 33). For many Black Americans, the means by which one demonstrated exceptional ability at the dawn of the twentieth century, in light of laws severely limiting or restricting the ability of Blacks to obtain education credentials, was through civil and human rights activities in defiance of insidious American apartheid. For example, men and women of exceptional ability such as Frederick Douglass and Sojourner Truth separated themselves from the masses through leadership activities directed at abolishing slavery and promoting human rights. This type of self-sacrifice in the face of potential physical and economic demise forms the very core of leadership Du Bois envisioned. Conclusively, one's admittance into the talented tenth is not singularly dependent on the acquisition of a college education, but, instead, on one's high accomplishments and willingness to engage in self-sacrificing and ethical leadership activities.

Du Bois's ([1903] 1970) third objective challenges the talented tenth to embrace their role in the struggle for the human rights of Blacks in America. He begins this section by asserting that the college-educated Negro "ought to be, the group leader, the man who sets the ideals of the community where he lives, directs its thoughts and heads its social movements" (p. 54). Although Du Bois highlights several immediate issues of concern to soon-to-be members of the talented tenth and simultaneously connects their relationship to the Negro problems, perhaps his most compelling data addressing why an exceptional cadre of Blacks serving in leadership positions is needed can be gleaned from some of the findings of the Atlanta University studies.

In January 1897, Du Bois began a 13-year tenure at Atlanta University where he directed the Atlanta University Studies on the Negro Problems. Although Atlanta University president Horace Bumstead and trustee George G. Bradford initiated the yearly investigations in 1895, the research program began its ascension toward becoming the first American school of sociology upon Du Bois's arrival (Wright 2002a; 2002b; 2002c; Wright and Calhoun 2006). Du Bois's research program at Atlanta University often uncovered data indicating the need for an educated cadre of Black Americans. For example, the 1898 Atlanta University publication, *Some Efforts of American Negroes for Their Own Betterment*, contains data indicating that Black Americans lost money to unscrupulous insurance companies who charged high principal and interest rates to Blacks since they were acutely aware that "the Freedman [was] noted for his effort to ward off accidents and a pauper's grave by insurance against sickness and death" (Du Bois 1898:19). According to Du Bois, a better educated Black populace would be less likely to succumb to such practices.

This philosophy is also evident in the 1899 Atlanta University publication, *The Negro in Business*. This study focuses on Black-owned businesses and readings of the data suggest that several Black entrepreneurs were vulnerable to racist Whites or deceitful Blacks who preyed on this relatively little-educated and exploitable population. Data indicate that of the twenty-five grocery store owners included in this investigation, only one had college training; nine had common school training; twelve could only read and write, but had no mathematic skills; and three had no education at all. For Du Bois, this case study provides sufficient evidence to support his belief that Black businesses should be controlled by liberal arts–trained persons who would be less likely than their peers to be victimized by deceitful and dishonest persons. While he argues that college-educated persons are the ideal choice to run the businesses discussed, Du Bois presents no data indicating that the businesspersons in the study had been duped out of any monies, nor does he conduct a follow-up investigation to that effect. Last, Du Bois believes an educated Black American populace would more efficiently and effectively operate the institutions within their community. Again, the 1898 study is instructive. In this inquiry Du Bois highlights the misuse of church funds that, if directed differently, could help uplift the Black American community. For example, the Nineteenth Street Baptist Church in Washington, D.C., reported a total 1895 income of $5,714.09. After expenses were subtracted the church was left with only $437. The data suggest that expenditures such as the $2,840 spent on building improvements were unnecessary and took away from the uplift mission of the church. A better use of the funds, according to Du Bois (1898), would include the establishment and support of much-needed social service programs such as orphanages and retirement homes for Black Americans.

Du Bois's principal objective in his original talented tenth essay is to provide a theory of leadership for Black Americans that can be used to improve the social, economic, and physical condition of the race. Ultimately, Du Bois's (1968) utopian vision of Black Americans dedicated to self-sacrifice and ethical leadership is betrayed by his beloved sons and daughters. This revelation leaves the renowned scholar disappointed in his select group of leaders whom he believed chose individual economic security over group uplift (Du Bois 1968). Contrary to criticisms leveled by Du Bois and subsequent scholars concerning the talented tenth's inability to fulfill the charge bestowed upon them, it is argued here that the talented tenth have been scapegoated for not providing leadership in their community because of the historic and inaccurate interchange of the terms "Black middle class" and "talented tenth."

'These criticisms [are] not fair to my meaning'

A popular criticism of the talented tenth is the notion that after obtaining a college education and ascending to middle- or and upper-class status they become primarily interested in their individual and familial condition with little regard to the masses of Black Americans in lower socioeconomic positions. This criticism is noteworthy insomuch as the term "talented tenth" has been historically and incorrectly used synonymously with the term "Black middle class" (referred to as BMC). Recent research suggests that accusations of elitism and adherence to rigid American individualism are more applicable to the BMC than talented tenth. Battle and Wright (2002), in the only quantitative test of the talented tenth theory to date, explore the notion that college-educated Black Americans reneged on the charge to engage in leadership activities in their community as Du Bois mandated. Key to answering this research question is their argument that "talented tenth" and "BMC" are not synonymous terms. According to the authors, the talented tenth, similar to Du Bois's ideal type, includes college-educated persons. The Black middle class refers to an individual's socioeconomic background, which encompasses education, income, occupation, or a combination thereof. Thus, according to the authors, one can be a member of the Black middle class without obtaining a college degree, but one cannot be a member of the talented tenth without a college degree. Battle and Wright (2002) conclude:

> [T]he multivariate findings of this investigation indicate that members of the talented tenth are currently and significantly engaged in political and community leadership activities in their respective communities. . . . These data indicate that the talented tenth are fulfilling Du Bois' charge to provide leadership for the masses, even in the presence of additional influences. (P. 670)

Battle and Wright effectively debunk the long-held notion that the talented tenth rejected their positions of leadership and abandoned the

Black community. According to the authors, and in defense of criticisms directed at Du Bois's cadre of leaders, the evidence suggests that the Black middle class actually abandoned leadership positions in the Black community, not Du Bois's talented tenth.

Aside from the questionable notion of its abandonment of the Black community, Du Bois's talented tenth has also been harshly criticized because many perceived that he wanted to create a Negro aristocracy. This accusation was a motivating factor in his decision to restate his theory on Negro leadership almost 50 years after his original essay. To criticisms that he desired his body of educated Blacks to be elitist and self-serving and that he was attempting to develop a Black aristocracy, Du Bois ([1948] 1980b) states, "neither of these criticisms were really fair to my meaning, although I can easily see today that it was perfectly natural for critics to draw these conclusions" (p. 1). Far from attempting to groom a brown-skinned cadre of individualistic-minded capitalists, what Du Bois actually has in mind was the amassing of a group of learned individuals who, although in positions of influence and relative power, will not regard themselves separate from the masses, but a part of the those prepared to fight for the human rights of Blacks in America. According to Du Bois ([1948] 1980b), "We [, the talented tenth,] did not regard ourselves as separate or superior to the masses, but rather as a part of the mass which was being equipted [*sic*] and armed for leadership and that leadership was of course for the benefit of the race" (p. 2). Du Bois even challenges the amusing notion that the talented tenth believed they were divinely selected to lead the Black community. He states ([1948] 1980b), "[the talented tenth] should be extremely humble[d] to think that by good fate they had the chance to be educated when others who deserved even more than they did, had no such opportunity" (p. 3). While Du Bois's 1948 rearticulation addresses several misconceptions of his theory, arguably, the most significant contribution of his revised theory of the talented tenth are the prerequisites for membership.

Prerequisites for talented tenth status include quality character and high ethical standards. Du Bois ([1948] 1980b) posits, "In this reorientation of my ideas, my pointing out the new knowledge necessary for leadership and new ideas of race and culture, there still remains that fundamental and basic requirement of character for any successful leadership toward great ideals" (p. 16). That members of the talented tenth, or those in any leadership position, possess quality character and high ethical standards is important to Du Bois because he believes an unethical leader can spoil a successful endeavor. Toward that end, Du Bois concludes that "honesty of character and purity of motive [are]

needed . . . without which no effort succeeds or deserves to succeed"
(p. 16). The "willingness to work and make personal sacrifice for solving
[the Negro] problems, [is] the first prerequisite [for the talented tenth]"
(Du Bois [1948] 1980a:3). Clearly, Du Bois calls on members of his
cadre to delay or forgo personal gains in favor of engaging in ethical
and self-sacrificing leadership activities for the race. Du Bois clearly states
this position in his 1948 rearticulation as he expresses dismay with some
members of his beloved group for not upholding this charge. Du Bois
([1948] 1980a) comes to a stark conclusion:

> I assumed that with knowledge [of the severity of the Negro
> problem], sacrifice would automatically follow. In my youth
> and idealism, I did not realize that selfishness is even more
> natural than sacrifice. I made the assumption of its wide
> availability because of the spirit of sacrifice learned in my
> mission school training. . . . It was from [my experience at
> Fisk University] that I assumed easily that educated people,
> in most cases, were going out into life to see how far they
> could better the world. (P. 3)

Du Bois's ([1948] 1980b) belief that most educated Black Americans had a duty to assist those less fortunate was instilled in him as an
undergraduate student at Fisk University. While at Fisk, Du Bois came
into contact with faculty who "developed in me, and I am sure the
majority of my fellow students, the idea of the Negro problem as being
an evangel, a gospel where chosen men were trained and armed, and
went out to take the leadership of the mass" (p. 2). Although Du Bois
fervently believes in his theory, he notes that his youth and naivety
prevented him from garnering a realistic assessment of the possible trappings of rigid American individualism and capitalism that were poised
to lure this group from its objective. Du Bois ([1948] 1980a) states:

> When I came out of college into the world of work I real-
> ized that it was quite possible that my plan of training a
> talented tenth might put in control and power a group of
> selfish, self-indulgent, well-to-do men, whose basic interest in
> solving the Negro problem was personal; personal freedom
> and unhampered enjoyment and use of the world, without
> any real care or certainly no arousing care as to what became
> of the real masses of American Negroes, or of the mass of
> any people. (P. 4)

Written several years before his public condemnation of the talent-ed tenth for their silence during his trial with the U.S. government, Du Bois ([1948] 1980a) foretells of the negative consequence of Black Americans becoming more concerned with ascending to middle-class status than engaging in ethical and self-sacrificing activities for the race: "My Talented Tenth, I could see, might result in a sort of interracial free-for-all, with the devil taking the hindmost and the foremost taking anything they could lay hands on" (p. 4).

Although some of Du Bois's talented tenth chose personal achieve-ments and rewards over self-sacrifice to help the race, he remained reso-lute in his belief that "the idea of the talented tenth was the idea of sacrifice for the mass of people who were worth the sacrifice and who were going to show the world what could be done by people who were released from slavery" (Du Bois [1948]1980b:3). Some 50 years after his original articulation, Du Bois recognized the need to provide a more coherent and applicable theory of the talented tenth. The result was a new theory on Negro leadership, which he called the "Doctrine of the Guiding Hundredth."

'Doctrine of the Guiding Hundredth'

In 1948 Du Bois unveiled his reexamined theory on Negro leadership. Describing his new theory, Du Bois ([1948]1980a) states:

> Here comes a new idea of a Talented Tenth: The concept of a group-leadership not simply educated and self-sacrificing but with [a] clear vision of present world conditions and dangers and conducting American Negroes to alliance with culture groups in Europe, America, Asia, and Africa, and looking toward a new culture. We can do it. We have the ability. The only question is, have we the will? (P. 11)

This new conceptualization extends the original charge bestowed on the talented tenth by combining the old principles of college educa-tion, self-sacrifice, and ethical leadership with new principles mandat-ing knowledge of world conditions and the development of alliances between Black Americans and the non-American world.

Du Bois's revised theory on Negro leadership, unlike his origi-nal articulation, proposes establishing a "talented tenth institute" to train potential members and serve as an organizational base for existing members. Such an organization will, according to Du Bois, provide members with an institutional base to promote a coherent and unified strategy for addressing issues of importance to Black Americans. Centralizing the mission and objectives of the talented tenth prevents individual members from engaging in fragmented and disjointed activities under the banner of the talented tenth. Instead, members will collectively engage in strategically designed and proactive campaigns to improve the social, economic, and physical condition of Blacks in America. Du Bois ([1948]1980a) argues that "a national organization of this sort must be prepared to use propaganda, make investigation, plan procedures and even finance projects" (p. 17). He also proposes creating "a directing council composed of educated and specifically trained experts in the main branches of the sciences and the main categories of human work, and a paid executive committee of five or six persons to carry out the program" (p. 11). Ideally, Du Bois champions establishing a new organization singularly focused on bettering the condition of Blacks in America through the development of self-sacrificing men and women of high ethical standards who embrace positions of leadership in their respective communities. However, after much consideration Du Bois ([1948] 1980a) concludes: "To launch such a scheme as a new organization would call for so much time, money and effort, that it would be more practical if an already existing body could be adapted to this work" (p. 11), prompting Du Bois to select Sigma Pi Phi, an existing exclusive fraternity of professional Black American men often referred to as the "Boule," to be the institutional home for his proposed institute. Du Bois briefly considered asking the collective of college-based Black American fraternal organizations to serve as hosts for his institute, but after some consideration he became firm in his selection of Sigma Pi Phi because it was a well-established fraternity of adult men that was not dominated by "rather youthful ideals of the mis-called college spirit" (p. 11). Du Bois was poised to turn over the training of his cadre of Negro leaders to Sigma Pi Phi despite deep concerns.

During a speech at the 44th national convention of Sigma Pi Phi in 1948, Du Bois reveals his new theory on Negro leadership and urges members of the organization to take an active role in developing this program and recruiting and training young members of the talented tenth for service in their respective communities. Du Bois, despite requesting assistance from the Boule in establishing the new talented tenth, delivers a speech highly critical of the aristocratic culture of Sigma Pi Phi. Referring to the elitism of the fraternity, Du Bois ([1948] 1980a) says:

> What the guiding idea of Sigma Pi Phi was, I have never been
> able to learn. I believe it was rooted in a certain exclusiveness
> and even snobbery for which we all have a yearning even
> if unconfessed. But such an object belongs to days of peace
> and security. Today is a time of crisis. (P. 12)

Continuing his critique of Sigma Pi Phi and, circuitously, some members
of his talented tenth, Du Bois ([1948] 1980a) states: "Our interests
then are not normally with the poor and hungry, yet we are not aware
of this; we assume on the one hand our identity with the poor and
yet we act and sympathize with the rich, an unconscious and dangerous dichotomy" (p. 14). Du Bois, somewhat surprisingly, continues his
speech by asserting, "Theoretically, then, this [Sigma Pi Phi Fraternity]
is not an ideal group for the kind of leadership which I have in mind"
(p. 14). Despite not being his ideal type, Du Bois continues his speech
by outlining the new talented tenth theory and urging the organization to assist him in his endeavor. The scholar concludes his speech by
pronouncing, "This, then, is my re-examined and restated theory of the
'Talented Tenth,' which has thus become the doctrine of the 'Guiding
Hundredth' " (Du Bois [1948] 1980a:20).

That Du Bois chose the national convention of Sigma Pi Phi Fraternity to outline his new theory on Negro leadership—a speech highly
critical of many talented tenth members in attendance—resulted in, at
best, a lukewarm reception from the audience and, in effect, his vir-
tual banishment from an organization that he had ties with since the
1920s. According to David Levering Lewis (2000), Pulitzer Prize–win-
ning author of two Du Bois biographies:

> It was a speech that would have been much better received
> by the Progressive Party delegates in Convention Hall. . . .
> [T]he "Talented Tenth Memorial Address" at Wilberforce
> seems to have marked the beginning of the end of Du Bois'
> purchase on the political loyalty of the class whose character
> was synonymous with his name. After the address, *Boule*
> members left him sitting alone on a campus bench. (P. 538)

In a manner befitting Du Bois, in his attempt to garner support for an
important endeavor, he alienates persons who can potentially play a vital
role in assuring its success. However, somewhat surprisingly, neither the
Boule nor any organization or institution to date has acted on Du Bois's
doctrine of the guiding one hundredth.

'Am I my Brother's and my Sister's keeper?'

To date the existing literature includes no scholarly works extending Du Bois's theory of the talented tenth. Quite possibly the ambiguity regarding the theoretical qualifications of Du Bois's offering on Negro leadership is one explanation for the lack of scholarly advances of this theory. If so, then questions concerning the theoretical merit of Du Bois's scholarship have been raised previously and refuted. Elliott Rudwick (1957), author of the singular scholarly analysis of the Atlanta Sociological Laboratory for almost 50 years, argues that a major weakness of this school under Du Bois's leadership was its lack of emphasis on theory. Wright (2002c) debunks this notion by arguing that Du Bois uses a grounded theoretical approach whereby the resolutions (theories) offered by this school emerge from the data collected and, therefore, qualify for theory status despite its nontraditional format. According to Wright, the resolutions Du Bois offered are consistent with contemporary conventions regarding how a theory is defined. Specifically, Wright argues (2002b):

> If one defines a theory as a set of interrelated statements that attempt to explain, predict, and/or understand social [facts], and that can be replicated and generalizable, then the resolutions offered in the conclusion of each Atlanta University Conference publication qualify as systematic theoretical constructions. Undoubtedly, the presentation of the Atlanta Sociological Laboratory theories did not mirror that of traditional scholars. Despite this fact, should Atlanta University's theoretical contributions be minimized or omitted because, although they qualify for theoretical status according to the strict definition of the term, they do not qualify ideologically? (P. 19)

Similar to the notion that the resolutions both Du Bois and the Atlanta Sociological Laboratory offered constitute legitimate theoretical offerings, I propose here that the talented tenth qualifies for theory status as defined above.

Du Bois's revised, synthesized, and clearly stated theory of the talented tenth, or the guiding hundredth, is defined as leadership by, ideally, college-educated men and women dedicated to engaging in ethical and self-sacrificing activities on behalf of the race. Members of this exceptional cadre should have superior knowledge of world conditions and its impact on Diasporic Blacks, while forming alliances with world neighbors in Africa, South America, Asia, and Europe. Importantly, contrary to traditional understandings, the lynchpin of Du Bois's theory hinges on leadership, not simply the acquisition of a liberal arts education. This point is clearly stated in his revised essay when he explains his motivation for developing the theory. Du Bois ([1948] 1980b), reflecting on the origin of his theory almost 50 years prior, states:

> It is clear that in 1900, American Negroes were an inferior caste, were frequently lynched and mobbed, widely disfranchised, and usually segregated in the main areas of life. As student and worker at that time, I looked upon them and saw salvation through intelligent leadership; as I said, through a Talented Tenth. And for this intelligence I argued we needed college-trained men. (P. 2)

After examining the above and earlier quotes, Du Bois's clarion call for a talented tenth clearly was based on data he uncovered that compelled him to champion the development of a group of persons to provide leadership in identifying and ameliorating the myriad problems Black Americans experienced in a manner that, ideally, can best be accomplished by college-educated persons. However, I maintain that whether or not one possesses a college education should not take precedence over his or her ability and willingness to engage in self-sacrificing and ethical leadership activities as Du Bois mandated. Unfortunately, Du Bois's emphasis on salvation of the race through intelligent leadership has been historically minimized in favor of interpretations that overly emphasize one's education credentials and the often class-based implications thereof. Although Du Bois was resolute in his belief that the best preparation for future leaders was through the acquisition of a liberal arts college education, more important than individuals' educational credentials is their understanding of the problems impacting Black Americans and their independent acceptance of leadership roles within their community to address those problems.

I extend the theory of the talented tenth by proposing that admission into this group be based on one's answer to the question, "am I my brother's and my sister's keeper?" While simplistic in nature, this prerequisite is essential in bringing to fruition the type of leadership Du Bois envisioned. An affirmative answer to the asked question signals that one voluntarily embraces the charge of the talented tenth as Du Bois proposed. Accordingly, membership into this group is not based on individuals' education credentials, but their willingness to engage in ethical and self-sacrificing leadership activities on behalf of the masses.

Since this extension of Du Bois's theory has no educational prerequisite, an opportunity is provided for nondegreed persons to gain full membership status into this once-exclusive fraternity of college-educated persons. While, as discussed previously, Du Bois's preferred mode of training is liberal arts education, this expansion of the talented tenth embraces the notion that multiple forms of knowledge and ways of knowing exist that may not be learned on a college campus and may be of importance in providing leadership for oppressed or minority groups (Collins 2000; Mannheim 1968).

Rejecting the question, "am I my brother's and my sister's keeper?" is useful in debunking the incorrect notion that all college-educated persons are automatically members of the talented tenth and are thus responsible for leading in their respective communities. One is mindful that in the present and in Du Bois's era, not all college-educated Black Americans embrace Du Bois's ([1948] 1980b) philosophy of leadership. Reflecting on this matter during his college years in the late 1800s, he concludes:

> Of course, as I look about me, I might have understood, that all students of Fisk were not persons [who felt compelled to act on behalf of the masses of Negroes]. There was no lack of small and selfish souls; there were among the student body, careless and lazy fellows; and there were especially sharp young persons, who received the education very cheaply at Fisk University, with the distinct and single-minded idea, of seeing how much they could make out of it for themselves, and nobody else. (P. 3–4)

This extension of Du Bois's theory is significant insomuch as it provides an escape route for those not interested in embracing his leadership charge. Additionally, I suggest that this new notion of the talented tenth helps eliminate charges of elitism that, however historically misconstrued as discussed earlier, have accompanied the theory for more than 100 years. By destroying the myth of elitism I believe that new relationships among disparate groups focusing on improving the condition of Blacks in America can be developed and existing relationships strengthened. Ultimately, this extended conceptualization of the talented tenth promotes the merging of like-minded individuals and institutions from different backgrounds (i.e., educators, grass-roots activists, politicians, church leaders, etc.) to engage in uplift activities to address the statistical and empirical data highlighting the grave contemporary plight of Black Americans, especially males. This extension of the talented tenth theory is also useful because it does not attempt to mandate membership status or leadership responsibilities upon those not willing to embrace the challenge. Also, it does not mandate that one possess a college education to be a member. Instead, this extended theory of the talented tenth rests on one's voluntary answer to the question, "am I my brother's and my sister's keeper?" Only after an affirmative answer is an individual expected to engage in proactive leadership activities as Du Bois mandated.

Conclusion

The objectives of this inquiry were to highlight the discrepancies between the ideal type talented tenth member and the many historical misinterpretations of Du Bois's concept; highlight Du Bois's 1948 revised theory on Black American leadership; and extend the theory beyond its present state. Some of the misconceptions addressed via the first objective include that the origin of the term "talented tenth" came from Henry L. Morehouse; that Du Bois did not champion the leadership of the race by an actual 10% of the population; that Du Bois was not completely opposed to the industrial and vocational philosophy of Booker T. Washington; that the talented tenth included non–college-educated persons; and, that Du Bois did not want to establish a Negro aristocracy. The second objective highlighted Du Bois's revised theory that explicitly focuses on ethical and self-sacrificing leadership, knowledge of world conditions, and the development of a talented tenth training institute. The third objective of this inquiry extended the theory of the talented tenth by basing admission into this group on one's answer to the question, "am I my brother's and my sister's keeper?" An affirmative answer to this question means that one accepts Du Bois's prophetic mandate to engage in ethical and self-sacrificing leadership activities on behalf of the race, be knowledgeable of world conditions and their impact on Diasporic Blacks, and form alliances with world neighbors in Africa, South America, Asia, and Europe. While some may question the relevance of advancing this theory, few can deny that most statistical data concerning Black Americans in general and Black males specifically are disconcerting. Contributions such as this query may quite possibly lead to barrier-breaking coalitions that address the many concerns of Black Americans. While Black Americans have made many social, economic, and political advances since the early 1900s when Du Bois ([1903] 1994) penned his original theory, it is eerily telling that his words in that seminal essay continue to ring true:

America, the problem is plain before you. Here is a race transplanted through the criminal foolishness of your fathers. Whether you like it or not the millions are here, and here they will remain. If you do not lift them up, they will pull you down. . . . The Talented Tenth of the Negro race must be made leaders of thought and missionaries of culture among their people. . . . The Negro race, like all other races, is going to be saved by its exceptional men [and women]. (P. 74–75)

Du Bois's words remind us of the significance of the prophetic research to the advancement of Black people in America. Moreover, by reconstructing an accurate articulation of his theory of the talented tenth and applying it to twenty-first–century models of leadership, we continue his prophetic directives for critically challenging racism and advocating for social justice for all marginalized peoples.

References

Battle, Juan and Earl Wright II. 2002. "W. E. B. Du Bois's Talented Tenth: A Quantitative Assessment." *Journal of Black Studies* 32(6):654–72.

Chudacoff, Howard P. and Judith E. Smith. 2005. *The Evolution of American Urban Society.* Upper Saddle River, NJ: Pearson Prentice Hall.

Collins, Patricia H. 2000. *Black Feminist Thought: Knowledge, Consciousness, and the Politics of Empowerment.* New York: Routledge.

Dennis, Rutledge. 1977. "Du Bois and the Role of the Educated Elite." *Journal of Negro Education* 46:388–402.

Du Bois, William Edward Burghardt. 1898. *Some Efforts of American Negroes for Their Own Social Betterment: The Atlanta University Publications, No. 3.* Atlanta, GA: Atlanta University Press.

———. 1899. *The Negro in Business: The Atlanta University Publications, No. 4.* Atlanta, GA: Atlanta University Press.

———. [1903] 1994. *The Souls of Black Folk.* New York: Dover Publications.

———. [1903] 1970. "The Talented Tenth." Pp. 31–76 in *The Negro Problem: A Series of Articles by Representative American Negroes of To-day*, edited by unknown editor. New York: AMS Press.

———. [1948] 1980a. "The Talented Tenth: The Re-Examination of a Concept." Reel 81, Frame 1090–100 in *The Papers of W. E. B. Du Bois*, edited by Robert W. McDowell. Sanford, NC: Microfilming Corporation of America.

———. [1948] 1980b. "The Talented Tenth." Reel 81, Frame 1101–20 in *The Papers of W. E. B. Du Bois*, edited by Robert W. McDowell. Sanford, NC: Microfilming Corporation of America.

———. 1968. *The Autobiography of W. E. B. Du Bois: A Soliloquy on Viewing My Life from the Last Decade of Its First Century.* New York: International Publishers.

Gates Jr., Henry L. and Cornel West. 1996. *Future of the Race.* New York: Knopf.

Lewis, David Levering. 2000. *W. E. B. Du Bois: The Fight for Equality and the American Century, 1919–1963.* New York: Holt.

Mannheim, Karl. 1968. *Ideology and Utopia: An Introduction to the Sociology of Knowledge.* New York: Harcourt, Brace, and World.

Morehouse, Henry L. 1896. "The Talented Tenth." *Independent* 48(April):1.

Rudwick, Elliott. 1957. "W. E. B. Du Bois and the Atlanta University Studies on the Negro." *Journal of Negro Education* 26:466–76.

Washington, Booker T. [1903] 1970. "Industrial Education for the Negro." Pp. 7–30 in *The Negro Problem: A Series of Articles by Representative American Negroes of To-day*, edited by unknown editor. New York: AMS Press.

Wright, Earl, II. 2002a. "The Atlanta Sociological Laboratory, 1896–1924: A Historical Account of the First American School of Sociology." *Western Journal of Black Studies* 26(3):165–74.

———. 2002b. "Using the Master's Tools: Atlanta University and American Sociology, 1896–1924." *Sociological Spectrum* 22(1):15–39.

———. 2002c. "Why Black People Tend to Shout: An Earnest Attempt to Explain the Sociological Negation of the Atlanta Sociological Laboratory Despite Its Possible Unpleasantness." *Sociological Spectrum* 22(3):325–61.

Wright, Earl, II and Thomas C. Calhoun. 2006. "Jim Crow Sociology: Toward an Understanding of the Origin and Principles of Black Sociology via the Atlanta Sociological Laboratory." *Sociological Focus* 39(1):1–18.

3

~

Blackening Up Critical Whiteness

Dave Chappelle as Critical Race Theorist

Robert L. Reece

Duke University

White criticisms of Black people and blackness have always been commonplace even though more contemporary critiques have opted to use seemingly race-neutral terms such as "urban," "inner-city," and "minority" to launch the same racialized objections. Similarly, many Blacks have observed whiteness, offering critiques of White structures and cultures. Yet, many Whites are overwhelmingly quite "shocked that Black people think critically about whiteness because racist thinking perpetuates the fantasy that the Other . . . lacks the ability to comprehend, to understand, to see the working of the powerful" (hooks 1992:167–68). I contend that this ignorance of the fact that critical whiteness theories have been, in some form, an ongoing topic of discussion among Blacks is what makes Dave Chappelle's *Chappelle's Show* such an important text. I further posit that the popularity of the program allowed Chappelle to make contributions to whiteness theory and bring those contributions into the living rooms of Whites and Blacks alike. To this end, Chappelle emerged as a prophetic popular leader in early twenty-first–century race theory. I demonstrate how his critical perspectives, drawn from the lived experiences of Black people in America, constitute a prophetic analysis of race that was in some ways ahead of its time.

This research attempts to evaluate Chappelle's contributions to critical race theory (CRT), the history of Blacks' critiques of whiteness, and popular discourses on race and racism. Content analysis of some of the comedic sketches in his television show is used to answer two research questions: (1) how is race in general and whiteness in particular portrayed on *Chappelle's Show*, and (2) how do these depictions inform our understanding of CRT?

Critical Race Theory, Whiteness, and Literature on Race

Whiteness theories are important "because the Black-White binary is so fundamental to our way of thinking in America" (Hunt 2005:4). Neither blackness nor whiteness can be understood without the other; traditional stereotypical descriptions of each (i.e., White as European, civilized, superior, and good; and Black as African, savage, inferior, and bad) have little meaning unless held against each other for comparison (Hunt 2005). As evidenced in this literature review, though theories of whiteness are not always congruent, the connection of whiteness to blackness is consistent throughout critical whiteness literature. W. E. B. Du Bois (1994) was one of the earliest scholars to investigate whiteness in relation to blackness. His concept of "double consciousness," introduced in 1903, continues to be widely used to understand and articulate the experiences of oppressed people. Du Bois (1994) asserts that being Black in the United States forces one to try to reconcile the whiteness in the country with one's blackness while dealing with the stress of being forced to assess one's self through the eyes of a people by whom he is despised. Implicit in his analysis is the need for Blacks to understand whiteness as a survival technique, although the need for Whites to understand the Black experience appears minimal. Du Bois (1994) postulates that Whites are free to impose their own views of blackness into Black consciousness and to use their power to create what becomes fundamental "truths" about what it is to be Black:

> . . . the Negro is a sort of seventh son, born with a veil, and gifted with second-sight in this American world,—a world which yields him no true self-consciousness, but only lets him see himself through the revelation of the other world. It is a peculiar sensation, this double-consciousness, this sense of

always looking at one's self through the eyes of others, of measuring one's soul by the tape of a world that looks on in amused contempt and pity. One ever feels his two-ness—an American, a Negro; two souls, two thoughts, two unreconciled strivings; two warring ideals in one dark body, whose dogged strength alone keeps it from being torn asunder. . . . (P. 2)

Du Bois (1994) describes how this paradox inevitably detracts from any activity in which Blacks choose to engage because of the contradiction of double aims, a desire to please one's people (i.e., Blacks) while simultaneously fighting White racism. This conundrum culminates in attempts to live up to two standards of humanity: one that emerges through the Black experience and the other Whites devised to suit their own needs:

Here in America, in the few days since Emancipation, the Black man's turning hither and thither in hesitant and doubtful striving has often made his very strength to lose effectiveness, to seem like absence of power, like weakness. And yet it is not weakness—it is the contradiction of double aims. The double-aimed struggle of the Black artisan—on the one hand to escape White contempt for a nation of mere hewers of wood and drawers of water, and on the other hand to plough and nail and dig for a poverty-stricken horde—could only result in making him a poor craftsman, for he had but half a heart in either cause. (P. 3)

Toni Morrison (1992) also addresses whiteness, arguing that it is predicated on blackness in the writings of several American writers. The scholar suggests that an "Africanist" presence is crucial to the definition of "Americanness" prominent American authors such as Edgar Allen Poe, Herman Melville, Willa Cather, and Ernest Hemingway presented. Morrison (1992) defines the term "Africanist" as "the denotative and connotative blackness that African peoples have come to signify as well as the entire range of views, assumptions, readings, and misreading that accompany Eurocentric learning about these people" (pp. 6–7) and further contends that "American means White" (p. 47). Moreover, she argues that what being American or White means emanates from and is amplified by what being non-Black means. Concepts that traditionally define Americanness, such as individuality and freedom, are and were reinforced by Blacks' historic lack of said qualities, both socially and legally:

> The concept of freedom did not emerge in a vacuum. Nothing highlighted freedom—if it did not create it—like slavery. Black slavery enriched the country's creative possibilities. For in that construction of blackness and enslavement could be found not only the not-free but also, with the dramatic polarity created by skin color, the projection of the not me. (Morrison 1992:38)

Morrison (1992) also blames classism for the persistence of racism and contends that race simply serves as a scapegoat.

Furthermore, Philosophers George Yancy (2004a, 2004b) and Robert Birt (2004) elaborate on Morrison's assessment by writing about the creation of the concept of blackness as the antithesis of whiteness. Birt (2004) posits:

> But it should be noted too that it was also themselves whom the Whites were inventing in and through their invention of the Negro. It was through the invention of the Negro as a degraded race that Whites invented themselves as an exalted race. Through the relegation of Blacks to bestiality they affirmed the elevation of Whites to divinity. From this process arose a common White identity (whether openly asserted or prereflectively assumed) and the illusion of an egalitarian community of Whites with mutual interests and common freedom. (P. 61)

And according to Yancy (2004b):

> The Black body is by nature criminal, because the White body is by nature innocent, pure, and good. Whiteness sets itself up as the thesis. Blackness, within the dialectical logic of whiteness, must be the antithesis. (P. 9)

However, Birt (2004) moves beyond explaining whiteness simply as a contrast to blackness. He also incorporates, as does Du Bois when describing double consciousness, a sort of double consciousness for Whites. He argues that "to embrace whiteness is to embrace the bad faith of privilege" (p. 58), and this innate privilege creates the conundrum for Whites. In response to the negativity associated with White privilege in America, Whites attempt to live a colorblind life, devoid of race and hoping that racism simply goes away while they continue to benefit from a system that is highly racialized socially, economically, and politically. Birt (2004) ponders whether these contradictions can ever allow Whites to live authentically.

Yancey (2003) also argues against claims that one day in the near future, often cited as 2050, Whites will no longer be the numeric demographic majority in America. He reminds us that racial categories are not static but malleable, and that that same claim was made in the early twentieth century—that by 1975, Whites would no longer be the statistical majority. Demographers then, just as now, failed to account for the changeability of racial categories. Yancy (2003) suggests that Whites have the ability to alter social reality for their benefit such that whiteness becomes an ever-changing entity that selectively subsumes other groups as necessary to maintain its majority position and power while continuously excluding Blacks, using them as the out-group against which other non-Blacks can rally. Though small pockets of non-Black minorities will continue to exist, Yancey (2003) argues that certain groups of light-skinned Hispanics and Asians are the next in line to become symbolically "White." His theory should be viewed cautiously because obvious phenotypic differences may not allow Hispanics and Asians, particularly dark-skinned ones, to be so easily accepted as White, save for Hispanics who are already allowed to self-identify as such. Instead, these two groups, especially Asians, may become White "affiliates" where they are not actually considered White, but receive some of the benefits of whiteness or, at a minimum, do not suffer the negative consequences of being Black.

Eduardo Bonilla-Silva (2006) echoes these sentiments based on his "triracial order" that includes " 'Whites' at the top, an intermediary group of 'honorary Whites' . . . , and a non-White group or the 'collective Black' at the bottom" (p. 179). He also supports Yancey's (2003) claim articulated above. Furthermore, Bonilla-Silva (2006) and Omi and Winant (1994) discuss colorblind ideology among many Whites as the belief that race as a social construction can be ignored as a factor in determining one's life chances and that one can make colorblind decisions. But these scholars suggest two contexts in which this dynamics emerges. Bonilla-Silva (2006) argues that though Whites may claim to be colorblind, they still embrace racist thoughts:

> I demonstrated how color-blind racism's frames, styles, and racial stories help Whites justify contemporary racial inequality. Whites use these components like "building blocks" to manufacture accounts on a variety of racial matters. In general, their accounts amount to, "Race does not matter that much today, so let's move on." For example, when Whites

are asked about affirmative action, they resort to the frame of abstract liberalism to oppose it: "Why should we use discrimination to combat discrimination? Two wrongs don't make a right. We should judge people by their merits and let the best person get the job or promotion, or be admitted into a good college." . . . When Whites are faced with evidence of discrimination, the[y] acknowledge its occurrence but label the episodes as "isolated incidents" and proceed to blame minorities for playing the "race card." Finally, when Whites are questioned about the Whites of their social networks, they rebut, "This has nothing to do with race. It's just the way things are." (Pp. 208–09)

Omi and Winant (1994) extensively chronicle racial formation from the 1960s to the 1990s and discuss how colorblind ideology has affected national politics to the detriment of minorities:

The "new Democrats" sought a way out of this pessimistic scenario [increasing residential segregation leading to the political ignoring of Blacks and Latinos living in the inner city] by simultaneously advocating universalistic reforms and blunting the wedge issue of race. The call for more jobs, better education, and increased social investment was especially well-suited for the benefits it offered to suburban, middle-class, White voters who had been battered—though not on the scale of inner city residents—by recession. To dismiss charges of catering to minorities, [President Bill] Clinton adopted the rhetoric of "personal responsibility" and "family values" which was so successfully utilized by the right. In order to win back the suburbanites, liberals too claimed the right to "blame the victim," to disparage the "dependence" or welfare mothers, and bemoan the disintegration of the family. In their use of racially coded language, the "new Democrats" chose to remain silent on any explicit discussion of race and its overall meaning for politics. (P. 112)

Writer and poet Langston Hughes (1995) and journalist and political activist Marcus Garvey (2004) write less about the social and historical construction of whiteness and more about how Blacks view Whites. Hughes (1995) primarily depicts Whites as a source of constant amusement for Black people, partly because of their ignorant and irrational application of racism. He also describes how White people claim to know Black people and Black culture, but consistently prove they lack even the most rudimentary knowledge about Blacks, a fact that he attributes to segregation. The other major source of Black amusement is Whites' constant and often comical instances of blatant and awkward racism. However, Marcus Garvey (2004) has a much more cynical and frightening view of White people. For him, there is nothing funny about a people who have built their history on the theft and destruction of the culture and history of others. He discusses how many Whites try to scientifically alter the racial makeup of non-American Blacks who become of significant use and fail to acknowledge the merits of most Blacks. According to Garvey (2004), such White scientists must define a Negro as "a person of dark complexion or race, who has not accomplished anything and to whom others are not obligated for any useful service" (p. 112). Although they reference different terminology and write during different epochs, Du Bois (1994), Morrison (1992), Yancey (2003), Birt (2004), Bonilla-Silva (2006), Omi and Winant (1994), Hughes (1995), and Garvey (2004) all use variants of CRT to provide important insight into American race relations and whiteness. These and similar theories will play a crucial role in determining the future of race in the United States and directing race-related political policy and activism. These scholars also inform the current study on contemporary CRT, the history of Blacks' critiques of whiteness, and popular discourses on race and racism by evaluating the comedic contributions of Dave Chappelle.

The Beginnings of Dave Chappelle and Chappelle's Show

Dave Chappelle was born in Washington, D.C., to two college professors and grew up in Silver Spring, Maryland, where he lived with his mother after his parents separated. He spent summers with his father in Ohio and after graduating from Duke Ellington School of the Arts in Washington, D.C., Chappelle New York City comedian. He landed small roles in film and television before the premiere of *"Chappelle's Show"* in 2003. The show was a 30-minute sketch comedy program for which he also served as executive producer. A total of 33 episodes were created. The original 28 episodes and specials, spanning two seasons, aired on Comedy Central at 10:30 eastern standard time on Wednesdays from January 22, 2003, to May 3, 2004. The remaining three episodes, dubbed the "Lost Episodes," aired in July 2006, after Chappelle departed the show. These were the only episodes not hosted by him (Zakos 2009). *"Chappelle's Show"* initially aired behind *"South Park,"* one of Comedy Central's highest rated shows in the 18–49-year-old demographic. It not only garnered the highest television rating premiere of any Comedy

Central show in that demographic, *Chappelle's Show* eventually gained higher ratings than *South Park* (Zakos 2009). The high ratings meant that Chappelle's critiques of social events in the United States and beyond would reach a broad audience, but also that the show would be expected to provide a brand of satirical and sometimes sophomoric comedy consistent with that of other Comedy Central shows.

I contend that Chappelle followed in the tradition of Garvey (2004) and Hughes (1995) in his construction of his critiques of whiteness. He builds an alternate to the standard racial vision by immediately reversing the social and power structure of America by depicting blackness as the norm. Katharine Zakos (2009) states:

> Most other television shows (notwithstanding those which air on the token minority friendly networks, the CW and BET) feature predominantly White characters unless the storyline specifically requires the presence of a Black character. On "Chappelle's Show," however, blackness is matter-of-factly depicted as the norm—for instance, if there is a sketch that requires a family, they will be presented as African American unless, of course, the script requires it to be played other-wise. (P. 33)

Although blackness is presented as the norm in his shows, there is not a complete reversal of the White-Black roles that are presented on traditional television programs. When Chappelle presents criminals or any other social deviants, they are not necessarily White. Instead, criminals are also presented as Black, a tactic that positions Blacks as both good and bad, allowing the audience to consider the normalcy of blackness in contrast to its stereotypical correlation with deviance. By depicting Blacks as "normal," he attempts to highlight the individuality of Black people. Instead of serving as affirmative action–style placeholders or representatives of the entire race, as is typically the case on most White television shows, Chappelle treats Blacks as individuals. This allows him to paint a diverse picture of blackness in contrast to the monolithic view on most White television shows. Formerly American individuality was reserved exclusively for White people who typically have had the luxury to refuse being considered representatives or spokespersons for all Whites. Chappelle extends this luxury to Blacks as well because each Black person is not required to be representative of all Blacks (McIntosh 1992; Morrison 1992).

Chappelle also eliminates Whites from sketches unless the script explicitly requires their presence; and even then they are included out of necessity to illustrate interracial interaction. By presenting Whites, as opposed to Blacks, as people outside the mainstream, Chappelle is able to intensify his cultural critiques of whiteness by not allowing White culture to hide behind a veil of normality. Instead, White culture is highlighted and critiqued because it becomes novel when placed against a background of Black normality. In addition to being highlighted, Whites, especially White men, are often presented stereotypically and generically. Furthermore, they do not exhibit cultural uniqueness. Their speech is dominated by monotones and a meticulous effort to avoid slang that may afford them cultural alliances. Their stereotypical distinguishing characteristic, so to speak, is *a lack of distinguishing characteristics*. Chappelle goes to great lengths to ensure that they appear nondescript and boring. Moreover, White men, when played by Chappelle in whiteface, are presented as timid, naïve, and lacking the assertiveness and masculinity of their Black counterparts. This pattern is also found in their interactions with Black characters, both male and female, who typically dominate them and further highlight their impotence. Chappelle's performances in whiteface also allow him to maintain complete control over these depictions of whiteness. By using whiteface to control the portrayals of White people, as opposed to using a White actor, Chappelle is able to directly show, for better or worse, what he believes many Black people think about many White people. When in whiteface, Chappelle goes beyond simply informing viewers about Black perspectives on Whites, and even further than entrusting the endeavor to a White performer. Instead, he attempts to provide a demonstration of whiteness as he contends it is understood by many Blacks.

Unfortunately, Chappelle's message was often misunderstood. During a taping session in his third season, Chappelle realized that some of his sketches were being misinterpreted, particularly by Whites, and thus deemed socially irresponsible by members of his Black audience. He later expressed regret at his failure to be more cautious with the direction of the show and its comedy. Chappelle recounted the moment that he decided he could not continue to perform on his show during an interview with Oprah Winfrey in 2006:

> But what I didn't consider was how many people watch the show and how the way people use television is subjective. . . . So then when I'm on the set and we're finally taping the sketch [the "Pixie sketch"] somebody on set, who was White, laughed in such a way; I know the difference in people laughing with me and people laughing at me and it was the first time I had ever gotten a laugh that I was uncomfortable

with. Not just uncomfortable, but like "Should I fire this
person?" . . . I know all these people who are watching TV
that there is [*sic*] a lot of people who will understand exactly
what I'm doing, but then there's another group of people
who are just fans that, the kind of people that scream "I'm
Rick James, b" at my concerts; they're just along for a different kind of celebrity worship ride; they're going to get
something completely different. That concerned me.

Although White misinterpretation[1] resulted in Chappelle's voluntary
departure from the show, his work is still telling of American race relations. The following sections explore some of Chappelle's contributions
to CRT and understanding whiteness as presented in his sketches during
which he addresses racial matters while simultaneously providing his
own cultural critiques.

Data and Method of Analysis

Chappelle's Show" contains 95 sketches.[2] For this study, I chose sketches
based on four criteria:[3] The sketch must (1) focus on the use of race
for humor; (2) focus primarily on structural critiques, whether racial or
nonracial (structural critiques center on institutions such as the government and corporations rather than individual actions); (3) concentrate
on cultural critiques that primarily analyze individual or group behavior or ways of being outside of the context of an institution; and (4)
depict Chappelle critiquing whiteness by playing a White person in some
form (although that form may not necessarily be in whiteface). Readers
should note that whiteface provides Chappelle's most telling critiques of
whiteness because he is able to show what he thinks of White people
by actually mimicking them. He is able to create a specific image of
whiteness, strip it of its individuality, and hold it up for critique as a
monolithic entity. I elected not to use sketches from the "Lost Episodes"
because Chappelle had left the show and requested that the episodes
not be aired. Moreover, these episodes reflect a lack of creative control
on his part and, thus, may not truly represent Chappelle's views on
race and whiteness.

   After selecting representative sketches, I systematically conduct a
content analysis by viewing the sketches, paying special attention to
instances when Chappelle's character is on the screen, noting his comments as well as the contexts in which statements are made. Interactions
between Chappelle's whiteface character and other Black characters are
especially important because Chappelle often reveals to the audience

what he thinks the White person being portrayed may be thinking. Sketches that allow comparisons of Chappelle's vision of White and Black culture are also important. This analysis positions Chappelle's contemporary comedic work in conversation with traditional academic race theorists such as Du Bois (1994), Morrison (1992), Yancey (2003), Birt (2004), Bonilla-Silva (2006), Omi and Winant (1994), Hughes (1995), and Garvey (2004) to situate his contributions as valid pictures of a racialized present and predictors of a racialized future. The subsequent section contains results from my content analysis of the following four sketches: "Frontline: Clayton Bigsby," "Reparations 2003," "Racial Draft," and "Trading Spouses," representative quotes as well as linkages to CRT.

Illustrating Whiteness Theory: *Chappelle's Show*

Sketch 1: 'Frontline: Clayton Bigsby'

This sketch follows the format of an episode of the PBS television documentary series, *Frontline*. The journalist has secured a rare and exclusive interview with reclusive, famed White supremacist, Clayton Bigsby. After making a dangerous journey to Bigsby's secluded home, the journalist is shocked to discover that the man dubbed the leader of the White supremacist movement in the United States is actually Black. Bigsby is blind and as a child attended an all-White school for the blind. For the sake of simplicity, the teachers told Bigsby that he was White. As a result, Bigsby was socialized under the impression that he was a White man and developed an intense hatred of Blacks. The obvious irony is the concept of a "Black White supremacist." Yet that is only one of several nuanced meanings Chappelle created including clever commentary on the arbitrary, socially constructed, and learned nature of race.

Most scholars agree that no significant genetic differences are found across racial groups and that genetically identifiable racial categories do not exist. Genetically, all humans are 95.38% identical (Graves 2004:7). Thus no innate reason exists to contest being placed in one racial category in the absence of visual confirmation. This means that as a child, despite his blackness, Bigsby had no inherent reason to suspect that he was any different from other children. He was socialized into whiteness (i.e., identity, views, behavior) and accepted it without question. Moreover, whiteness is made most evident via use of extreme, highly absurd examples of bigotry. Even after Bigsby learns that he is Black, we see no indications that he has changed or will change his beliefs or

behavior. In fact, he suggests his intent to remain a White supremacist as he divorces his White wife, explaining that "she's a ['N-word']
lover." The Bigsby sketch suggests that racial identity is dependent on
socialization, a primary sociological tenet based on the social constructions called blackness and whiteness that have been created through a
process of sociohistorical reification—with no meanings other than those
society ascribes and perpetuates through cultural transmission and social
and political phenomena to create difference. Furthermore, "although
the concept of race invokes biologically-based human characteristics
(so-called 'phenotypes'), selection of these particular human features
for purposes of racial signification is always and necessarily a social and
historical process" (Omi and Winant 1994:55). The inherent strength
of racial socialization is so ingrained that it seems natural, and when
a character such as Bigsby shatters that notion of intrinsic race-based
behavior, the results can be challenging for audiences to accept.

This sketch also provides commentary on the irrationality of stereotypes attributed to Blacks. As a blind man, Bigsby does not have
the benefit of ascribing a behavior to a racial group after he has deter-
mined the race of the person performing the action. For example, he
cannot witness a Black person playing loud music. In his example, he
simply assumes the person is playing loud music because he is Black.
His blindness forces him to do the opposite. He must gauge the action
and use existing stereotypes to determine the race of the person by
their behavior. The arbitrary nature of these stereotypes often leaves
him incorrectly discerning the race of characters. Zakos (2009) notes:

> This sly removal of the visual aspect from the performance of
> race is truly one of the most sophisticated facets of "Chap-
> pelle's Show's" commentary on race. Chappelle's clever use
> of a blind man to hold up the mirror for the dominant
> framework so that White society can see the incongruities in
> its notions of race is the sharpest, most pointed bit of social
> commentary on "Chappelle's Show." (P. 44)

For example, at one point in the sketch Bigsby is being driven to a
White supremacist rally. He encounters a carload of White male adolescents dressed in baggy clothes that would be associated with hip-hop
culture and they are playing rap music loudly. When Jasper (Bigsby's
driver) pulls next to the car, Bigsby, mistaking the occupants for Black,
says, "Why don't you jungle bunnies turn that music down? ['N-word']
make me sick." After Bigsby is driven away, one of the young men
turns to another and says, "Did he just call us ['N-word']? Awesome!"

Based on the blaring rap music as a prevalent stereotype for young Black men and because Bigsby is blind, he assumes the young men are Black. Yet Chappelle challenges this stereotype by depicting the boys as White. His challenge is deepened by the widely accepted fact that suburban White adolescents continue to be the largest consumers of hip-hop music. Given this purchasing trend, we may reasonably assume that one's chances of encountering Whites in a similar situation is just as likely as encountering Blacks. Also implicit is the White males' overwhelming desire to identify with stereotypes of Black people, specifically urban Black youth (West 1993).

The car scene also continues a commentary on the "N-word" that is embedded in the sketch. The reporter initially promises that the sketch will contain "gratuitous use of the 'N-word,' and by 'N-word,' I mean [actually states the 'N-word']. There, I said it" (Cundieff 2003). The White reporter's use of the word in a seemingly inoffensive manner seemed to lessen its offensive nature as laughs are heard from the live audience. However, the caveat, "There, I said it," also signifies that some cultural line has been crossed or some social taboo has occurred. Use of the racial slur takes an ironic turn given that Bigsby is Black. He is the only person to use the word in a manner associated with its historic use by racist, belligerent Whites. This dynamic raises the question, when is use of the "N-word" acceptable? If it is based on the speaker's race, Bigsby is within his social rights (even though he does not realize he is) to use the word. If appropriateness is situational and the word is only offensive when meant to be, those who are usually offended by its use by a White person should also be offended by its use by Bigsby as it is intended to be equally derogatory.

In the final scene at a book signing during which attendees realize that Bigsby is Black (when his imitation Ku Klux Klan robe equipped with the pointed hood that masks his face is removed), the White supremacist crowd is shocked. One woman starts to vomit and one man's head appears to explode. The reactions to Bigsby's unveiling reflect Chappelle's way of showing how difficult it is for many Whites to completely accept the socially constructed, non-biological nature of race. The strain can be literally mind-blowing. Their acceptance of the fact that race is a social construction would also increase White guilt. White people would be forced to accept that the larger structural and institutional forces that prevented many Black people from advancing in society in the past still impede significant Black collective progress today. The cataclysmic reaction to Bigsby's unmasking represents the reluctance of White rally participants—and by extension White viewers—to acknowledge, "Yes, I am racist." Bigsby's life story greatly deviates from the "script" that is prescribed to Black men. Even though he is blind, he is still expected to behave in a manner representative of the collective Black identity—and any behavior outside of this model constitutes a problem that is initially paradoxical and humorous, but that has serious undertones for audiences willing to venture beyond the superficial (Appiah 2009).

Sketches 2 and 3: 'Reparations 2003' and 'Racial Draft'

Chappelle's "Reparations 2003" sketch depicts a scenario in which the U.S. government has passed legislation to award Blacks monetary reparations for slavery. Blacks are subsequently shown spending their newfound wealth in stereotypical ways such as buying pricey sport utility trucks, eating fried chicken, and starting record labels. There are also hundreds of delinquent phone bills being paid and a merger between Kentucky Fried Chicken (KFC) and the urban clothing line For Us By Us (FUBU), creating the largest corporation in the world (i.e., because the value of chicken has skyrocketed). Chappelle plays two newscasters covering the story—Chuck Taylor, who is White, and Big Al, a heavyset, apparently whitewashed Black weatherman. Next, in the "Racial Draft" sketch, Chappelle presents a scenario in which Blacks, Whites, Asians, Latinos, and Jews have grown tired of debating the racial and ethnic categories of mixed-race celebrities and the extent to which celebrities' success is attributable to one aspect of their heritage. The groups collaboratively decide to sponsor a racial draft, akin to drafting professional athletes, to resolve the identities of celebrities such as Tiger Woods, Halle Berry, and Mariah Carey. Chappelle plays three characters: the draft representative for the Whites (in whiteface), Tiger Woods, and a Black draft analyst who offers play-by-play reports alongside two White analysts.

Chappelle's White characters in the two sketches are so similar that they appear identical. Additionally, he does not alter their voices or mannerisms and they have the same blonde hair. Even these simple similarities are a cultural critique about the supposedly generic nature of whiteness. Yet his critique expands as one considers the behavior of the two White draft analysts he portrays in tandem with the White men he portrays in the two sketches. A significant feature all of these characters share is their not-so-subtle racist commentary. They all make racist jokes and then attempt to dismiss them with laughter. For example, one analyst comments that since Blacks have received reparations, "The crime rate has fallen to zero percent. How could that be? Did the Mexicans get money today, too?" (Allen 2003). After realizing that he should not have made such a statement on air he attempts to backtrack, but quickly gives up, concluding, "Mexicans don't watch the news. Now if this were Telemundo . . ." (Allen 2003). Again, the characters mask their racist commentary with laughter.

Another similarity shared by Chappelle's two White characters in the two sketches is their lack of assertiveness. For example, in "Racial Draft" as the White representative approaches the podium to announce the Whites' draft selections, the Black representative refers to him as a "Cracker." Although the epithet does not carry as much weight as other racial slurs, it is still disrespectful. Moreover, he is unable to quiet the crowd although, paradoxically, he feels a sense of entitlement:

[The White representative approaches the podium.]

Rondell (Black representative): Cracker.

White representative: Very mature, Rondell. Thank you all. Good afternoon.

[Boos from the crowd]

White representative: Excuse me. Ahem. Pardon me. Hey, will you cut the malarkey? Ok, I'm talking! There's a White man talking up here. (Cundieff 2003)

Tiger Woods, played by Chappelle, can also be considered a form of whiteface. Because Woods is often popularly associated with whiteness, Chappelle's portrayal of the golfer is akin to "acting" White. Interestingly, Woods makes a brief acceptance speech then returns to the podium to say, "I always wanted to say this: fo shizzle [for sure]" (Cundieff 2003; *Urban Dictionary Online*). The comment suggests that Woods has been secretly envious of Black culture and is excited that he can now openly participate in it. The entire sketch is a commentary on the pliable and shifting nature of racial categories. It differs from the Bigsby sketch that simply asserts that race is socially constructed. The "Racial Draft" sketch implies that racial categories are socially constructed, changeable, and that their meanings are constantly being altered and reinforced. Yancey (2003) comments on this dynamic: "Future researchers must build upon the understanding that race is a social construct and majority group status is permeable. Those who study issues of race and ethnicity must not make the mistake of perceiving race as a static concept" (p. 151). This concept is also expressed explicitly when the Latino representative "drafts" Elián González[4] because she "wanted to do this before the

White people try to adopt him as one of their own—Again." This is commentary on the incorporation of Latinos as "proxy Whites" which, according to Yancey (2003), may represent America's future:

> We have been told that Whites will be close to being a numerical minority by 2050, and that there will be about 95 million Hispanics in the United States at that time, about 24 percent of the population. Yet projections from the census indicate that while the number of individuals who have a Latino heritage will increase, the percentage of those individuals who are first-generation Hispanics will steadily decline. . . . If these projections are correct, then by 2050 the number of native-born Hispanics in the United States will be about four times higher than the number of foreign-born Hispanics, a great enough difference that the typical Hispanic will be seen as one who is acculturated. Americans who encounter Latinos will be much more likely to encounter a Latino who exhibits the cultural aspects of the United States than the cultural aspects of Latin America. At that point, majority group members will find it much easier to accept Hispanics as "White." (Pp. 129–30)

As the sketch continues, the Whites draft Colin Powell, a selection that stumps the analysts because he has no known White heritage. This selection is reminiscent of Garvey's (2004) claims that Whites often attempt to claim that accomplished Blacks are not authentically Black:

> The *New York World* under the date of January 15, 1923, published a statement of Drs. Clark Wissler and Franz Boaz (the latter a professor of anthropology at Columbia University), confirming the statement of the French that Moroccan and Algerian troops used in the invasion of Germany were not to be classified as Negroes, because they were not of that race. How the French and these gentlemen arrive at such a conclusion is marvelous to understand, but I feel it is the old-time method of depriving the Negro of anything that would tend to make him recognized in any useful occupation or activity. . . . Let us not be flattered by White anthropologists and statesmen who, from time to time, because of our success here, there or anywhere try to make out that we are no longer members of the Negro race. (Pp. 119–20)

The Whites not only adopt Colin Powell, they trade for Condoleezza Rice from the Blacks and return O. J. Simpson to the Blacks. The Blacks also attempt to acquire prominent White rapper Eminem but the Whites refuse this trade. When the analysts comment that "O. J. is Black again" (Cundieff 2003), the two White analysts exchange a subtle handshake signaling their approval that Simpson has been abandoned by White society. The analysts then comment that, if Whites could openly select a Black person, they would have chosen Oprah Winfrey because she has "thick thighs, no felonies" (Cundieff 2003 ""), and thus would have made an excellent addition to their race. These seemingly comical events further illustrate Garvey's (2004) point; Whites have claimed a high-achieving Black person (i.e., Rice) while rejecting a former high-achieving Black whose reputation has plummeted dramatically (i.e., Simpson). Yet they refuse to trade Eminem, who exhibits characteristics often associated with blackness, but who has the prestige and wealth that make him attractive to Whites. Lastly, Oprah Winfrey is not taken by the Whites, but as an influential multibillionaire, they consider her desirable. I contend that these sketches illustrate the often subtle, yet troubling racial interactions in society that often result in deleterious outcomes for Blacks. Chappelle uses comedy to confront such controversies in an attempt to challenge the audience to reflect upon contemporary issues of whiteness, racism, and inequality.

Sketch 3: 'Trading Spouses'

This sketch is a parody of the FOX reality show *"Trading Spouses: Meet Your New Mommy,"* in which two families swap mothers for a week under the stipulation that the woman gets to decide how the family spends $50,000 in prize money. This is the only sketch where Chappelle directly contrasts Black and White culture. However, in his sketch, two families, one White and one Black, switch fathers, both played by Chappelle. The swap facilitated cultural contrasts. The White man, Todd Jacobson, follows the pattern of other whitefaced characters on the show. He is timid in his interactions with other family members and exhibits cultural distance implicit in other sketches. He disrupts the Black household due to his lack of cultural capital to fit in this new space. Nor is his own culture impressive or interesting enough to garner the respect of his temporary family. In contrast, Chappelle places the Black man, Leonard Washington, in a position of normalcy despite his misogyny and violent temperament.

Leonard attempts to "fix" the White household—his vices only compound the apparent abnormality of the White home. In Chappelle's world, this home is so dysfunctional that even someone as problematic as Leonard is qualified to enhance it. For example, when he walks into the house, after locking the door suspiciously and looking out a window to check the surroundings, he hugs his new White wife, Katie, and remarks that he does not smell any dinner cooking. He says she should "go on and make some grits" (Allen 2003). This introduction signals the start of Leonard's process of restoring order and routine to the household. He is also asserting his patriarchal dominance, a position that, judging by Katie's facial expression when she is commanded to cook dinner, Todd does not assume very often if ever. And by taking control of this household, Leonard is restoring "normal" (albeit problematic) gender roles. Meanwhile, Todd is disrupting the "normalcy" of the Black household. The Black son, T-Mart, immediately takes advantage of Todd's naivety and ignorance of Black culture by making an offensive joke at his expense:

> Todd: You must be little T-Mart? Would you like to call me daddy?
>
> T-Mart: Is it okay if I call you Mr. Dez [pronounced d z]?
>
> Todd: Mr. Dez?
>
> T-Mart: Dez Nuts! [while grabbing his groin, implying that he is referring to his genitalia.]
>
> Todd: I . . . I don't understand. (Allen 2003)

Todd does not realize that the joke is offensive, which is presumed to be a critique of White ignorance of Black culture.

During dinner at the Washington residence Todd further disrupts the setting by preparing food, a reversal of the expected gender roles that Leonard demands, and by cooking "strange" foods—cauliflower, corn beef hash, and parsnips. The Black wife, Sharron, remarks, "What the [expletive] is a parsnip?" (Allen 2003). In this setting created by Chappelle in which Black is the norm, Sharron's lack of knowledge about parsnips does not reflect negatively on her, but implies that White people eat "strange" foods. At the Jacobson house Katie informs Leonard that Todd usually washes dishes after dinner. Leonard quickly reminds her that he is not present and that it is her responsibility to wash dishes. After Katie sarcastically asks Leonard if he would like her to light his cigarette as well he abruptly responds, "You better check your tone girl.

Put your inside voice on before I put your ass outside" (Allen 2003). Leonard's aggressive assertion further establishes him as the new patriarch of the household.

The subsequent scene provides two critiques of whiteness. In simultaneously cut scenes, Todd and Leonard sit on the toilet reading fictional magazines. Todd peruses *Mahogany* magazine and Leonard reads *White People*. Both men discover something new about each other's culture—and what is realized is most significant for this analysis. Todd reads about racial profiling for the first time and is shocked. Leonard's discovery is much more superficial as he is introduced to the actress Renee Zellweger. The dramatic contrast between the two realizations is significant and not lost on the viewer—the Black man discovers a popular-culture icon and the White man discovers a reality that threatens Black lives every day. Several other family scenes provide comic relief as well as similar outcomes that remind the audience of the dramatically different cultural, social, and economic spaces in which many Blacks and Whites navigate.

Conclusion: Contemporary Critiques of Whiteness

This study focuses on Dave Chappelle's cultural critiques that reflect examinations of racism, whiteness, and blackness. Regarding blackness, Chappelle specifically focuses on how Blacks must navigate a world filled with White racism by either conforming to what Whites expect or hiding their "true" identities in an attempt to emulate whiteness and thus seem less threatening. These results also illustrate that Dave Chappelle's show provides a significant contribution to critical whiteness theories by telling and showing viewers how segments of the Black community often view Whites via the use of whiteface and controversial, often comical, yet thought-provoking skits. I contend that Chappelle contributes in a nontraditional, contemporary way to CRT and informs existing discourses on race and racism by providing a lens "inside" the minds of White America to illumine how stereotypes, prejudices, and other outcomes of systemic racism can manifest. He is able to comically articulate broad notions of whiteness and the negative Black experiences that often follow. Moreover, by depicting them in extreme fashion, Chappelle confronts common images and interactions between many Whites and Blacks to challenge the audience in controversial ways. The pointed nature in which he uses comedy to consider the dangers of unchecked race-based attitudes and actions are akin to academic endeavors by scholars such as Du Bois (1994), Morrison (1992), Yancy (2004a), Birt

(2004), Hughes (1995), and Garvey (2004). Like Bonilla-Silva (2006), Chappelle illustrates the existence of colorblind racism, White hegemony, and societal complicity. His sketches also present varied "racial projects" that have legitimized oppression and inequality in the United States (Omi and Winant 1994). Furthermore, his comedy allowed Chappelle to reach the masses in a way that academia cannot. For these reasons, a strong argument can be made that Chappelle's manipulation of popular culture to inform audiences about race and race matters positions him as a current-day example of a prophetic critical race theorist, particularly for Black audiences.

However, one must wonder about the effectiveness of Chappelle's message given that his lack of comfort in performing such sketches ultimately led to the voluntary cancelation of the show. This sobering fact raises questions about whether Chappelle was foiled by his humor and whether effective social commentary can ever be funny. Without his humor, Chappelle would have probably been denied the opportunity to make such commentary. Or maybe Chappelle ruined himself by peppering his socially relevant sketches with sophomoric jokes (Chappelle 2006). This has been one of academia's primary critiques of Chappelle— that if he desired to provide a serious forum for social dialogue, he should have omitted jokes that did not fit that mold. But Chappelle is, after all, a comedian, not an academic. Importantly, Chappelle's sketches can certainly be read in varied ways and the meanings are debatable. Yet his attention to racial themes is clear. For his Black fans, Chappelle "defuses the power of popular stereotypes and allows people to laugh at the absurdities and irrationalities of American racism" (Jackson 2008:xi). Yet White viewers possibly used Chappelle's humor to reinforce existing stereotypes and as a "license to laugh away their own racism" (Jackson 2008:xi). Additional studies are needed to consider Chappelle's legacy as well as to identify and describe other nonacademic avenues by which CRT is being presented in contemporary spaces. Only by doing so can we better gauge whether and how race and racial issues are being presented in mainstream spaces in general and via the media in particular.

Notes

1. Though this misinterpretation is only speculative, Jackson (2008) might argue that as a Black man, Chappelle had enough experience with race to recognize the difference between being laughed with and being laughed at. His sense of racial paranoia is a real result of the state of race relations and is justification for

leaving the show. This is a reality that, given his state of racial paranoia and the racialized and polarizing nature of Chappelle's work, may have been inevitable.

2. If the "Lost Episodes" are included, there are 108 sketches.

3. All of the sketches are available to readers on request.

4. Elián González is a young Cuban who was at the center of a U.S.–Cuba controversy in 2000. His mother died as fourteen Cubans attempted to reach Florida in an aluminum boat. Only Elian and two others survived by floating on an inner tube until they were rescued by two fishermen who turned them over to the U.S. Coast Guard. Relatives in Miami welcomed Elian and planned for him to remain in the United States but his father demanded his return to Cuba and eventually won what became an intense international custody battle that engulfed both U.S. and governments. As a result, Elian was returned to his father in Cuba ("Elian Timeline in Pictures" 2000).

References

Allen, Andre. 2003. "Episode #1.4" *Chappelle's Show*. MGM Television. March 1, 2010.

Appiah, K. Anthony. 2009. "Racial Identity and Racial Identification." Pp. 669–77 in *Theories of Race and Racism*, edited by L. Back and J. Solomos. New York: Routledge.

Birt, Robert E. 2004. "The Bad Faith of Whiteness." Pp. 55–64 in *What White Looks Like: African American Philosophers on the Whiteness Question*, edited by G. Yancy. New York: Routledge.

Bonilla-Silva, Eduardo. 2006. *Racism without Racists: Color-Blind Racism and the Persistence of Racial Inequality in the United States*. Lanham, MD: Rowman and Littlefield.

Chappelle, Dave, interviewed by James Lipton. 2006. *Inside the Actor's Studio*, YouTube Website. Retrieved March 12, 2010 (http://www.youtube.com/watch?v=SvH_XBht-Ok).

Cundieff, Rusty. 2003. "Episode #1.1" *Chappelle's Show*. MGM Television. March 1, 2010.

———. 2003. "Episode #1.12" *Chappelle's Show*. MGM Television. March 1, 2010.

———. 2004. "Episode #2.1" *Chappelle's Show*. MGM Television. March 1, 2010.

Comedy Central Presents: Chappelle's Show, Season One: Uncensored! 2003. [Motion picture].

Du Bois, W. E. B. 1994. *Of Our Spiritual Strivings*. New York: Dover.

"Elain Timeline in Pictures." 2000, June 28. Retrieved March 12, 2010 (http://news.bbc.co.uk/2/hi/americas/625829.stm).

Garvey, Marcus. 2004. *Selected Writings and Speeches of Marcus Garvey*, edited by B. Blaisdell. Mineola, NY: Dover.

Graves, Joseph L., Jr. 2004. *The Race Myth: Why We Pretend Race Exists in America*. New York: Dutton.

"His First Interview: Why Comedian Dave Chappelle Walked Away from $50 Million," interviewed by O. Winfrey. *The Oprah Winfrey Show*, Buzznet. com. Retrieved March 12, 2010 (http://vj2006.buzznet.com/user/video/2504/).

hooks, bell. 1992. *Black Looks: Race and Representation*. Boston: South End Press.

Hughes, Langston. 1995. *Langston Hughes and the Chicago Defender*, edited by C. C. De Santis. Urbana: University of Illinois Press.

Hunt, Darnell. M. 2005. "Making Sense of Blackness on Television." Pp. 1–24 in *Channeling Blackness: Studies on Television and Race in America*, edited by D. M. Hunt. Urbana: University of Illinois Press.

Jackson, John L. 2008. *Racial Paranoia: The Unintended Consequences of Political Correctness*. New York: Basic Civitas.

McIntosh, Peggy. 1992. "White Privilege and Male Privilege: A Personal Account of Coming to See Correspondences through Work in Women's Studies." Pp. 70–81 in *Race, Class, and Gender: An Anthology*, edited by M. L. Anderson and P. H. Collins. Belmont, CA: Wadsworth.

Morrison, Toni. 1992. *Playing in the Dark: Whiteness and the Literary Imagination*. New York: Vintage Books.

Omi, Michael and Howard Winant. 1994. *Racial Formation in the United States from the 1960s to the 1990s*. New York: Routledge.

Urban Dictionary Online. "Fo Shizzle." Retrieved March 12, 2010 (http://www.urbandictionary.com/define.php?term=fo-shizzle).

West, Cornel. 1993. *Race Matters*. Boston: Beacon Press.

Yancey, George. 2003. *Who Is White: Latinos, Asians, and the New Black/Nonblack Divide*. Boulder, CO: Lynne Rienner Publishers.

Yancy, George. 2004a. "A Foucauldian (Genealogical) Reading of Whiteness." Pp. 107–42 in *What White Looks Like: African American Philosophers on the Whiteness Question*, edited by G. Yancy. New York: Routledge.

———. 2004b. "Introduction: Fragments of a Social Ontology of Whiteness." Pp. 1–23. in *What White Looks Like: African American Philosophers on the Whiteness Question*, edited by G. Yancy. New York: Routledge.

Zakos, Katherine P. 2009. *Racial Satire and Chappelle's Show*. Master's thesis, Georgia State University, Atlanta.

Part II

~

Daily Experiences and Implications of the Postracial Obama Age

The election and reelection of Barack Obama as president of the United States in 2008 and 2012 did not dramatically alter the daily lives of Blacks who are experiencing poverty, racism, or both. The historic election and reelection events were inspirational, and their emotional and psychological significance are inestimable. In addition to evidencing that the United States has become more racially tolerant, several changes, including health-care reform; passage of the Civil Marriage Protection Act in Maryland, Maine, Minnesota, and Washington; and the capture of Osama Bin Laden ensure that Barack Obama's presidency will hold an indelible place in U.S. history. Yet, by and large, most people who were poor, experienced racial discrimination, or both before Obama's election continued to be poor, discriminated against, or both following each election. Importantly, African Americans who recognize the importance of the recent presidential elections dismiss notions of racial betrayal and become comfortable honestly assessing social problems that continue to plague the Black community despite and because of the historic Obama elections.

The two chapters in this section enable readers to assess some of the real-world local, regional, and national implications of race and race matters that are theoretically illumined in part I of this volume and prepare them for further research on such subjects from an international frame of reference in part III. Moreover, they reflect prophetic work in their ability to empirically and directly consider some of the implications of the paradigms detailed in the initial section of this volume. Thus the two chapters illustrate the importance of providing empirical results to augment theoretical work and anecdotes (Bonilla-Silva 2001, 2010; Feagin 2006, 2010; Gallagher 2003). Furthermore, they show how contemporary forms of racism still undermine the quality of life and lived experiences of segments of the Black community during a historical moment in which whether and how race matters are up for debate.

In Chapter 4, "Race, the Great Recession, and the Foreclosure Crisis: From American Dream to Nightmare," Cedric Herring, Loren Henderson, and Hayward Derrick Horton rely on quantitative findings to suggest that the recent Great Recession disproportionately affected people of color. They contend that this approximately four-year nationwide economic downturn was more reminiscent of a depression for many Blacks and Latinos. The authors reference various secondary data sources, including the U.S. Census Bureau and the Bureau of Labor Statistics, to evidence how segments of these two racial and ethnic groups were more apt to experience home foreclosures, unemployment, poverty, and health-care inequities.

Their findings illustrate how historic economic and racial oppression can render groups that have made notable advancements (for example, Blacks who now have a representative who is the U.S. president) more relatively vulnerable to socioeconomic travail than other groups. Moreover, they contend that the "American Nightmare" that many Blacks and Latinos are experiencing indirectly suggests some of the contemporary, unfavorable implications of race matters that may be more difficult to identify and acknowledge—particularly for persons who espouse a colorblind racial posture—continue to exist. Because race tends to be negatively associated with class, particularly for persons of color in the United States, blaming social problems such as poverty and unemployment on class considerations rather than racial dynamics may be more palatable for some people. In addition to their empirical analysis, the authors provide strategies and policy suggestions to combat some of the economic challenges Latinos and Blacks are experiencing to ultimately combat ethnic and racial disparities associated with the Great Recession.

Some of the contemporary economic implications of historic racial inequities are documented in chapter 4. Chapter 5, "Black Experiences, White Experiences: Why We Need a Theory of Systemic Racism," examines present-day manifestations and implications of historic racial inequality as well as the importance of establishing concepts and perspectives that accurately convey the severity and pervasiveness of racial divisiveness and racism in our society. Louwanda Evans and Joe Feagin introduce the concepts "White racial frame" and "systemic racism" to describe and understand why they contend that many White Americans understand Blacks and historically Black colleges and universities. Both phrases convey the entrenched nature of contemporary manifestations of racial discrimination and how it shapes White identity as well as White-Black encounters where negative comments and behavior by members of the former group toward members of the latter group on several college campuses seem normative.

Evans and Feagin rely on interview and survey data to convey that systemic racism, driven by a White racial frame, undermines the potential for racial equality, racial reconciliation, honest self-assessments by many Whites, and safe spaces for many Blacks who attempt to negotiate predominately White college spaces. Their sobering results show how some Black students on predominately White college campuses endure microaggressions and, in some instances, physical danger as they endeavor to earn an education. This empirical analysis confirms theories used to explain colorblind racism as well as the systemic nature of negative social forces.

The two chapters reflect prophetic work in the manner in which they provide direct evidence to challenge postracial perspectives as well as strategies and best practices to stem the tide of economic- and race-based social problems. Their evidence-based findings question prevailing sentiments that race no longer matters in influencing life chances and quality of life indices. The authors illumine results that clearly contradict this stance. Although results from the two studies do not contradict the history-making reality of what the presidential election and reelection of Barack Obama signify, they do illustrate that we still have a long way until racial parity is realized in the United States.

References

Bonilla-Silva, Eduardo. 2001. *White Supremacy and Racism in the Post–Civil Rights Era*. Boulder, CO: Lynne Rienner Publishers.

———. 2010. *Racism without Racists: Color-Blind Racism and the Persistence of Racial Inequality in the United States*. Lanham, MD: Rowman and Littlefield.

Feagin, Joe R. 2006. *Systemic Racism: A Theory of Oppression*. New York: Routledge.

———. 2010. *The White Racial Frame: Centuries of Racial Framing and Counter-Framing*. New York: Routledge.

Gallagher, Charles A. 2003. "Color-Blind Privilege: The Social and Political Functions of Erasing the Color Line in Post-Race America." *Race, Gender and Class* 10(4):1–17.

4

~

Race, the Great Recession, and the Foreclosure Crisis

From American Dream to Nightmare

CEDRIC HERRING

University of Illinois at Chicago

LOREN HENDERSON

Wright College

HAYWARD DERRICK HORTON

State University at New York at Albany

Research suggests that between 2007 and 2010, the United States experienced one of the worst economic crises since the Great Depression. This period is often referred to as the Great Recession. Although most Americans directly or indirectly experienced implications of this nationwide economic precariousness, the consequences of the economic crisis were not evenly distributed. Based on analyses of secondary data from the General Social Survey (GSS), this study considers how the recent economic recession affected foreclosure rates and other economics indices for the Black and Latino communities. Specifically, we ask, were racial and ethnic groups such as Blacks and Latinos disproportionately affected by the recent recession and if so, how? What types of factors exacerbated their negative experiences? What types of strategies and solutions can be forwarded to help Americans in general and racial and ethnic minorities in particular bounce back? This largely applied research project considers why, in light of singular changes such as the election and reelection of the country's first African American president, growing segments of the Black community continue to face chronic economic challenges. Moreover, we consider implications for social policy and practical suggestions based on the growing belief that the United States is now experiencing a postracial Obama age. By empirically examining some of the economic inequalities that continue to persist across various racial groups, we endeavor to add to a prophetic query that focuses on pragmatic issues that impact the daily lives of people of color in particular and the larger society in general. Furthermore, our findings will inform a more comprehensive dialogue that includes qualitative, quantitative, and theoretical work on the subject of race and racial matters in the United States.

From Recession to Depression?

A "recession" is a slowing of the economy for an extended period. According to the National Bureau of Economic Research, the United States began experiencing a recession in December 2007 (National Bureau of Economic Research 2012). When an economic downturn is sustained and severe, economists often refer to it as an economic depression. For many Americans of color, the economic downturn has been more severe than a recession. Indeed, some have argued that Americans of color are already experiencing "a silent economic depression that, in terms of unemployment, equals or exceeds the Great Depression of 1929" (Rivera et al. 2009:iii). Considered a rare and extreme form of recession, a depression is characterized by its length and abnormal increases in unemployment, scant availability of credit, shrinking output and investment, high bankruptcy rates, and reduced amounts of trade and commerce. By all these criteria, one could argue that Blacks and Latinos are in the midst of an economic depression. Rather than debate the appropriate term to use, we focus an empirical lens on some of the economic indices and implications for Blacks and Latinos of what we are calling the Great Recession.

The unemployment rate is a key indicator of economic well-being. Long periods of high unemployment indicate economic weakness and distress. The Great Recession has increased unemployment rates for all racial and ethnic groups. Since the start of the recession, an estimated 8.1 million jobs have been lost. But because higher unemployment rates for people of color than those for Whites are an enduring part of the U.S. economy, people of color normally face catastrophic recession levels of unemployment. We know that even during periods of economic growth and expansion, the unemployment rates for Blacks and Latinos are consistently higher than those for Whites. During periods of economic downturn, the gaps between Whites and other groups increase even greater. For example, GSS data from 1980 to 2010 suggest that during times of national economic hardship, Blacks and Latinos experience a disproportionate increase in unemployment. Moreover, the highest point for annual unemployment among Whites of 8.6% was still lower than the lowest unemployment rates for Blacks in all but three years since 1980 (Romer 2009).

Furthermore, as of the first quarter of 2010, the official unemployment rate for Blacks of 16.3% was more than 85% higher than the 8.7% rate for Whites. Latinos had an unemployment rate of 12.5% (U.S. Bureau of Labor Statistics 2011). And when we factor in the underemployed (i.e., the broad group of people who have been unable to locate full-time work and are either working part-time or not at all) and discouraged workers who no longer search for employment and thus are not included in unemployment statistics, the gaps between Blacks (23.8%), Latinos (25.1%), and Whites (14.2%) are even greater. The economy negatively affected the profits of many businesses, and unemployment rates for all groups increased. Furthermore, the Great Recession has had a human toll that goes beyond unemployment. Jobless people cannot fully contribute to the economy as taxpayers or as consumers. Indeed, among those without jobs, meeting basic economic needs associated with food and shelter often becomes difficult. Moreover, such persons are often negatively affected emotionally. For example, in 2008, 14.6% of U.S. households experienced "food insecurity" or difficulty providing enough food for all family members. More than 4 million families faced a more severe disruption in the normal diet for some members (Nord, Andrews, and Carlson 2009). These numbers increased through 2010 as unemployment remained high and incomes continued to fall. According to GSS data, 56% of Blacks without jobs reported bankruptcies or property losses compared to 13% of Whites without jobs. Among Whites, 28% of the jobless experienced housing problems. In comparison, 44% of jobless Blacks reported housing difficulties. Similarly, the results also show that 52% of unemployed Whites said they are worse off financially. This compares with 81% of unemployed Blacks who report that they are worse off financially. The above-noted standard indices for broadly assessing quality of life suggest that, although large segments of the U.S. population experienced negative repercussions from the recent recession, people of color such as Blacks and Latinos appeared to feel the brunt of the economic downturn.

From American Dream to Nightmare?

The term "American Dream" is rooted in a phrase from the Declaration of Independence that all men have inalienable rights, including life, liberty, and the pursuit of happiness. Home ownership is often considered a symbol of the American Dream because it suggests that one has achieved a certain level of prosperity. But given the ongoing mortgage crisis, the dream of home ownership has become a nightmare for millions of Americans. According to a 2010 *U.S. Foreclosure Market Report*, more than 2.3 million families have had their homes repossessed since the Great Recession began (RealtyTrac 2010). Nearly 1 million additional foreclosure filings—default notices, scheduled auctions, and bank repossessions—were reported in the third quarter of 2010 alone. This represented about one in every 130 housing units and more than a 20% increase over the same period in 2008. These figures reflect the third highest numbers of foreclosures in a given quarter since such data have been collected. Moreover, August 2010 represented the ninth consecutive month that the pace of homes lost to foreclosure had increased annually. At the same time, the number of families in homeless shelters increased by more than 20% between 2007 and 2009.

Why are the numbers of foreclosures and repossessions growing so dramatically? Who experiences foreclosures and related housing problems and why? Millions of homeowners owe more on their mortgages than their homes' current market values (i.e., often referred to as being "under water"). Government programs aimed at aiding the jobless may do little to assist those who believe they have little choice but to walk away from such housing situations. The following section provides information about the contours of the mortgage crisis. We present a profile and overview of the characteristics of those who have experienced foreclosure and related housing problems since the Great Recession began. We also examine the determinants of foreclosure. Finally, we offer some policy recommendations to stem the tide of housing foreclosures and repossessions and to soften the blow for those who undergo such experiences.

Contours of the Mortgage Crisis:
The Reality of Real Estate 101

The mortgage crisis is an ongoing real estate and financial crises triggered by a dramatic rise in mortgage delinquencies and foreclosures in the United States. For example, the price of U.S. homes peaked in 2006 and began a steep decline thereafter (Federal Housing Finance Agency 2011). High default rates on "subprime" and adjustable rate mortgages (ARMs) began to increase quickly and exacerbated these problems. Arguably, the steep drop in housing prices also resulted in homes being worth less than the amount owed on mortgage loans. This situation undoubtedly provided financial incentive for some borrowers to enter foreclosure.

What are some of the events that precipitated the current crisis? From 2003 to 2006 unusually low interest rates and buyers' expectations of double-digit increases led to new records in the volume of home mortgages being written by U.S. lenders (Johnson and Kwak 2010). About 20% of such loans could be considered "subprime"—that sector of the mortgage industry that serves borrowers with poor credit histories at higher interest rates. One of the major developments leading to the increase in subprime lending was the adoption of new credit scoring techniques that allowed lenders to sort applicants by creditworthiness and to set risk-based loan interest rates. A large percentage of these subprime loans were subsequently sold to Wall Street investment banks. The investment banks, in turn, packaged these loans into debt obligations and sold them to investors around the world.

From 2002 to 2005 rising home prices usually allowed subprime borrowers the opportunity to refinance their loans or to sell their properties when they were unable to make their monthly payments. In addition, many loans were offered with low "teaser" interest rates that would convert later to higher interest rates (Porter 2010). When teaser rates expired and resulted in higher mortgage payments, families that were paying for homes they could barely afford were suddenly required to make mortgage payments that were substantially more than when they first moved into the homes. Such families typically had to cut back on other expenses to pay their mortgages. In many cases, these families turned to credit cards and accrued other debt in order to maintain their lifestyles. By 2007, the U.S. economy was ensconced in a mortgage crisis that led to financial panic and other financial problems. Moreover, unemployment, reduced incomes, and other economic woes exacerbated foreclosures and repossessions.

In September 2010 several mortgage companies put a moratorium on foreclosure sales and evictions in 23 states when the Public Broadcast Service disclosed that much of the information in the legal documentation for foreclosures was not being verified for its accuracy and in some cases documentation was being fabricated (Caldwell 2010). As a consequence, every state attorney general in the United States participated in an investigation into the flawed paperwork and questionable methods behind many foreclosures. Such illegitimate practices are tantamount to lenders rubber-stamping foreclosures without providing due process to homeowners. The practice became known as "robo-signing"—a term that reflects the lack of human review of foreclosure documentation. It also pointed to misbehavior on the part of mortgage servicers that needs to be monitored more carefully. The short-lived moratoria on foreclosures did have an effect, at least temporarily. Foreclosures slowed in several states. However, the damage had been done.

National Policy Responses to the Foreclosure Crisis

Policymakers have stepped in to attempt to soften the economic blow of the foreclosure crisis. A wide variety of proposals have been introduced and adopted. In 2008, for example, some in the investment community feared that the Federal National Mortgage Association (Fannie Mae) and the Federal Home Loan Mortgage Corporation (Freddie Mac)—two government-sponsored enterprises that are the largest mortgage backing entities in the United States—would run out of money. In July 2008 President G. W. Bush signed the Housing and Economic Recovery Act of 2008 that authorized the Federal Housing Administration (FHA) to guarantee up to $300 billion in new 30-year fixed-rate mortgages for subprime borrowers. It was intended to restore confidence in Fannie Mae and Freddie Mac by strengthening regulations and injecting capital into mortgage funding. However, these actions proved to be inadequate and by September 2008 the Bush administration announced that both Fannie Mae and Freddie Mac would be placed into conservatorship—a quasi-nationalized status in which the federal government promised to maintain their solvency by adding new equity on demand and taking over management of them.

In order to impede the downward economic spiral, the Bush administration also proposed and signed into law the Emergency Economic Stabilization Act of 2008. This legislation, commonly referred to as a bailout of the U.S. financial system, was also enacted in response to the subprime mortgage crisis. It authorized the U.S. Secretary of the Treasury to spend up to $700 billion to purchase distressed assets, especially mortgage-backed securities. But many had concerns about such initiatives. To the degree that alteration of loan contracts came to be viewed as bailouts in situations of excessive risk taking, some were concerned that lenders that had taken on unsafe risks would be emboldened to assume even riskier borrowers if they came to believe that they were insulated from the consequences of risky behavior because of such government bailouts.

With the election of Barak Obama as president in 2008, policy shifts occurred with respect to the deepening foreclosure crisis. The Obama administration introduced several initiatives to tackle the crisis. For example, in February 2009 the administration introduced the Financial Stability Plan to address key problems at the heart of the mortgage crisis that it hoped would also help revitalize the economy. A critical piece of that effort was Making Homes Affordable (MHA), a plan to stabilize the housing market and to help struggling homeowners get relief and avoid foreclosure. A central component of MHA was the Home Affordable Modification Program (HAMP) (Gordon 2010), created to provide eligible homeowners the opportunity to modify their mortgages to make them more affordable. Moreover, the Second Lien Modification Program (2MP) offered homeowners with second mortgages a way to modify their second mortgages to make them more affordable when their first mortgage is modified under HAMP. Similarly, the Home Affordable Refinance Program gave homeowners with loans owned or guaranteed by Fannie Mae or Freddie Mac the opportunity to refinance into more affordable monthly payments. Lastly, the Home Affordable Foreclosure Alternatives Program provided opportunities for homeowners who could no longer afford to stay in their homes but wanted to avoid foreclosure to transition to more affordable housing through a short sale or deed-in-lieu of foreclosure. More than 1.3 million homeowners have received help under these programs, but nearly half of those who enrolled in this mortgage relief program have fallen out because of their inability to pay their mortgages even under more favorable terms. Still, with all of these proposals, programs, and attempts to assist homeowners, the scale of the foreclosure crisis continued to grow. The next section explains foreclosure experiences and related housing problems and some of the consequences minorities experienced.

Who Experienced Foreclosure? Groups Most Affected

According to data from the 2007–2009 Panel Study of Income Dynamics (PSID 2009), 5.8% of those who owned homes in 2007 had experienced foreclosure by 2009. Who are these families and individuals who have been foreclosed on, and how do they compare to other homeowners? About 1 in 13 Blacks (7.9%) and Latinos (7.7%) lost their homes to foreclosures. This compares to 1 in 22 Whites (4.5%). In other words, Blacks were 76% more likely than Whites to undergo foreclosures, and Latinos were 71% more likely than Whites. These results suggest that Black and Latino homeowners were hit particularly hard by the foreclosure crisis. The disparity in the foreclosure rates among Blacks, Latinos and Whites is not simply the result of differences in income. Homeowners with incomes of less than $50,000 were the least likely to undergo foreclosure (5.6%); those with incomes in the $50,000–$100,000 range (6.9%) were the most likely to have undergone foreclosure; and 6.3% of those with incomes in excess of $100,000 underwent foreclosure. The pattern of racial disparity is found for all income categories.

The likelihood of undergoing foreclosure increases slightly as education increases: 5.6% of those with less than a high school education underwent foreclosure, as did 6.1% of those with a diploma, and 6.4% of those with more than a high school education. The likelihood of foreclosure decreases slightly with age, as 6.8% of those younger than 35 years, 6.2% of those between the ages of 35 and 50 years, and 5.6% of those over 50 years old have undergone foreclosure. In terms of marital status, divorcees (6.7%) were the most likely to undergo foreclosure. They were followed closely by married couples (6.6%). Families headed by men (6.4%) were slightly more likely to undergo foreclosure than those headed by women (5.7%). Unemployed homeowners (8.1%) were more likely than were other homeowners (5.6%) to have experienced foreclosure. Lastly, the unemployed (28%) were also substantially more likely than others (11%) to have missed mortgage payments in the past year.

Gordon (2010) notes, "some observers have claimed that unemployment is the root cause of the foreclosure crisis. To consider the validity of this claim, it is useful to examine historical trends—that is, to review how the housing market typically behaves during periods of high job losses" (p. 14). Over the past four decades the link between unemployment and foreclosures has been weak. Foreclosure rates have generally climbed over the past four decades, and they have not typically risen more during periods of high unemployment nor declined when unemployment rates have fallen. This suggests that unemployment, while potentially exacerbating foreclosure problems, is not the cause of the problem.

In addition to these basic sociodemographics, other characteristics apparently distinguish between individuals who have been foreclosed on and those who have not. For example, while those with ARMs represented 9.9% of those with mortgages, they represented nearly 3 in 10 (29%) of those foreclosed on. Similarly, those with no (or negative) equity in their homes represented less than 2% of homeowners in 2007. By 2009, they constituted more than 35% of homeowners. During this same time period, 51% of homeowners had lost equity in their homes. In addition to increased foreclosure rates, the toll the Great Recession took is evident in other indices such as poverty rates, income loss, and loss of health insurance. We briefly consider these challenges and their implications for remedying the broader economic malaise.

Poverty and Income Differentials

The poverty line or threshold is the minimum level of income deemed necessary to achieve an adequate standard of living based on government estimates of the amount of money needed to purchase basic goods and services. We consider changes in the poverty rates for various racial and ethnic groups in the United States from 2007 to 2009 based on census data. It suggests that during the Great Recession, poverty levels increased for all groups in the nation. For example, in 2007–2008, poverty rates for Whites increased from 12% to 16%. Blacks saw an increase from 33% to 36%. And for Latinos, the poverty rate increased from 21% to 22%. These figures also parallel income differentials. According to Lin and Bernstein's (2008) calculations, a basic budget required for a family with two adults and two children was $48,778 in 2008. This is well above the median income of Black ($38,269) and Latino families ($40,000). The median income of White families was $61,280. This means that more than 50% of Black and Latino families fall below the basic family budget, as compared with 20% of White families. Furthermore, between 2007 and 2009, the real median U.S. household income fell from $52,163 to $50,313. All racial and ethnic groups experienced large declines in income in 2008. For example, the median White income declined by 2.6% from 2007 to 2008, while Black households experienced a decline of 2.8%. The median Latino household income declined 5.6% during that same period. In 2000, the median Black family earned 63.5% of what the median White family did. By 2009, that ratio had dropped to 62.4%.

Loss of Health Insurance

The Great Recession has affected the health insurance coverage of various groups differentially. According to census data, the number of uninsured adults grew by more than 1.5 million between 2007 and 2008. As the unemployment rate grew, all racial and ethnic groups experienced a decline in employer-sponsored insurance. This drop was partially offset by increases in Medicaid and Medicare. For Whites and Blacks, however, the uninsured rates increased from 13.9% to 14.7% for Whites, and from 25.3% to 25.4% for African Americans. More Latinos turned to public coverage in 2008. So, despite a decrease in employer-sponsored insurance, their uninsured rate declined slightly. However, because of growth in the Latino population, the number of uninsured Latino adults increased by 100,000. One should also note that because of the increase in the size of the low-income population, the number of uninsured, low-income Americans increased by 1.4 million in general.

These findings detail some of the primary economic and non-economic factors that precipitated and exacerbated the current U.S. foreclosure crises. We also illustrate systemic reasons why this national problem disproportionately affected Latinos and Blacks. Beyond statistical profiles, considering some of the sentiments of persons whose lived experiences were inestimably changed as a result of the Great Recession is important. Despite the scope and scale of the mortgage crisis, public opinion about government intervention in the housing market is mixed. For example, according to data from a 2009 *CBS News Survey on the Economic Crisis* (CBS 2009), 38% of Americans say that they are resentful because policies could benefit irresponsible lenders and homeowners. Similarly, 45% believe that problems facing homeowners who are having difficulty paying their mortgages are mostly the result of the homeowners' own financial decisions. Moreover, 40% believe that providing government support to people who are having trouble paying their mortgages is not necessary to help improve the housing market because the housing market will probably improve without such interventions. Such public opinion may make policymakers reluctant to take more action than they already have to respond to the mortgage crisis.

Strategies and Solutions: Combating the Mortgage Crises

In addition to documenting some of the effects of the Great Recession and its implications, we present several strategies and best practices that can be implemented to help keep families in their homes. For example, states and local governments could implement a voluntary property tax "escrow exchange" in which property taxes held in escrow for home-owners by mortgage companies would be released to the mortgage company in exchange for 1.5 times their equivalent in principal and interest payments owed to the mortgage company. When mortgagor and mortgagee agree to this escrow exchange, instead of mortgage payments immediately going into arrears, additional months might be gained by applying would-be tax payments to principal and interest. Instead of mortgage companies receiving none of the revenue during a foreclosure process, they would receive two-thirds of the payment due them by having access to payments from tax escrow accounts. And for local taxing authorities, rather than having local property taxes going unpaid, as is usually the case with foreclosures and repossessions, the payments would be deferred. In short, this escrow exchange would buy time for homeowners, provide additional revenue for lenders, reduce many of the problems associated with foreclosure, and provide the possibility of taxing authorities recouping revenue when homeowners are better able to pay. Second, under a Deed-for-Lease Program, qualifying homeowners facing foreclosure may be able to stay in their homes if they sign a lease and voluntarily transfer the deed of the property back to the lender. This program, while not preventing families from losing their homes, would alleviate the problems associated with foreclosure, such as uprooting families, decaying neighborhoods, and other related hardships. This program would also provide revenue to lenders over the alternative of no revenue for the nine months that a typical repossession takes in a judicial foreclosure.

The Center for Housing Policy (2008) suggests that helping former homeowners return to renting after they have been foreclosed upon is also necessary. High security deposits and the loss in credit rating can make the transition back to the rental market a difficult one. The organization outlines these recommendations:

- Adopt a first-time homebuyer tax credit in jurisdictions with high foreclosure rates and extend eligibility to those who have lost their home to foreclosure in addition to first-time homebuyers.

- Create a preference for housing vouchers to go to families at risk of losing their homes or who have already been foreclosed upon.

- Provide funding for land banks to buy foreclosed properties and rent them back to the former homeowners.

- Provide funds for credit repair counseling.

- Provide assistance with first and last months' rent, security deposits, and the housing search process.

In addition to these ideas, other broader options are possible. One consideration involves expanded spending on education programs so that the unemployed can be better prepared to work at available jobs when jobs reappear. Relatedly, another option is expanding programs that encourage education and skills enhancement, public service, and education debt forgiveness such as AmeriCorps. AmeriCorps members, for example, are involved in service to communities all across America in activities such as tutoring and mentoring disadvantaged youth, fighting illiteracy, improving health services, building affordable housing, teaching computer skills, cleaning parks and other public lands, managing after-school programs, helping communities respond to disasters, and helping build organizational capacity. Such programs, if engaged on a large enough scale, can do much to expand our economy and to soften the impact of the Great Recession. Additionally, proactively responding to the foreclosure crisis could include our aforementioned proposals such as: participating in a voluntary property tax "escrow exchange"; instituting a Deed-for-Lease Program; offering a first-time homebuyer tax credit in jurisdictions with high foreclosure rates and extended eligibility; offering housing voucher preferences to families at risk of losing their homes or who have already been foreclosed upon; providing funding for land banks to buy foreclosed properties and rent them back to the former homeowners; providing funding for credit repair counseling; and, providing assistance with first and last months' rent, security deposits, and the housing search process for persons searching for rental property.

The housing market failure is responsible for more than $1 trillion dollars in lost wealth, severe cuts in state and municipal services, lack of affordable housing for hundreds of thousands of families, tightening of credit markets, and a great decrease in disposable income. As the number of foreclosures grows, the size and scope of these associated costs will escalate. Policymakers have taken action, but the crisis continues, and the public's patience for ineffective policies is waning. Despite the extent of the mortgage crisis, a segment of the public clearly does not want additional bailouts. But policymakers must be steadfast in their search for solutions because homeownership represents not only an individual good, but also the common good. Encouraging homeownership and offering carefully targeted programs and strategies to ensure that this symbol of the American Dream remains attainable and sustainable for as many families as possible is in the best interest of the community, the state, and the nation.

Conclusions and Policy Recommendations: What's Next?

Experts expected that many people would worry about their economic well-being and security during economic downturns; however, the consequences of the recent economic crisis were not evenly distributed. This chapter examines how the Great Recession (2007–2010) took its toll disproportionately on Americans of color and offers possible solutions for short- and long-term redress. Some readers may wonder how our analysis constitutes a prophetic query. We contend that prophetic thinking must also include pragmatic studies focused on issues such as quality of life, lived experiences, and life chances that complement more unconventional theoretical and empirical studies on the implications of race, racial matters, and postracial beliefs. This chapter provides such an analysis. Economic recessions are at times portrayed as short-term events. However, they can and do have harmful lasting effects. For example, job loss and falling incomes can force families to delay or forgo a college education for their children. Recessions also bring about economic hardships, rising poverty, and the inability for families to purchase necessary food and medicine. They are associated with lower levels of insurance and deleterious health outcomes.

As we have shown throughout this chapter, the effects of recessions are not borne equally. People of color such as Blacks and Latinos often experience the brunt of economic downturns. Economic indicators that were negative for such groups before the recession tend to get worse. Indeed, one may reasonably argue that during the Great Recession, communities of color have actually been experiencing an economic depression. Unfortunately, racial inequality in the economy, education, criminal justice, and health-care arenas prevent many people of color from achieving their potential. When these individuals fail to prosper, the nation as a whole is less prosperous as well. Such economic travail may seem particularly troubling given the singular political and economic strides we've made as a nation.

What can be done? And how can we better understand the situation based on the postracial rhetoric so common today? When jobs disappear, public jobs programs and the direct intervention of government in the private labor market may go a long way toward the creation of jobs and the reduction of the harmful effects of the Great Recession. But such programs are often politically unpopular and raise concerns about too much government intervention. They are also an expensive remedy that may not offer a cure. For example, on the national front, the American Recovery and Reinvestment Act—otherwise known as the $787 billion economic stimulus act—and other efforts to stimulate the economy and job growth have and will continue to add to the fiscal deficit. Those costs should be viewed as necessary to provide the short-term boost that allows us to avoid even greater long-term damage to families and to the economy. Stimulus proposals based on tax cuts for the wealthy or for business owners are not likely to provide immediate relief to the unemployed, especially people of color. Consider the now-infamous case of Caterpillar in Illinois. President Obama suggested that passing the stimulus package would help Caterpillar avoid laying off additional employees and even hire back some of those who had recently been laid off. Caterpillar CEO Jim Owens subsequently contradicted these comments and announced that Caterpillar would need to lay off an additional 2,500 workers. The total number of layoffs at Caterpillar exceeded 20,000 (Kelleher 2009; Travers 2009).

These sobering findings also call into question beliefs that we now live in a postracial age. Despite the election and reelection of the first Black U.S. president in 2008 and 2012, respectively, many of the economic remnants of historic and systemic racial discrimination continue (Bonilla-Silva 1996; Feagin and Feagin 1978; Gallagher 2003; Oliver and Shapiro 1995; Omi and Winant 1994). Moreover, belief that racial and ethnic discrimination and inequities no longer exist in the United States stymie both concerted efforts to combat chronic conditions that disproportionately impact people of color and acknowledgement by Whites who directly or indirectly benefit from such inequality (Bonilla-Silva 1996, 2006; Feagin 2006; Gaertner and Dovidio 1986; Gallagher 2003). Importantly, we must applaud the noteworthy advances we have made in the United States economically, politically, socially, and culturally. Equally important is admitting the challenges still yet to conquer. One such challenge includes combating economic inequality in all its forms. The Great Recession and its side effects pose some formidable challenges to policymakers. It will test the nation's values and priorities. Such an economic crisis will not just let us wait and let the market correct itself. Rather, we must prudently consider the pros and cons of concrete policies and proposals, such as those discussed in this chapter, that can be implemented to help stimulate economic growth and help reduce racial and ethnic disparities.

References

Bonilla-Silva, Eduardo. 1996. "Rethinking Racism: Toward a Structural Inter-pretation." *American Sociological Review* 62 (June):465–80.
———. 2006. *Racism without Racists: Color-Blind Racism and the Persistence of Racial Inequality in the United States.* Lanham, MD: Rowman and Littlefield.
Caldwell, Phyllis. 2010. "Testimony before the Congressional Oversight Panel Hearing on the Troubled Asset Relief Program Foreclosure Mitigation Program." Washington, DC.
CBS News. 2009. "Economic Crisis Survey." Storrs, CT: Roper Center for Public Opinion Research. Retrieved on August 28, 2010 (http://www.ropercenter.uconn.edu.proxy.cc.uic.edu/CFIDE/cf/action/catalog/abstract.cfm?).
Center for Housing Policy. 2008. "Foreclosure Living: Resources and Advice for a Good Life after Foreclosure." Retrieved November 4, 2010 (http://www.foreclosureliving.com/tag/return-to-renting/).
Feagin, Joe R. and Clairece B. Feagin. 1978. *Discrimination American Style: Institutional Racism and Sexism.* Englewood Cliffs, NJ: Prentice Hall.
———. 2006. *Systemic Racism: A Theory of Oppression.* New York: Routledge.
Federal Housing Finance Agency. 2011. "House Price Index Falls 0.8 Percent in Fourth Quarter 2010; House Prices Decline in Most States." Washington, DC: Federal Housing Finance Agency.
Gaertner, John and Samuel Dovidio. 1986. *Prejudice, Racism, and Discrimination.* Orlando, FL: Academic Press.
Gallagher, Charles A. 2003. "Color-Blind Privilege: The Social and Political Functions of Erasing the Color Line in Post Race America." *Race, Gender and Class* 10(4):1–17.
Gordon, Julia. 2010. "Testimony before the Congressional Oversight Panel Hearing on HAMP, Servicer Abuses, and Foreclosure Prevention Strate-gies: Hearing Before the Congressional Oversight Panel for the Troubled Asset Relief Program, 111th Congress. Retrieved on November 1, 2010 (http://cybercemetery.unt.edu/archive/cop/20110402015801/http://cop.senate.gov/documents/testimony-102710-gordon.pdf).
Johnson, Simon and James Kwak. 2010. *13 Bankers: The Wall Street Takeover and the Next Financial Meltdown.* New York: Pantheon Books.
Kelleher, James B. 2009. "Caterpillar Sets More Layoffs; Week's Total 22,000." Reuters (syndicated). Retrieved March 14, 2012 (http://www.reuters.com/article/2009/01/30/us-caterpillar-idUSTRE50T41K20090130).

Lin, James and Jared Bernstein. 2008. "What We Need to Get By: A Basic Standard of Living Costs $48,778, and Nearly a Third of Families Fall Short." Economic Policy Institute Briefing Paper. Washington, DC: Economic Policy Institute. Retrieved December 16, 2010 (http://www.epi.org/files/page/-/old/briefingpapers/224/bp224.pdf).

National Bureau of Economic Research. 2012. *NBER Business Cycle Dating Procedure.* Retrieved October 20, 2012 (www.nber.org/cycles/recessions_faq.html).

Nord, Mark, Margaret Andrews, and Steven Carlson. 2009. *Household Food Security in the United States, 2008.* Darby, PA: Diane Publishing.

Oliver, Melvin L. and Thomas M. Shapiro. 1995. *Black Wealth/White Wealth: A New Perspective on Racial Inequality.* New York: Routledge.

Omi, Michael and Howard Winant. 1994. *Racial Formation in the United States: From the 1960s to the 1990s.* 2nd ed. New York: Routledge.

Panel Study of Income Dynamics, Foreclosures, 2007–2009 Public Use Dataset (PSID). 2007–2009. Ann Arbor: University of Michigan.

Porter, Katherine. 2010. "Testimony before the Congressional Oversight Panel Hearing 14 on the TARP Foreclosure Mitigation Program." Washington, DC, HAMP, Servicer Abuses, and Foreclosure Prevention Strategies: Hearing before the Congressional Oversight Panel for the Troubled Asset Relief Program, 111th Congress. Retrieved November 1, 2010 (http://cybercemetery.unt.edu/archive/cop/20110402015351/http://cop.senate.gov/documents/testimony-102710-porter.pdf).

RealtyTrac. 2010. "Foreclosure Activity Increases 4 Percent in Third Quarter." U.S. *Foreclosure Market Report.* Irvine, CA: RealtyTrac. Retrieved on November 8, 2010 (http://www.realtytrac.com/content/press-releases/q3-2010-and-september-2010-foreclosure-reports-6108).

Rivera, Amaad, Jeannette Huezo, Christina Kasica, and Dedrick Muhammad. 2009. *State of the Dream, 2009: The Silent Depression.* Boston: United for a Fair Economy.

Romer, Christina D. 2009. "Lessons from the Great Depression for Economic Recovery in 2009." Paper presented at the Brookings Institution, Washington, DC, March 9.

Travers, Karen. 2009. "CEO Contradicts Obama on Rehiring Employees." *ABC News.* Retrieved January 31, 2013 (http://abcnews.go.com/Politics/story?id=6866995&page=1).

U.S. Bureau of Labor Statistics. 2011. *Employment and Earnings, January 2011.* Washington, DC: U.S. Bureau of Labor Statistics.

5

~

Black Experiences, White Experiences

Why We Need a Theory of Systemic Racism

LOUWANDA EVANS

Millsaps College

JOE FEAGIN

Texas A&M University

In the past century, social science research has made pivotal gains in understanding the nature of race, racism, and racist ideologies (Bonilla-Silva 2010; Feagin 2006, 2013; Gaertner and Dovidio 1986; Gallagher 2003). As a result, increasing numbers of scholars suggest that many long-held understandings and conceptualizations of racial issues need to be theorized in ways that reposition and reconceptualize vital racial realities (Bonilla-Silva 2003, 2010; Feagin 2006, 2013; Gallagher 2003). Much social science research is seriously weakened by using concepts such as "prejudice," "stereotype," "bigotry," "intolerance," and "individual discrimination," which insufficiently describe and explain the scope and nature of race and contemporary racial matters. In truth, a major conceptual and theoretical problem exists in American social science because of the commonplace use of these relatively weak analytical terms. Social science concepts such as "bigoted discrimination," "prejudice," and "stereotyping" are often used generically in ways that suggest all people can be major discriminatory actors and take part equally in creating a racially troubled society. Moreover, because such concepts have tended to focus on individual, microlevel situations, they suggest that all people can experience negative outcomes associated with race similarly. Yet such concepts, without an analysis of the historical and systemic nature of racism in the United States, often become vague concepts that some scholars can use to downplay the significant costs and consequences of systemic racism (Lewis 1966; Mead 1992; Moynihan 1967; Murray 1984; Myrdal 1962; Ogbu 1978, 1991; Wilson 1978). Our prophetic intervention addresses these prevailing problematic epistemologies of race through attention to racism as a fundamental systemic process and the development of concepts that more thoroughly account for the experiences of minority groups. As we posit in this chapter, conventional concepts such as "bigoted discrimination," "prejudice," and "stereotyping" are inadequate for understanding the everyday experiences of people of color. We contend that the development of stronger theoretical concepts—such as "systemic racism" and the "White racial frame"—need to be put in the forefront of social science conceptualizations to fully comprehend the everyday racist realities many people of color face.

We rely on in-depth interview and survey results analyzed using Burawoy's (1991) extended case method to address the following questions: What are the current racial realities facing Black students at predominately White colleges in the American southwest?[1] What do White students think about HBCUs in particular and Black students generally? Are current mainstream social science concepts such as prejudice, individual discrimination, and stereotyping useful in adequately capturing the everyday racial experiences of such students? Lastly, will findings illustrate that concepts such as "White racial frame" and "systemic racism" more comprehensively and appropriately illustrate contemporary race-related dynamics in the postracial Obama age? Studies show that racial oppression remains well-imbedded in major U.S. institutions—including higher education (Feagin 2006, 2013; Gallagher 2003; Omi and Winant 1994). Though progress has been made to dismantle legal segregation and overt racism in certain areas of higher education, many less obvious racial barriers and discriminatory practices remain part of such spaces in significant and sustained ways. Furthermore, student inquiry is encouraged in collegiate spaces and many students may not have learned to be politically correct when discussing race-related topics

(Bonilla-Silva 2003; Bonilla-Silva and Forman 2000; Gaertner and Dovidio 1986). Thus we focus on higher education as a research site here. This chapter examines the important social contexts and experiences of Black and White university students to better assess how historic social science concepts used to understand racialized experiences and racism are inadequate to fully gauge and challenge many current racist realities.

Central to this analysis is the concept "White racial frame," which we contend incorporates each of the dimensions of stereotypes, narratives, images, emotions, and inclinations to discriminate—and more accurately explains contemporary racial dynamics in the United States. In light of continued racism in this country, we further posit that the White racial frame includes historical, foundational, and institutional aspects of racial oppression and the consequences of these actions to Whites and people of color. In the United States, racial oppression has been demonstrated to be both foundational and systemic (Feagin 2006, 2013). This racial oppression involves much more than a set of competing and balancing "racial formations" (Omi and Winant 1994) or some social cancer on the side of an otherwise healthy U.S. society. Building upon developed theories of systemic racism and the White racial frame, we highlight the experiences of Blacks at predominately White universities and then examine White students' perspectives to better understand the college worlds in which Black students must navigate, survive, and thrive.

Race Theories and Concepts: The White Racial Frame

One primary assertion here is that many mainstream social science concepts have become too limited to adequately detail the racial realities of people of color in White-dominated institutions (Bonilla-Silva 1996; Feagin 2006, 2010, 2013; Feagin and Feagin 1978). Terms such as "prejudice," "stereotyping," and "(individual) discrimination" have become common phrases used in everyday conversation. These terms are now used interchangeably by many people outside academia. For example, prejudice is defined as "the negative evaluation of a social group, and individuals within that group, based upon conceptions held about the group despite facts that contradict them" (Anderson and Taylor 2008:276). In other words, prejudice usually involves an individual's negative attitudes toward an entire category of people (Schaefer 2011). Similarly, stereotypes are often believed to be individuals' oversimplifications or beliefs about members of a social group that are usually incorrect, but are nonetheless used to describe the typical member of some social group (Anderson and Taylor 2008). These concepts have long remained an important aspect of the social science literature and have helped move discussions of racial and ethnic relations forward. However, as documented racial experiences of people of color and the methods of racial discrimination against them continue to change, a reconceptualization should also occur to adequately document the continuing struggles of people of color—one that encompasses the systemic and foundational nature of racism and racial oppression accented from a strong (non-White) counterframing.

Moreover, contemporary discussions of discrimination, or the "denial of opportunities and equal rights to individuals and groups because of prejudice or other arbitrary reasons" (Schaefer 2011:36), do not capture well the collective consequences of a long history of discrimination. In all their basic forms, these concepts obscure the larger relationships to society and how they function to maintain the racial status quo. In everyday usage of these terms, we posit that the historical and systemic underpinnings often remain hidden and inconspicuous. This observation does not imply that members of all racial groups cannot face stereotypes, prejudice, and individualized discrimination, but rather it suggests that the historical and systemic foundation of racialized experiences differs among U.S. racial groups and with vastly different consequences. At face value, the contemporary use of these particular concepts assumes a zero-sum, colorblind formulation that fails to account for the historical experiences of minority groups as well as White dominance (Bonilla-Silva 2010; Gallagher 2003). As formulated in this research, continually calling attention to White dominance and inequality by framing inequality based on a systemic perspective is important.

On one hand, academicians widely accept that "race" is a social construct, and is therefore a category that can shift and be rearticulated across time. Omi and Winant (1994) sought to enhance our understanding of race using their racial formation thesis. Racial formations, or the sociohistorical process by which racial categories are created, inhabited, transformed, and destroyed, seek a rearticulation of "race" by emphasizing "the social nature of race, the absence of any essential racial characteristics, the historical flexibility of racial meanings and categories, the conflictual character of race at both the 'micro-' and 'macro-social' levels" (p. 5). Although this theory continues to be a pivotal work in social science, it "overemphasizes the racial projects of certain actors, thus obscuring the general character of racialized societies" (Bonilla-Silva 1996:466). Because of this tendency, many scholars have instead underscored the foundational and systemic nature of race and racism (Bonilla-Silva 1996; Carmichael and Hamilton 1967; Feagin 2006, 2010, 2013; Feagin and Feagin 1978).

The White Racial Frame Detailed

In closely examining the contours and realities of U.S. racial oppression, some researchers (Feagin 2006, 2013; Moore 2008; Picca and Feagin 2007) have shown that a dominant, White-created racial frame provides an overarching and generally destructive worldview of racial matters that extends across White social divisions of class, gender, and age. This concept—"White racial frame"—is foundational to this analysis and thus detailed in the next several paragraphs. Since its early and full development over the seventeenth century, studies show that this powerful racial frame has provided the vantage point from which the vast majority of White Americans has constantly viewed North American society. The centrality of this centuries-old frame in the mind of most Whites makes it a dominant societal frame. Over time, it has expanded, nuanced, and imposed on the psyches of most Americans of all races, ages, classes, and other demographic groupings, thereby becoming the country's dominant racial frame of mind and frame of reference.

Feagin (2013) notes that Whites have historically combined several important features in this broad racial frame: racial stereotypes (a belief aspect); racial narratives and interpretations (integrating cognitive aspects); racial images (a visual aspect) and language accents (an auditory aspect); racialized emotions (a "feelings" aspect); and, inclinations toward discriminatory action. The frame results in both a strong positive orientation toward Whites and whiteness and a negative orientation toward those racial "others" who are exploited and oppressed. Due to its indelible nature, many Whites employ these features in their everyday actions and decisions as they relate to people of color. The contemporary White racial frame encompasses concepts about what is racially desirable and undesirable. This White racial frame serves as an important aspect of systemic racism because it "does not exist apart from everyday experience, and racist practices flowing from it are essential parts of the larger system of racial oppression" (Feagin 2013:13).

The contemporary racial framing of Blacks by such Whites includes notions of colorblindness and the tendency to minimize the racial inequality that the former group collectively experiences (Bonilla-Silva 2003). Respondents in this study provide sobering examples of resulting negative outcomes. By showing how the White racial frame has evolved over time, yet endured because of its deep connections to systemic racism, we assess more recent expressions and attitudes of White college students. While our White racial frame concept acknowledges the vacillating nature of racial framing, its long-standing systemic nature is apparent. Using the concepts of "systemic racism" and the "White racial frame," this chapter examines the experiences of Black students on predominantly White campuses and then contrasts those with the views of White students about Blacks and HBCUs. In our examination of Black experiences, we show that moving beyond concepts such as "individualistic stereotyping" and "prejudice" and repositioning Black and White experiences within the conceptual context of the White racial frame to better understand contemporary racial interrelationships and realities is important.

Race and Racism on College Campuses

Until recent decades, Black students were excluded from virtually all historically White institutions of higher education. HBCUs were created to redress this exclusion (Bennett and Xie 2003). Even as predominantly White institutions of higher learning continue to increase their enrollment of Black students, the latter's experiences on those campuses have often been plagued with feelings of alienation, discriminatory mistreatment, and overt and covert expressions of racial prejudice (Swim et al. 2003). Because of the historical nature of exclusionary practices against many Black students, as key societal institutions, predominantly White college campuses are fundamentally racialized and "function to reproduce racist social relations and ideologies that support these relations as institutions" (Moore 2008:24). While many Black students continue to bear the burden of dealing with racism on White college campuses, others turn to HBCUs for increased integration in campus life, reduced racism, and more satisfying interpersonal relationships (Allen and Jewell 2002; Bennet and Xie 2003; Swim et al. 2003). Studies designed to understand the racial climate at historically White universities show that many White students openly state that they do not hold negative views about Blacks or their academic abilities. Moreover, they do not consider racial discrimination to be a major problem (Bonilla-Silva 2010; Feagin, Vera, and Imani 1996; Picca and Feagin 2007). Norton and Sommers (2011) also found that although Blacks continue to believe societal racism is a problem, Whites believe anti-Black racism no longer exists. Furthermore, many Whites believe that anti-White racism is now a serious concern that requires a change in political discourse and policy. These types of disparate attitudes and experiences provide the context for the current study.

Methodology: Studying Controversial Issues

Burawoy's (1991) extended case method guides this analysis. This method takes existing social theory and examines its usefulness for making sense of new data and then alters or replaces that extant theory if it does not offer a full explanation of the new data. The extended case method allows us to examine the value of newer theoretical contributions in the area of systemic racism and the White racial frame against the more heavily used social science concepts such as racial prejudice, stereotyping, and bigotry. This method also examines how external forces from the larger social structure shape students' social situations. Using this approach, we argue that the racialized experiences of Black college students cannot be fully understood apart from considering individual agents of discrimination, their social group, and certain important institutions in the larger society. Because the language surrounding racial inequality has become much more covert—often concealed in colorblind ideologies—uncovering racial attitudes and how these attitudes contribute to the racialized environments of Black students remains of utmost research and policy importance (Allen 2007; Allen and Jewel 2002; Bonilla-Silva and Forman 2000; Feagin et al 1996). Burawoy's (1991) extended case method enables us to identify and describe some of these situations.

The field research was conducted at several Southwestern universities between 2006 and 2009 as part of a larger study. Face-to-face in-depth interviews were conducted with 35 Black students between the ages of 18 and 31 concerning their experiences at two predominately White universities in 2006–2007. Of the total, 18 Black (African American can be used interchangeably) students were male and 17 were female. Each university had a Black student population that represented less than 15% of the student body. The first university boasted one of the more diverse student populations in the nation, with White students comprising just over 50% of the population; 12 Black male and 13 Black female students were interviewed from this site. At the second school, which has a student population of about 48,000, about 3% of the student body self-classified as Black; Whites constitute the majority at 69%. A total of 10 Black students were interviewed at the second site—6 males and 4 females. Snowball sampling, a methodology used to gain entry into difficult-to-reach social networks, was used at each site to obtain interviewees. Snowball sampling remains a viable qualitative method to reach often hidden populations (Noy 2008). Each interview lasted between 45 and 90 minutes and was audiotaped.

The third college in the sample, also in the Southwest, had a student population of more than 12,000 in 2009; Black students represented just 5% of the student body. About 150 open-ended anonymous surveys were distributed to students between ages 18 and 29 enrolled in social science courses. Sociology and psychology courses were chosen based on the likelihood that such students would be more than familiar with concepts such as "prejudice," "stereotyping," "discrimination," and "bigotry." The surveys were constructed to better understand the perspectives of White students toward Blacks and HBCUs. Open-ended questions enabled participants to elaborate on their responses. Students also provided demographic data including gender, age, racial identity, and primary residence. Of the 150 students, 8 self-identified as Black (or African American), 12 were Latino, and 3 were Asian American; 3 participants did not provide a racial identity and were excluded from the analysis. White students were the major members of this convenience sample (n=124). Sixty percent of the sample was female. Because we anticipated that many Whites are aware that expressing overtly negative attitudes toward people of color, even in anonymous surveys, is not socially desirable, we elected to assess their racial attitudes by asking them about perceptions of educational institutions associated with Blacks. In doing so, we expected results to also inform us about their views about Blacks as well.

Several additional statements about our methodology are in order. The sensitive nature of the subject matter warrant certain data-collection processes to garner the views of as many students as possible. Thus we intentionally relied on convenience and snowball sampling rather than random sampling during the interview phase. Despite its limitations, convenience sampling, a sampling method in which participants are selected because of availability, "provides an important opportunity to examine contemporary racial attitudes" (Bonilla-Silva and Forman 2000:54). Furthermore, we realize that students in sociology and psychology courses may have different views about racial issues than their peers in courses such as chemistry and mathematics because of the former students' exposure to the social sciences. However, we do not know how these differences in views might manifest. We acknowledge these limitations and their impact on the ability to generalize our findings (Babbie 2002; Bickman and Rog 1998). However, our sample selection and results are not intended to be generalizable to the larger U.S. student population, but will be used as a guide to assist theory building and illume the attitudes and experiences of a set of students. The next sections include our analysis and representative quotes.

Black Students: Views and Experiences at HWCUs

The alienating experiences of Black students on White college campuses have and continue to be researched (Allen 1992; Allen and Jewel 2002; Allen, Jewel, Griffin, and Wolf 2007; Bennett and Xie 2003; Bonilla-Silva and Forman 2000; Feagin et al. 1996). We further assess their experiences here and contend that these representative quotes inform a more comprehensive understanding of racism, its embeddedness in society, and the implications for many Blacks in particular and the larger society in general. Although Black and White college students maneuver similar academic environments, their socioracial experiences are indeed contrasting and often opposite in effect (Allen 2007; Bennett and Xie 2003; Bonilla-Silva 2000; Feagin et al. 1996). Black students are often forced to live in and understand the context of institutional racism and suffer its significant consequences that can take the form of stereotyping. However, here we stress in our conceptualization of stereotypes the more deleterious influence of the White racial frame from which they usually stem. By referencing the historic and foundationally racist derivations, contexts, and connotations of stereotypes, the transparency and impact of even seemingly "minor" stereotypes aimed at Blacks becomes clearer, as do their links to the deeper White racial framing that informs our racist history. For example, John, a 21-year-old Black education major, describes his job near one historically White campus:

> The White people here are kinda set back in their ways so we have issues. It's a lot of racist people over here. From the way they treated me out here by school and on the job, I mean, I started to see—wait, that is true, they do grab their pocketbooks and purses or clinch their pockets when I get on the elevator with them. . . . I work at a fast food restaurant up the road, and we have people here that don't want me to fix their food—or they want to watch you wash your hands and ask you outright if you and the facilities are clean.

Some of the oldest anti-Black stereotypes, dating back to Thomas Jefferson's era, are apparent in this account (Feagin 2006; Gaertner and Dovidio 1986). The stereotypical perception of Blacks as dirty and criminal is not a recent invention, yet this entrenched historical framing can be missed if we examine stereotypes as mere surface-level cognitions or as specific, individual incidents distinct from a broader racialized context as they are customarily understood. For minority members, group stereotypes of this nature result in a collective remembrance of subordinate social positions and a long-standing racial hierarchy—which most Whites do not appear to have. Based on the above painful account, continual exposure to these deeply embedded stereotypes by Whites can carry significant emotional, psychological, and physical consequences.

Negative racial imagery as well as mistreatment associated with this imagery and associated ideologies are a major aspect of the White racial frame, which in turn, is a key component of systemic racism. Consider another telling account from Darryl, an 18-year-old mechanical engineering major attending a historically White university: "I am new here to the school and I already want to leave. It is hard being here. I have been called a nigger three times and I have only been here a little over a month." In this example, considering use of the "N-word" an example of mere stereotyping or prejudiced is an inadequate assessment. Such experiences do not reflect a few deranged Whites with momentary lapses of morality, but are rather part of the culture in the larger society in which such language is tacitly condoned. To many Blacks, this racist epithet serves as a blatant reminder that "one's humanity is automatically devalued because of one's race" (Cose 1993:43). Recognizing the historical and institutional foundation of the White racial oppression from which this word emerged and its oppressive nature is important; inherently attached to it are many damaging meanings that are evoked to signify Black inferiority in the minds of many Whites. The constant social reproduction ("three times" in this case) of this systemically racist language—and a much broader anti-Black racial framing—is indeed a process that is intended to maintain the existing racial hierarchy. This type of incident reflects the negative outcomes associated with a White racial frame. Although he has only been matriculating one month, the actual event, its frequency over a relatively short period of time, and ease with which it occurred, all illustrate the embeddedness of a White racial frame and that its existence has already begun to have a deleterious effect on Darryl.

Darryl's desire to exit the hostile space and the gravity and heaviness of having such racialized experiences is one that White administrators, faculty, and students typically fail to acknowledge. In researching Black males on college campuses, Smith, Allen, and Danley (2007) conceptualize these experiences and the ensuing responses as "racial battle fatigue"—the "physiological and psychological strain exacted on racially marginalized groups and the amount of energy lost dedicated to coping with microaggressions and racism" (p. 555). The concept of "microaggressions" also helps inform our understanding of the critical distinction between mere prejudices and individualized racist encounters and those linked to a White racial frame. Microaggressions describe a continual barrage of slights, brief encounters, and short-lived, but negative experiences that, over time, amass and result in long-term detrimental effects on recipients. The frequency of such aggressions, meted out by myriad Whites over time supports claims that their impetus is systemic.

Furthermore, the overt use of a racial epithet can place Blacks in an agonizing dilemma: Is speaking out against racist behavior in an atmosphere where color-blind ideologies suggest the slur is an isolated instance appropriate or necessary? Whites use colorblind notions of meritocracy and equality, accusations of reverse racism, and the fact that some Blacks use the "N-word" to accuse Blacks of being hypersensitive or playing the race card (McKinney 2005). Over time, Darryl's failure to respond can result in his becoming more accepting of such encounters and ultimately losing his "voice" to these controlling images (Collins 2000). Such Whites fail to recognize the deep structural context and significance of such oppressive language or the larger collective meaning to Blacks when they hear this racial epithet. Whites' attempts to redefine and minimize the negativity associated with the "N-word" reflect their belief in White authority and superiority to dictate its use—and represent an example of the dangerous implications of the White racial frame.

In addition to racial slurs, Black students can be subject to other taunts in spaces where such behavior is often expected and accepted. For example, Carlos, a 22-year-old kinesiology major, poignantly describes the experiences of students near campus:

> Some students of color live in the area near campus, and they get water balloons thrown at them; they get harassed. You know when some people get drunk, I mean when some White people get drunk[—]that's just the kinda stuff they do, and I would hate for an individual like myself or my roommate to come about it [*sic*]. I mean, we are not fighters, but some stuff you gotta make a stand against. You hear the word "nigger" shouted out of windows like it's an everyday word. Come on—really!

In this account, Whites physically and verbally abuse students of color. For Carlos, a common tactic is to ignore verbal assaults. However, he suggests a "tipping point" (Smith et al. 2007) after which a response by the oppressed person is necessary (Collins 2000). Although the nature of much White-racist behavior has changed to more covert and subtle methods, some Whites still rely on historical methods of blatant intimidations to remind people of color of their "place" in the racial system "drawn from a legacy of White racial oppression, exclusion, and violence" (Moore 2008:29). Experienced Black students at historically White universities or in other traditionally White spaces become very familiar with White-racist slurs, learn how to avoid becoming lost and isolated, and learn methods to protect themselves from the harm that comes from enduring or confronting negative racial climates (Stewart 2008). This necessary ability to cope with racial experiences comes from a tradition of collective memory for most Blacks. And by extension, Whites who engage in such behavior are also informed by another dimension of this same collective memory.

Traditional social science conceptualizations of individual stereotyping, prejudice, and bigoted discrimination do not adequately explain the character and sources of the deep emotions felt by Whites who repeatedly resort to yelling racist epithets and throwing objects at students of color. These tendencies should be understood based on the long-standing historical and hierarchical positions of power and domination held by Whites that has been designed to elicit fear and intimidation in Blacks and other people of color. Concepts to replace traditional conceptualizations must reflect the severity, magnitude, embeddedness, and potentially devastating nature of systemic racism for people of color as well as the loss of humanity both Whites and Blacks ultimately experience as a result. Most racial stereotyping and prejudice are part of this broad White racial frame that portrays racial minorities summarily negatively and imbeds a learned predisposition to act in a negative way toward such minorities (Feagin 2006, 2013).

As shown in the following excerpt, young Black men are often considered "criminal" or "looking for trouble" by Whites in power (Feagin 2006, 2013). Will, a 20-year-old political science major at a historically White campus, recounts a common story for Black men:

> I had just got a new car. I was leaving my girlfriend's house at about midnight to head back towards campus. A [White] cop kept trailing me and he turned on his lights, pulled out a bullhorn and start saying, "Pull over." He came to my passenger window and knocked. I did not have automatic windows, so I leaned over to roll it down and he gripped his gun. He took out his flashlight and started looking in the car and asked if he was going to find marijuana. I said, "I don't smoke, my asthma pump is right there." . . . He said, "Don't get smart with me son." So again, he said, "If I search your car, I won't find any marijuana?" I said, "No sir, but I don't think you can just search my car." He said, "Hold on, I'm the law. . . ."

While this is an example of White racial stereotyping, the social science concept of "stereotyping" does not adequately communicate the deeper social reality and magnitude of the encounter. In this instance, we need to note the very old, systemic, and foundational aspects of the officer's White-framed stereotypes, their creation, and their purpose. "Stereotype," as used currently in most social science literature, fails to capture and encompass the impactful reality and countering perspective of Blacks who are routinely and severely targeted. In addition to profiling Will, the campus policeman overgeneralizes about Black males, assuming that the student will be in possession of marijuana. Moreover, because he is assumed to be guilty, the student is forced to experience a harassing search. Furthermore, studies suggest that White actors constantly use the larger White racial framing from which these racist ideas and ideologies are constructed to justify the racial status quo and protect White group interests (Bonilla-Silva 2003). As evidenced in the following multilayered incident that Steven, a 21-year-old business major, experienced on a major street near his historically White campus, historic anti-Black stereotypes do not exist in a vacuum, but are part of a generalized White collective framing of Black men:

> My roommate and I were coming from the grocery store, heading back to campus and all of a sudden, its [*sic*] two cop cars on us. Next thing you know, me [*sic*] and my roommate both; mind you, we are about 300 feet away from our destination; both of us layin' in the dirt, handcuffed; four cop cars down there; guns drawn. . . . So, they stood us up, and, naturally, I was pissed off 'cause they didn't tell us anything and so he goes, "Do you know why we pulled you over? We got a report that two Black males committed a robbery." So, apparently we fit the description; two Black males in an older model sedan and so they decided to handcuff us and look through our bags and look in his trunk. They made us spin around and stuff. I mean, I called my dad, I called everybody I know. That has never happened to me. In this area, I realize I am always gonna fit their description.

The idea of "fitting the description" has been documented in the work of Smith et al. (2007), who note that Black men have often been constructed in a way that defines them as "out of place" and "fitting the description" of illegitimate nonmembers of the campus community (p. 552). Steven continues: "My world came crashing down. . . . I began to see all the things that had been happening to me all along that were racist." Emotionally traumatized, this new experience was devastating for Steven, but resulted in an epiphany after which he was cognizant of prior personal racist experiences. His previous desire to view the social world as a postracial or nonracist space provided an escape from imagining and acknowledging the everyday racist realities that many Blacks face (Bonilla-Silva 2010; Collins 2000; Feagin 2013). Moreover, the incident solidified a sobering reality for Steven—that his educational attainment or future successes would never nullify the negative opinion most White persons would have about him. In this instance, this type of racial profiling incident results in recollections of past injustices and the reality of the additional societal burden such students of color usually carry and from which they can never escape.

For Blacks and other students of color, experiences of everyday racism in and around historically White campuses can lead to stress, psychological problems, anger, fear, bitterness, excessive alcohol consumption, and numerous problems with classes and grades (Bynum, Burton, and Best 2007). In these predominately White environments where everyday racism is common, Black students often suffer from lower achievement and problems coping with constant affronts to their racial identity (Tatum 1997). Additionally, they often believe that they have little choice but to accept the racist epithets and episodes as part of the personal and psychological price they pay for securing certain societal opportunities (Cose 2011; Picca and Feagin 2007). Dealing with recurring feelings of social isolation and exclusion becomes a huge personal and peer group burden. Tatum (1997) corroborates this sobering reality: "White students and faculty frequently underestimate the power and presence of the overt and covert manifestations of racism on campus, and students of color often come to predominantly White campuses expecting more civility than they find" (p. 78). Several respondents mentioned leaving their universities or wondered, "Is it really worth it?" Understanding the recurring and chronically racist experiences of Black students on predominately White campuses across the country means understanding well the systemic nature of White racial framing and its ideologies, emotions, and inclinations. In these institutions that often stress the necessity of a campus "community," students of color are often reminded that they are largely isolated and subjugated.

White Students Views about Black Students and HBCUs

As a result of the White racial frame, the negative experiences of Blacks respondents shared in this study are usually unknown, misunderstood, or downplayed in most White's minds (Picca and Feagin 2007). We contend that this tendency is a result of the White racial framing process. Because the White racial frame is perpetuated by Whites who either willingly condone or reinforce it or by those who tacitly ignore it, this study considers the views and experiences of persons from this group. Results here are based on White students who reside in the same Southwestern schools as the Black respondents. Yet their views are generally very different from their Black counterparts. Conventional survey research suggests that among Whites, racial stereotypes, ideologies, and inclinations to discriminate have declined significantly since the 1960s Civil Rights movement (Feagin 2013; Gaertner and Dovidio 1986). Yet others' research based on in-depth interviews and diaries shows that Whites still harbor extremely negative attitudes toward people of color (Bonilla-Silva 2010), but are openly and routinely expressed in settings when only Whites are present (Moore 2008; Picca and Feagin 2007). In addition to documenting their perspectives on this controversial subject, the perceptions of White students also serve to reveal important aspects of the White racial frame.

In discussions about HBCUs, many White respondents fail to acknowledge historic as well as current racial discrimination and oppression. A central aspect of maintaining the White racial frame associates images of Whites as virtuous and involves collectively forgetting about how many Whites have historically and systematically oppressed people of color or benefited from such incidents (Feagin 2013). White respondents here tend to embrace belief in a colorblind society. Yet their often scathing comments reflect White racial framing that includes the age-old stereotypically racist notions of Blacks and predominately Blacks institutions of higher learning. Consider this statement by Tony, a 20-year-old White male business administration student:

> I feel that it is ridiculous that there are colleges that are for minorities specifically when we are talking "affirmative action" in colleges. If they are creating universities for minorities only, why are they not making universities for the majority? Or, at least stop giving less qualified applicants spots because they are a minority and give them to those who deserve it!

Tony's comment moves beyond simple stereotyping and relies heavily on old stereotypical notions of Blacks. Tony has embraced incorrect definitions of both HBCUs and affirmative action. Furthermore, by stating that many Blacks are less qualified than Whites, he reproduces generationally derived racial beliefs about the inferiority of Black intelligence and abilities that is a deeply embedded aspect of the White racial frame that views Whites as superior and even virtuous and benevolent as they bestow opportunities on less qualified Blacks (Bonilla-Silva 2010). By adhering to a meritocratic ideal as well as an ethnocentric view of Blacks and places associated with them, such White students deny the structural nature of racial inequality and instead rely on a discourse that emphasizes Black cultural deficiencies and ignores White racial privilege (Bonilla-Silva and Forman 2000; Feagin 2010, 2013; Gallagher 2003).

White assumptions about Black favoritism based on athletic skills or affirmative action (Feagin et al. 1996) rather than merit (Picca and Feagin 2007) can seriously undermine Black progress, reinforce faulty thinking among Whites, and on historically White campuses, constantly remind Black students of their inferior racial position. David, a 19-year-old White education major, states:

> These [historically Black] schools are a cop-out for minorities to go to college because they have a better chance of getting in. They are unnecessary. If you can't get into a normal university because you are impassable [*sic*], then tough shit. But, they do have good drum lines and marching bands. I would say athletes, but that's not true. One positive is that HBCUs keep minorities together and away from the majority.

The White racist frame allows this respondent to embrace old, false White notions of superiority. Suggesting that HBCUs are "not normal" illustrates belief in the inferiority of institutions associated with Blacks. Moreover, he contends that such schools accept "impassable" students. The tendency to generalize and assume with certainty in the absence of valid information entrenches this frame in the minds of such Whites. In addition to the use of profanity to emphasis his disdain, David decries the legacy of White privilege and posits several additional stereotypes that associate Blacks with entertainment and sports. Another important aspect of this comment is the openly expressed desire to keep people of color away from Whites. The belief that Blacks do not belong in the same educational environment as Whites undoubtedly continues to serve as a catalyst for White discrimination and racial oppression.

A key factor of the White racial frame reflects what Vera and Feagin (2001) term "social alexithymia," that is, the ingrained inability of a great many Whites to understand the perspective and experiences of Blacks and other people of color. The White frame–related disconnection that results from delegitimizing both past and present racism in the United States fosters continued hostility toward and mistreatment of students of color. This social alexithymia also enables many Whites to believe that they are now the key victims of mistreatment and discrimination, primarily at the hands of people of color. An 18-year-old White female biology major, Kathy, vitriolically comments: "I think HBCUs are bullshit! Everyone should have the same opportunities. These colleges are completely unnecessary—do we have any historically White colleges/ universities? This seems prejudice and is reverse discrimination." Kathy's belief in "reverse discrimination" against Whites is grounded in a colorblind racial framing and does not incorporate the reality and historical significance of racial discrimination. White use of this oxymoronic concept dilutes or removes the oppressive nature of discrimination by suggesting a commonality of discriminatory experiences between Whites and people of color in general and Blacks in particular (Bonilla-Silva and Forman 2000; Feagin 2000, 2010; Gallagher 2003). Despite the disproportionate percentage of predominantly White colleges and universities, a White racial frame means such students fail to recognize their majority position in these spaces. To them, in a postracial context, "everyone" can be prejudiced or participate in discrimination in a similar fashion. Such beliefs support our contention that these concepts are no longer sufficient or appropriate for social science purposes. It suggests that Whites are no longer responsible for most of the continuing racial discrimination, but have become part of the racially oppressed.

One strong commonality among White respondents is the tendency to ignore, delegitimize, or both the racial past and present in the United States. They tend to refer to the distant past when describing racism and remain far removed from accenting the not-so-distant past of Jim Crow racism or current racial challenges. Consider the following excerpt from an 18-year-old White female nursing student: "Certain people have made it so easy for minorities to get into school just because they are a minority and not because of their grades that they are taking the spots of others who are not minorities but are more qualified. If anything we need historically White colleges." She relies heavily on aspects of the White racial frame in her description of minority and White intellects. Her statement, like those of many others here, continues to marginalize and devalue the abilities of Blacks and other people of color, thereby highlighting again White superiority and accomplishments. Moreover, she critiques Whites who she considers complicitous in making it "easy" for minorities and discounts the reality that the majority of institutions of higher learning are historically White settings. This common racial narrative is used to legitimate White anger, animosity, and resentment toward racial minorities (Bonilla-Silva 2010). The anger numerous White respondents displayed as they discuss HBCUs is evident in the response from a 20-year-old White male general studies student, Dale:

It's bullshit. You don't see HWCUs around. Slavery's dead and gone; show the equal treatment they cried for! I guess that this is inspiration to African Americans that think the U.S. is still racist. Wait. . . . Hmmm. . . . I don't recall receiving a scholarship for being White!

A central theme in this account is the belief that racial equality has been achieved, but that Blacks rather than systemic racism hinder their progress. Dale's statement also suggests that Blacks continue to play the race card, and scholarships at historically White universities and the presence of HBCUs evidence the absence of systemic racism. Furthermore, statements such as "slavery is dead" enable White students to exonerate themselves from responsibility for contemporary discrimination students of color face, their silent complicity in the process, their failure to participate in redress, or a combination of these. Such statements also illustrate the inability or refusal to acknowledge White privilege and the historic benefits it has accrued (Oliver and Shapiro 1995). An important aspect of the contemporary White racial frame buttressing systemic racism is the omnipresent notion of White innocence and virtue. As noted in the above representative statements, many Whites continue to regularly deny the seriousness of anti-Black racism in the past or the present reality of racial oppression of people of color in the United States (Bonilla-Silva 2010; Feagin 2013). These findings illustrate how the White racial frame reifies and reinforces racist attitudes and actions and fosters hostility toward Black students, making the latter group vulnerable to continued negative onslaughts while simultaneously exonerating the former group from the role in and benefits from the process. And doing so undermines equality, racial reconciliation, and self-reflection needed to eliminate systemic racism.

Conclusion: Accurately Understanding and Describing Racism

Most of the White students in this study incorporated many aspects of the White racial framing to make sense of U.S. racial matters in general and Black experiences in particular. Their Black counterparts bore the brunt of such sentiments. For most Whites, this White racial frame is more than one significant ideological perspective among many; it has routinely defined a way of being, a broad perspective on life, and language and interpretations that help structure, normalize, and make sense out of society (Feagin 2013). This commonplace framing continues to give White students who embrace it the ability to live in an altogether separate psychological and racial reality—one that constantly perpetuates the notion of White virtue and superiority. At the same time, in their everyday lives, Black young people and other young people of color have to navigate these precarious, troubled, and often dangerous spaces.

The Black students here are daily fighting an uphill battle perpetuated by a great many White students' denial of their experiences and achievements. The resilience of these Black students constitutes prophetic lifestyles that should be applauded. However, imbedded in colorblind notions are the beliefs that color and race are no longer issues unless people of color continue to make them so. Intentionally ignoring systemic discrimination and its consequences helps perpetuate a burdensome system of White normalcy and virtuousness. Moreover, the everyday psychic toll of battling systemic racism and its rationalizing White racial frame on the part of students of color in historically White academic environments will continue unchecked if we do not include historical and systemic perspectives in discussions about stereotyping, prejudice, and discrimination. By co-opting some of these as individualistic concepts, like "reverse 'discrimination,'" many young Whites use them to explain and describe their experiences at institutions of higher education (Bonilla-Silva and Forman 2000; Feagin 2010, 2013; Gallagher 2003). Their suggestions that institutions of higher education now employ such reverse discrimination confirms the weakness of concepts such as "discrimination" and "prejudice" when used to examine the experiences of racial discrimination and related oppression their Black peers face. Thus such terms have been co-opted by members of the larger White society and incorporated into part of the storytelling of the White racial frame such that it prevents self-reflection, justifies existing White privilege, and exonerates them from working to dismantle systemic racism.

As this chapter illustrates, the White racial frame incorporates each of the aspects of stereotypes, narratives, images, emotions, and inclinations to discriminate and includes historical, foundational, and institutional dimensions of racial oppression as well as their consequences for Blacks and Whites. We envision the concept of the White racial frame as a prophetic corrective to dominant analyses of discrimination in its centering of the structures that undergird discrimination and de-centering of individual attitudes. Scholars are compelled to continue research to identify and uproot these structural scourges. Doing so requires nontraditional, compelling academic and applied studies that can inform and compel White and Black people to proactively fight against this new manifestation of racism. Only prophetic research, teaching, and community service will uproot this systemic scourge. Studies are also needed that focus on these dynamics in other social settings (i.e., job spaces, religious institutions, and neighborhoods), detail Black responses and coping strategies, and profile the experiences of Whites who reject the White racial frame. Our findings highlight the continued existence of these deleterious dynamics. Research, community activism, and other proactive steps are mandatory to stem the tide of the devastating effects of systemic racism and the White racial frame on people of color such as Blacks in general and on young people in particular.

Notes

1. Here we define predominately White colleges as those in which White, non-Hispanic students exceed 50% of the student population. Furthermore, the terms "Black" and "African American" are used interchangeably here and refer to people of African descent who are residents in the United States.

References

Allen, Walter A. 1992. "The Color of Success: African American College Student Outcomes at Predominantly White and Historically Black Public Colleges and Universities." *Harvard Educational Review* 62(1):26–44.

Allen, Walter R., Joseph O. Jewell, Kimberly A. Griffin and De'Sha Wolf. 2007. "Historically Black colleges and universities: Honoring the Past, Engaging the Present, Touching the Future." *Journal of Negro Education* 76(3):263–80.

Allen, Walter A. and Joseph O. Jewell. 2002. "A Backward Glance Forward: Past, Present, and Future Perspectives on Historically Black Colleges and Universities." *Review of Higher Education* 25(1):241–61.

Anderson, Margaret L. and Howard F. Taylor. 2008. *Sociology: Understanding a Diverse Society.* 4th ed. Belmont, CA: Thomas Higher Education.

Babbie, Earl. 2002. *The Basics of Social Research.* 2nd ed. Belmont, CA: Wadsworth/Thomson Learning.

Bennett, Pamela R. and Yu Xie. 2003. "Revisiting Racial Differences in College Attendance: The Role of Historically Black Colleges and Universities." *American Sociological Review* 68(4):567–80.

Bickman, Leonard and Debra Rog, eds. 1998. *Handbook of Applied Social Research Methods.* Thousand Oaks, CA: Sage.

Bonilla-Silva, Eduardo. 1996. "Rethinking Racism: Toward a Structural Interpretation." *American Sociological Review* 62 (June):465–80.

———. 2003. "Racial Attitudes or Racial Ideology? An Alternative Paradigm for Examining Actors' Racial Views." *Journal of Political Ideologies* 8(1):63–82.

———. 2010. *Racism without Racists: Color-Blind Racism and the Persistence of Racial Inequality in the United States*. Lanham, MD: Rowman and Littlefield.

Bonilla-Silva, Eduardo and Tyrone A. Forman. 2000. "'I Am Not a Racist but, . . .': Mapping White College Students' Racial Ideology in the USA." *Discourse and Society* 11(1):50–85.

Burawoy, Michael. 1991. *Ethnography Unbound: Power and Resistance in the Modern Metropolis*. Berkeley, CA: University of California Press.

Bynum, Mia S., E. Thomoseo Burton and Candace Best. 2007. "Racism Experiences and Psychological Functioning in African American College Freshmen: Is Racial Socialization a Buffer? *Cultural Diversity and Ethnic Minority Psychology* 13(1):64–71.

Carmichael, Stokely and Charles V. Hamilton. 1967. *Black Power: The Politics of Liberation in America*. New York: Random House.

Collins, Patricia. 2000. *Black Feminist Thought: Knowledge, Consciousness, and the Politics of Empowerment*. New York: Routledge.

Cose, Ellis. 1993. *The Rage of a Privileged Class*. New York: Harper Collins.

———. 2011. *The End of Anger: A New Generation's Take on Race and Rage*. New York: Ecco Press.

Feagin, Joe R. 2006. *Systemic Racism: A Theory of Oppression*. New York: Routledge.

———. 2010. *Racist America: Roots, Current Realities, and Future Reparations*. New York: Routledge.

———. 2013. *The White Racial Frame: Centuries of Racial Framing and Counter-Framing*. 2nd ed. New York: Routledge.

Feagin, Joe R. and Clairece B. Feagin. 1978. *Discrimination American Style: Institutional Racism and Sexism*. Englewood Cliffs, NJ: Prentice Hall.

Feagin, Joe R., Hernán Vera and Nikitah Imani. 1996. *The Agony of Education: Black Students at White Colleges and Universities*. New York: Routledge.

Gaertner, John and Samuel Dovidio. 1986. *Prejudice, Racism, and Discrimination*. Orlando, FL: Academic Press.

Gallagher, Charles A. 2003. "Color-Blind Privilege: The Social and Political Functions of Erasing the Color Line in Post-Race America." *Race, Gender and Class* 10(4):1–17.

Lewis, Oscar. 1966. "The Culture of Poverty." *Scientific American* 115 (October):19–25.

McKinney, Karyn D. 2005. *Being White: Stories of Race and Racism*. New York: Routledge.

Mead, Lawrence. 1992. *The New Politics of Poverty: The Nonworking Poor in America*. New York: Basic Books.

Moore, Wendy Leo. 2008. *Reproducing Racism: White Space, Elite Law Schools, and Racial Inequality*. Lanham, MD: Rowman and Littlefield.

Moynihan, Daniel Patrick. 1967. "The Negro Family: The Case for National Action." Pp. 41–124 in *The Moynihan Report and the Politics of Controversy*, edited by L. Rainwater and W. L. Yancey. Cambridge, MA: MIT Press.

Murray, Charles. 1984. *Losing Ground: American Social Policy, 1950–1980*. New York: Basic Books.

Myrdal, Gunnar. 1962. *An American Dilemma: The Negro Problem and Modern Democracy*. New York: Harper and Row.

Norton, Michael I. and Samuel R. Sommers. 2011. "Whites See Racism as a Zero-Sum Game that They Are Now Losing." *Perspectives on Psychological Science* 6(3):215–18.

Noy, Chaim. 2008. "Sampling Knowledge: The Hermeneutics of Snowball Sampling in Qualitative Research." *International Journal of Social Research Methodology* 11(4):327–44.

Obgu, John U. 1978. *Minority Education and Caste*. New York: Academic Press.

———. 1991. "Low Performance as an Adaptation: The Case of Blacks in Stockton, California." Pp. 249–85 in *Minority Status and Schooling*, edited by M. A. Gibson and J. U. Ogbu. New York: Grand Publishing.

Oliver, Melvin L. and Thomas M. Shapiro. 1995. *Black Wealth/White Wealth: A New Perspective on Racial Inequality*. New York: Routledge.

Omi, Michael and Howard Winant. 1994. *Racial Formation in the United States: From the 1960s to the 1990s*. New York: Routledge.

Picca, Leslie Houts and Joe R. Feagin. 2007. *Two-Faced Racism: Whites in the Backstage and Frontstage*. New York: Routledge.

Schaefer, Richard T. 2011. *Racial and Ethnic Groups: Census Update*. 12th ed. Upper Saddle River, NJ: Pearson Education.

Smith, William A., Walter R. Allen and Lynette L. Danley. 2007. " 'Assume the Position . . . You Fit the Description': Psychosocial Experiences and Racial Battle Fatigue among African American Male College Students." *American Behavioral Scientist* 51(4):551–78.

Stewart, Dafina Lazarus. 2008. "Being All of Me: Black Students Negotiating Multiple Identities." *Journal of Higher Education* 79(2):183–207.

Swim, Janet K., Lauri L. Hyers, Laurie L. Cohen, Davita C. Fitzgerald and Wayne H. Bylsma. 2003. "African American College Students' Experiences with Everyday Racism: Characteristics of and Responses to These Incidents." *Journal of Black Psychology* 29(1):38–76.

Tatum, Beverly Daniel. 1997. *"Why Are All the Black Kids Sitting Together in the Cafeteria?" and Other Conversations about Race*. New York: Basic Books.

Vera, Hernán and Joe R. Feagin. 2001. "Human Empathy." Department of Sociology, University of Florida, Gainesville, unpublished manuscript.

Wilson, William Julius. 1978. *The Declining Significance of Race: Blacks and Changing American Institutions*. Chicago: University of Chicago Press.

Part III

~

Diasporic Black Identities in International Contexts

In an increasingly globalized world, a multiplicity of experiences in varied national contexts often inform theoretical and empirical analyses of race. Through legal and social processes, racial identities are inscribed within national identities and cannot be easily understood or analyzed without consideration of place. Furthermore, in addition to national contexts, regions and cities, and their concomitant social and topographical features, affect how race is experienced. For instance, racialized experiences cannot be understood without an accounting of how the particular characteristics of rural and urban, North and South, Detroit and Accra, matter. Because multiple configurations of the intersections of race, space, place, and nation exist, as well as because of the fluidity of identity, when we discourse broadly about Black experiences, we must attend to important experiential differences within the group of people who are identified as Black or African-descended. And in doing so, we further illustrate how the prophetic research theorized in part I of this volume and empirically examined in a U.S. context in part II can inform some of the race-based trials and triumphs on the global scene.

While we acknowledge these nuances in identity and the manifestation and experience of inequality, highlighting the vast similarities of the experiences of African-descended people in the Diaspora, no matter their geographical location, across time and space is important. People of

African descent are more likely to experience poverty, chronic illnesses, brutality at the hands of police or other government representatives, and shorter life expectancies compared to their White or majority counterparts in any nation-state. These similar outcomes are a result of the nearly indistinguishable deployment and arrangement of power across place, and even across race. That is, the experiences of African-descended people are a mirror that tends to reflect the experiences of racial, ethnic, gender, religious, sexual, and other minorities globally. Although the methods range from segregation, marginalization, and disinvestment in vital human and social resources, to mass incarceration, enslavement, and genocide, the consequences for African-descended people are separated less by type and more by degree. In short, we can find similar patterns of inequality for people of color across the globe. Through sociological analysis of Black experiences in the aggregate, we are more equipped to understand how oppression operates in multiple arenas and to foresee how oppression and resistance will unfold. This is one of the central gifts of the Black radical and prophetic tradition in sociology: by illuminating the experiences of U.S. Blacks by analyzing the workings of racial structures, we can examine the experiences of marginalized people globally. Part III features chapters that reflect the U.S. experience in familiar and divergent ways in Haiti and the Dominican Republic; examine the United States through the eyes of Brazilian return migrants in Governador Valadares; and look out from the United States to Africa and back through the eyes of Black-centered museums.

Black sociologists in the United States have often used the American experience, and diversity within the American experience, to understand the lived experience of race in varied national contexts. Furthermore, Black sociologists integrate international perspectives into their epistemological and methodological positions, speaking through and for Black Americans as members of the African Diaspora. This tradition in Black sociology, like several others, counts the work of sociologist W. E. B. Du Bois amongst its intellectual antecedents. Additionally, it is one of the most robust examples of prophetic scholarship in the Black sociological tradition because its direct core concern is eradicating the oppression of marginalized peoples globally.

Du Bois's work on oppressed and colonized peoples, and the relationship between the freedom struggles in Africa and America, spans the course of his lifetime beginning in the Reconstruction era of post–Civil War America and concluding at the zenith of the modern Civil Rights movement led by Martin Luther King Jr. Not as widely recognized as a Pan-African internationalist in some U.S. scholarship (Provenzo and Abaka 2012), Du Bois was not only an early Pan-Africanist, but arguably the first. Moreover, Du Bois turned toward Africa after disaffection with America's lack of racial progress. However, Du Bois's theoretical and epistemological tendencies did not actively separate Africa from the experiences of African Americans, even as he conducted studies that accounted for the effect of place—whether Farmville, Virginia, or Philadelphia, Pennsylvania—on Black life.

Shortly after the publication of *Souls of Black Folk* ([1903] 1996), Du Bois wrote about the global color line in the 1906 *Collier's Weekly* essay, "The Color Line Belts the World." Du Bois ([1906] 2000) argues, "The Negro problem in America is but a local phase of a world problem," thus linking "the problem" to the imperialistic expansion practices of countries including England, France, Belgium, and Russia. Du Bois's characterization of America's race problem as a "local phase" undergirds much Black sociological scholarship on race. By highlighting the experiences of Black folk in multiple local locales, the United States in particular, the prophetic scholarship of Black sociologists provide vivid description and analysis of the function, deployment, and consequences of oppression in all of its forms for all marginalized peoples.

The chapters in this section follow in the Black sociological tradition of investigating race in Diasporic contexts while highlighting the importance of global epistemologies to understanding how race works across space and place. They also demonstrate how critical race analyses based on the experiences of African Americans in the United States inform investigations of race, whiteness, blackness, and identity in global contexts. Like Du Bois, the authors in this section analyze the color line that belts the world. Yet, they also move beyond a simple discussion of inequality to demonstrate the dialectical relationship between Black identities and the experience of oppression.

Each chapter examines key questions about the relationship between identity and oppression. Antonio D. Tillis's chapter, "Contextualizing 'Race' in the Dominican Republic: Discourses on Whitening, Nationalism, and Anti-Haitianism," asks how the Dominican Republic's institutionalized efforts to whiten itself affect constructions of racial identity among Dominicans and Haitians. Specifically, Tillis documents how the Dominican Republic has historically attempted to excise blackness from its genealogy and how this practice manifests in its pathological and oppressive treatment of Haitian immigrant workers. Tillis's findings on the relationship between Dominicanness, whiteness, and anti-Haitianism mirror processes of racialization in the United States, from slavery through the Jim Crow era. Furthermore, his chapter also reflects the neoliberal, multinational conflicts over race, labor, whiteness, and Otherness that have undergirded U.S. discourses on immigration since the nineteenth century. Through his research, Tillis conjures questions about the value of blackness as an enduring repository of Otherness on the global stage.

Whereas Tillis focuses on the blatant and invidious oppression of Haitians by structural racism in the Dominican Republic, Tiffany D. Joseph's research centers on subtleties in cross-national perceptions of racial identity and experience. Her chapter, " 'U.S. Blacks are beautiful but Brazilian Blacks are not racist': Brazilian Return Migrants' Perceptions of U.S. and Brazilian Blacks," examines how Black folk from outside America both understand and navigate the U.S. racial hierarchy. Joseph uses the narratives of Brazilian return migrants from Governador Valadares—the Brazilian city with the highest rate of Black immigration to the United States—to show how race, blackness, and class identity operate within a country with a similar history in the African Diaspora as the United States. Ultimately, Joseph's research demonstrates that class distinctions are increasingly significant in the making and remaking of racial identity and perhaps especially so when immigrants from more impoverished places in the African Diaspora encounter America's growing, if delicate, Black middle classes.

Derrick R. Brooms's chapter delves further into the nuances of African American identity through an analysis of the function of Africa as idea and ideology in African American museums. Brooms argues that in Black-centered museums, the use of depictions of Africa to culturally and genealogically root African Americans constitutes a counterframed "racial project" (Omi and Winant 1994). This racial project, Brooms asserts, is intended to challenge White supremacist notions of Black culture and to articulate a positive history for Black people outside of the history of oppression and slavery. This racial project is both literally and figuratively curated by Black-centered museums, which shape and reflect Black Americans' conceptions of their cultural relationship to Africa. Brooms's chapter brings us back to questions about the cultural, blood, and social ties that bind us together across the Diaspora, despite and because of our shared African ancestry. Former National Basketball Association player turned TNT sports commentator Charles Barkley once quipped that the "Motherland" is his hometown of Leeds, Alabama. That is, for Barkley, like many African Americans, Africa is too distant, perhaps temporally and geographically, to constitute an ancestral homeland. The museums Brooms investigate deliberately situate Africa to problematize sentiments such as Barkley's, whether made in jest or sincerity, and to create a sense of collective history and identity rooted in Africa.

While each of these chapters address distinct questions about Black Diasporic identities, together they inspire us to ask broader questions about the relationship between Black identities, experiences, and the Diaspora. Is the unifying force in Diasporic Black identities the common experience of oppression and suffering? Does blackness have ontological or metaphysical status, and if so, are we unified across space, place, and time despite and because of those shared experiences of suffering? As we work for social justice in communities in the United States and beyond, will Black intellectuals and other members of the global Black bourgeoisie resist "the pitfalls of national consciousness," as revolutionary philosopher Frantz Fanon ([1963] 2005) implored? Or will our efforts only temper the amount of oppression we personally experience while contributing to the further marginalization of the global lumpenproletariat? We must more consistently address these and other questions about Diasporic Black identities and experiences to operate more consistently and squarely within the Black sociological tradition of prophetic scholarship and justice.

References

Du Bois, W. E. B. [1903] 1996. *The Souls of Black Folk.* New York: Modern Library.

———. [1906] 2000. "The Color Line Belts the World." *Collier's Weekly*, October 20, p. 30. Reprinted in pp. 40–42 in *W. E. B. Du Bois: A Reader*, edited by D. L. Lewis. New York: Holt.

Fanon, Franz. [1963] 2005. *The Wretched of the Earth.* New York: Grove Press.

Omi, Michael and Howard Winant. 1994. *Racial Formation in the United States: From the 1960s to the 1990s.* 2nd ed. New York: Routledge.

Provenzo, Eugene F. and Edmund Abaka, eds. 2012. *W. E. B. Du Bois on Africa.* Walnut Creek, CA: Left Coast Press.

6

~

Contextualizing "Race" in the Dominican Republic

Discourses on Whitening, Nationalism, and Anti-Haitianism

ANTONIO D. TILLIS

Dartmouth College

The ideology of race is often configured and contextualized within national frameworks. While global discourses on race and racial identity necessarily inform the racialized experiences of global citizens, the specifics of racialization are constructed within national contexts. This chapter explores how race is configured within the national framework of the Dominican Republic vis-à-vis its island neighbor, Haiti. Like most binary constructions of race, dominance is defined with and against Otherness as Dominicanness is set against an Othered Haiti. Specifically, in an effort to distinguish itself from its island neighbor, as well as its neighbor's blackness and poverty, the Dominican Republic constructed a genealogical history that tied the nation firmly to a Spanish-speaking, European-descended, White identity. The refractory ideological material of this contemporary crucible in Dominican society has calcined and erupted into a nationalistic performative display that marginalizes Haitianism in order to solidify Dominicanness and Dominican national identity. Yet, despite its similarities to global racial hierarchies, the social construction of race in Hispaniola has features endemic to postcolonial Black republics that inform Diasporic Black experiences. These methods of racial construction reflect the past and prophetically point toward the future of racialized experiences for marginalized Black populations globally.

The historical and evolutionary development of national and racial identity in the Dominican Republic has fostered a present-day vilification of Haiti in everyday racial discourse in the Dominican Republic. This paradigmatic iteration implicates the manner in which the average citizen sees himself or herself vis-à-vis the rest of the global world, and in particular in relation to her conjoined neighbor, the Republic of Haiti. Indeed, Dominicans forge a national discourse that centers prejudicial hostility toward Haiti. This discourse manifests within the imagined borders of the neoslave sugar cane community, or *batey*—an intra-Dominican community of Haitian migrant workers. This chapter examines the historical development and structural organization of the *batey* in order to unpack how this "imagined" community of the *batey* serves as the geopolitical space where Dominican discourses on race, whitening, nationalism, and anti-Haitianism converge.

In his exegesis on nationalism, entitled *Imagined Communities* (2006), Benedict Anderson states the following in the revised edition relative to the limited-spatial conceptualization of defined national territories: "The nation is imagined as *limited* because even the largest of them, encompassing perhaps a billion living human beings, has finite, if elastic, boundaries, beyond which other nations lie. No nation imagines itself coterminous with mankind" (p. 7). In the painstaking process of mapping, cartographers are challenged when it comes to the axis of geospatial boundaries as one community distinguishes itself from another topographically and territorially. In terms of coterminality, as Anderson evokes, of particular intellectual concern is the encounter, or exchange, that occurs at the bordered-space in mediated articulations of national culture and understandings of geospatial proprietorship. The island of Hispaniola stands as a testament to Anderson's postulation of the spatial configuration of nation-building in that an essential understanding of "nation" is conceptualized within the context of presumed geographical boundaries that separate one from the other. In terms of North America, the United States, Canada, and Mexico have constructed such boundaries to protect the confines of the autonomous rule of each nation state. These "gated national communities" have for centuries attempted to define and contain the core attributes that have distinguished one nation from its bordering neighbor. An observation of note in this play of "nationalizing" one's spatial domain is the length to which one nation will go to differentiate itself from the other, especially when they share a common land mass. Scholars generally agree that the concept of "nation-building" in the Americas has its genesis in the eighteenth century with the American Revolutionary War, followed by the Haitian Revolution. As these new nations began to free themselves from colonial enterprise, they engaged in the arduous task, one akin to launching a new commercial product for global consumption, of "packaging and selling" themselves and their new economies as they entered the marketplace of independent state-building.

In an attempt to construct a national identity subsequent to liberation from Haitian rule in 1844, the Dominican Republic formulated a history lodged in the myths of a selectively imagined identity that valorized certain moments spanning from the nation's pre- to postcolonial history. The outcome of such a historical narration of nation engenders a predilection that supports an imagined classification of "race" that has at its ideological center an anti-Black resonance. Thus, the racial politics of the contemporary Dominican Republic are steeped in the ideology of historical *blancamiento*, or whitening. From its adoption of a Hispanic-Indigenous identity and discriminating immigration policies under the early Trujillo reign to the current situation with Haiti, this Spanish-speaking Caribbean Island has for its few centuries of existence promulgated a national racialized identity that has not been congruent with the racial background of the majority population. Mythologized for national and global consumption is the idea that the Dominican Republican is a White nation, infiltrated by Blacks, or in today's context, Haitians. Interestingly, during the late 1840s following the 22-year Haitian rule of Hispaniola, the Dominican Republic, in an effort to seek recognition in the international community, appealed to the United States for solidarity within the region along racial lines. Rayford Logan notes in *Haiti and the Dominican Republic* (1968):

> During the late 1840s the Dominican government appealed to the United States for recognition, largely on the ground that it was a "White" nation. But American special agents, even after counting "White Negroes" and "Negroes with a White heart" were unable to find enough White people to justify recognition. One agent, obviously seeking to support the request for recognition, guessed that in 1845 that there were 40,000 Negroes, 90,000 coloured people, and 100,000 Whites. (P. 13)

However, noted Latin American historian George Reid Andrews (2004) in *Afro Latin America, 1800–2000* indicates that Blacks or people of African ancestry in the Dominican Republic constituted 66% of the total population at the beginning of the nineteenth century. In 2000, Reid Andrews states that Blacks and mulattoes constitute 84% of the total Dominican population. Yet, the myth of "Hispanidad" and whiteness remains pervasive in the Dominican concept of national and cultural identity. To unpack these ideologies, the notion of Hispanidad in the Dominican Republic is the nation's effort to preserve its colonial Spanish heritage in terms of language, Spanish; religion, Catholicism; and presumed race, Caucasian, or their iteration of White. Eclipsed is the memory of African and Black migration to the region from colonialism and slavery to the present. Additionally, the desire to portray itself as a non-Black nation-state has surpassed the once-coveted indigenous-based national identity conceptualized on the ancestry of the native Taíno people. Thus, like many emerging nations in the Americas during the nineteenth century, ontological iterations of subjecthood became an exercise in construing mythologies that would come to define a people, a geographical territory, a culture, and a nation-state.

In *Myths and Memories of the Nation* (1999) Anthony D. Smith engages the importance of myth and memory in the creation of national identity. Smith (1999) argues, " . . . what gives nationalism its power are the myths, memories, traditions, and symbols of ethnic heritages and the ways a popular living past has been, and can be rediscovered and reinterpreted by modern intelligentsias" (p. 9). Smith's (1999) assertion contextualizes the Dominican Republic's production of a national discourse that facilitates its attempts to market itself globally as a largely White, Spanish-Caribbean nation, under the guise of the ethnic myth of Hispanidad. Consequently, the Dominican Republic erects an illusionary border from its neighboring Haiti that reinforces the binary, instead of moving beyond it. The contextualized construction of an anti-Haiti nationalist discourse is created in the Dominican national imaginary, as the Dominican Republic imagines itself to be that which the perception of Haiti is not in the Western Hemisphere and beyond: White and catholic. Regarding the anti-Haitian sentiment that shapes contemporary race discourse, Latin American political scientist Ernesto Sagás (2000) states:

> The case of *antihaitianismo* in the Dominican Republic is particularly poignant, as it has added an intra-island dimension to these Hispanophile dominant ideologies. *Antihaitianismo* ideology combines a legacy of racist Spanish colonial mentality, nineteenth-century racial theories, and twentieth-century

cultural neoracism into a web of anti-Haitian attitudes, racial
stereotypes, and historical distortions. Not only does this
ideology affect Haitian migrants in the Dominican Republic,
but it has also traditionally been employed as an ideological
weapon to subdue the Black and mulatto Dominican lower
classes and maintain their political quiescence. (P. ix)

This mid-nineteenth century national ideological posture set into play
the relationship that is reflected in today's context between these two
sister-nations. The *batey* community, replete with its complex historical
development, is the crucible where race relations between these two
nations are hyperbolically played out. However, in order to understand
the contemporary racial politics of the twenty-first century Dominican
Republic, we must journey very briefly to two significant conjoined periods in the country's history: the emancipation of slaves and Dominican
Independence.

The abolition of slavery and the presumed Dominican Independence are two historic moments that are met with competing emotions
and sentiments of nationalism. Historians such as Frank Moya Pons
(1995) contend that Haitian rule of the Dominican Republic in 1822
accompanied the emancipation of the enslaved. Dominican alignment
with Haiti was a result of joined forces responding to fear of potential
French opposition within the Caribbean basin, in addition to the desire
for liberation on the part of Dominicans from Spanish colonial rule.
However, the Dominican Republic soon found itself under direct rule
for the next 22 years—until February 27, 1844. In the cerebral imagery
that shapes the political ethos, the 22 years of Haitian rule was a persistent threat to Dominican sovereignty and served as a basis for what
has become a national racialized discourse that continues to separate
the two sister island-nations.

Haitians are contextualized in the Dominican psyche as that barba-
rous element, a symbolic reminder of its Black African heritage, of which
the Dominican Republic tried to rid itself. An acknowledgement of its
African past would be counterintuitive to its present discourse relative
to the national epistemology of Dominicanness. That which manifests
in present-day Dominican Republic is the residual of what Cornel West
(1993) might call "psychological violence," whereby Dominicans have
been socialized to repudiate a central component of their racial heritage
in light of how that component has been vilified globally. Thus, the
treatment of "blackness" in the Dominican Republic can be reduced to
the manner in which Africa has been mythologized by Western imperial
powers. So powerful are these conceptualizations that they dictate the

global understandings ascribed to Africa and its Diaspora. These power-ful discourses contribute to a self-fulfilling prophesy as African descen-dants in nations such as the Dominican Republic began to incorporate such epistemologies into their nationalistic comprehensions of blackness. That is, Dominicans have come to believe that blackness is equated with barbarism, that element in modern and postmodern societies that impedes further civilization. Thus, in their attempt to evade the truth of their miscegenated African heritage, the Dominican Republic, as a nation, has engaged in psychological projection whereby the burden of its disdain has been cast upon those deemed to be the true "Blacks" of Hispaniola: Haitians. Furthermore, the contemporary presence of Haitians in the country fuels this anti-Black discourse as the projected discordant image of Haitians in the Dominican public sphere incites an antagonistic reception.

As alluded to earlier, the evolutionary history of the contextu-alization of race and discourses on whitening and anti-Haitianism in the Dominican Republic is evidenced within the intranationalist bor-ders of the constructed *batey* communities. One can argue that the creation of this intranation space is purposed to contain that which has contaminated the purity of Dominican national and cultural identity. This constructed intranation space has been explored in several venues, including a YouTube clip that offers an indelible introduction to the *batey* community in the Dominican Republic. The short, entitled "A Batey in the Dominican Republic," (2010) provides the viewer with a personalized account of life in this neoslave community. Furthermore, an Al Jazeera–produced segment, "Haitian Exploitation in the Dominican Republic" (2007), examines the structural inequalities inherent in the relationship between Haitian labor and the Dominican state. Addition-ally, Bill Haney's 2007 documentary, *The Price of Sugar*, chronicles the efforts of Father Christopher Hartley, a Spanish priest who protests the inhumane treatment of Haitian immigrants in the Dominican Republic. In the film, Father Hartley exposes the exploitation and social margin-alization of subjects. The film brings to the fore the existence of gen-erational subjects of Haitian ancestry born in the Dominican Republic who exist without a defined national citizenship within the contentious borders of the *batey*.

With regard to the historical development of the *batey*, it is impor-tant to understand that both governments, through the signing of the 1952 bilateral *acuerdo,* or agreement, legitimated the entrance of Hai-tians into the Dominican Republic for the purpose of working in the sugar cane fields. Under this agreement, Haitians were to be imported as seasonal workers for a five-year period. Records show that both governments signed two additional five-year agreements in 1959 and 1966, respectively. The latter of these agreements expired in 1971 and no new bilateral agreement has been established. Instead, the Dominican government entered into an annual contract with migrant Haitian workers that lasted until 1986, the downfall of the Duvalier dictatorship. However, despite the lack of a signed agreement or an annual contract, thousands of Haitians are smuggled into the Dominican Republic to work the cane fields as depicted in the clips and film alluded to earlier in this analysis.

Under the official bilateral agreements of 1952, 1959, and 1966, the Haitian government was to supply transportation for migrant workers while the Dominican government provided housing and a base salary for their labor. Haitians were to reside near the fields in camps that consisted of dwellings that were to be furnished with beds, chairs, tables, electricity, running water, sanitary facilities, and common dining grounds. At the end of the harvest season, Haitian migrant workers were to be repatriated until the beginning of the next harvest season. For many Haitians who were brought or smuggled illegally into the Dominican Republic, their fate was to endure slavelike conditions that bear testament to the nation's view of Haiti and Haitian migrants.

In her 1989 Human Rights Watch report, *Haitian Sugar Cane Cutters in the Dominican Republic*, Maryse Fontus states the following:

> Although slavery in the Dominican Republic was formally abolished over a century ago, Haitians in that country continue to be delivered at gunpoint to work on government-run plantations. Like their ancestors brought from Africa, they are forced to labor against their will, cutting sugar cane for armed Dominican masters. (P. 1)

The metaphor Fontus's initial comments evoke is that of neoslavery in the Americas, sanctioned by government-run facilities that exploit people for economic gain. In this scenario, Haitians are the enslaved and Dominicans become the masters in the reenactment of the colonial master-slave paradigm of old. Bearing numerous similarities of the chattel slave system, Haitian sugar cane workers in the Dominican Republic find themselves relegated to the restricted confines of their neoslave quarters, referred to in Spanish as *el batey*: a concentration camp–like community constructed specifically for sugar cane workers proximate to the cane field and sugar mill. These communities exist in isolation from mainstream Dominican society where forced segregation between the Haitian workers and Dominicans is the rule. The Jim Crow–like and neoapartheid political structure of the *batey* engenders the physical segregation of Haitians in the Dominican Republic and further advances the historical relationship between two people and two nations sharing one island with common histories.

Due to the sociopolitical and economic situation in Haiti, hundreds of thousands of Haitians are lured to the Dominican Republic in an effort to work and find economic gain. Haitians are enticed to illegally enter the Dominican Republic with promises of well-paying jobs. Once they arrive to the *batey* they find themselves imprisoned within this neoslavery system with little to no chance of escape. They are recruited in Haiti by *buscones*, long-time Haitian workers who can no longer cut cane. Once in the Dominican Republic these Haitian migrants are subjected to subhuman living conditions, disease, continued poverty, social marginalization, economic exploitation, and national displacement as they become subjects without a nation to claim as their own. Generations of these cane cutters exist in the Dominican Republic as *sin patria*, country-less subjects belonging to neither Haiti nor the Dominican Republic. Although born and raised in the Dominican Republic, many who comprise this disenfranchised population today are not provided documentation that would allow civil status as Dominican nationals. Haitian workers remain confined to the *batey*, caught within a vicious cycle of systemic poverty, hopelessness, and abuse. Once they are brought to or born on these plantations, physical force, like that used during slavery, is used to compel them to cut cane and to submit to the Dominican power-based hierarchy.

The structure of the *batey* community consists of two types: the *central* and *agrícola*. As an extension of the cane field, the *batey central* is the community largely for those who process sugar cane once cut and weighed. Typically, a majority of the inhabitants of the *batey centrales* are Dominicans. Those who actually do the cutting of the cane live in the *batey agrícola*, where Haitian migrants and their descendants are estimated to comprise approximately 85% of the population. The *batey agrícola* is also stratified and consists of three classifications of workers: (1) the *viejos*, former cane cutters who have lived in the Dominican Republic for many years and are now too old for such strenuous labor; (2) the *congos*, or recent recruits; and (3) the *braceros*, the seasoned cane cutters, many of whom were born in the Dominican Republic. They live in *barracones*, or barracks, consisting of a long row of single rooms made of concrete or wood with no electricity or running water. Many of the *barracones* date from the colonial era when they served as slave quarters. The hygienic conditions with which the workers are forced to contend are a focus of discussion among countless human rights groups. These communities are laden with tuberculosis, diarrhea, and malaria, all resulting from unsanitary conditions. Haitian children working the cane fields are in violation of Dominican child labor laws, which forbid minors younger than age 14 to work. Additionally, Article 229 of the Dominican labor code provides that "the employment of minors less than 18 years old in dangerous or unhealthy labor is prohibited." Thus, the condition of the average Haitian found in the Dominican Republic is peppered by historical and ideological iterations that can be attributed to how Dominicans have contextualized understandings of race and nation. Cemented within their constructions lies Haiti, the geofractional denominator testifying vehemently to the amnesiac historical identity of the Dominican Republic that is steeped in blackness.

In short, what exists today in the psyche of most Dominicans is the notion that the nation-state ideologically represents one whose heritage is largely Hispanic, namely White. Such a position has caused a sense of self-hatred among many Dominican people that fosters a selective amnesia relative to the overwhelming history of Africans and Africa-descended people within the nation. This ideological *blancamiento*, or whitening, has created a racial politics with a Black-White binary: Dominicans are White, and by extension Haitians are Black. The psychological projection of blackness onto the Haitian population in the Dominican Republic has afforded a slippery slope for contemporary Dominican national identity formation that resonates with historical anti-Haitianist discourse. The current neoslavery situation in the *batey* fuels the perennial racial fire and further divides two people and two nations who inhabit one island. Furthermore, the current-day *batey* becomes the locus where Dominican race and nation performativity morphs into a national and racial discourse that has at its core anti-Black and anti-Haitian sentiments. Thus, the contextualization of "race" in the Dominican Republic, engendered by the historical moment of 1822, becomes a nationalist project constructed within a historical binary. Since 1844, Dominican nation-building has emerged as a project that necessitates the eradication of blackness from epistemologies of nation and national identity. The ideological mechanism used for this undertaking is ensconced in the historical whitening of the nation in terms of how Dominicans see themselves and how they wish to project a reflection of self onto the global world. The nucleus of the protoplasmically constructed nation is iterations of anti-Haitianist discourse.

The Dominican response to contextualizations of race and discourses on nation, national identity, and Haiti are best illustrated visually in political caricatures extracted from the leading national newspaper, *El Nacional*, in Ernesto Sagás's highly referenced *Race and Politics in the Dominican Republic* (2000). In "Appendix B: Anti-Haitian Political

Cartoons from the Dominican Press," Sagás offers critical commentary regarding how these images reflect the national discourse regarding Dominican attitudes toward Haiti, representing the overarching
sentiment of Dominican political officials and laypersons alike.[1] The
first caption Sagás uses demonstrates the sentiment of anti-Haitian discourse as a big "White" Dominican hand impedes the migration of
the poorly depicted Haitian migrant. Resonating within the caption is
the ideological leitmotif of Latin American Romanticism, civilization
verses barbarism. This ideology is "clothed" in the construction of the
vestment adorning the Dominican arm in contrast to the scantily clad
Haitian speeding out of poverty, desolation, and disdain into a salvific
Dominican Republic. In the second caption, the nationalistic fear of that
which is Haitian is hyperbolically presented and raced as the "Black"
feet carrying the cartographic body of the Haitian people runs after a
fleeing "White" Dominican nation in fear of invasion. The third caption
vividly illustrates the fear of Haitian encroachment on the Dominican
Republic. A further deconstruction of this political caricature reveals the
racial dichotomy that influences the nationalist politics of the Dominican Republic in terms of its being a "White" nation and Haiti being
"Black." Such political propaganda reinforces the *blanqueamiento*, or
whitening aesthetic that has come to "color" Dominican racial politics
with regard to how this nation of "coloreds" self-views. Furthermore,
this iconography speaks to the public and official stance regarding Haitian immigration. The final caption attests to the Dominican regard of
Haitians in a racial hierarchy as the "White" Dominican man points to
the adult male Haitian with a pacifier in his mouth. This visual emotes
the position that Haitian cane workers, in juxtaposition to Dominicans,
are viewed as childlike, possessing the intellect and aptitude of infants.
We should note, as does Sagás (2000), that this visual was used to make
mockery of allegations by human rights organizations regarding Haitian
children working in Dominican sugar cane fields.

    While I have highlighted the idiosyncrasies of the construction of
race on Hispaniola, the Dominican stance toward Haiti is not unlike the
position of other dominant nations toward their poorer neighbors, particularly when those neighbors are seeking economic security within their
borders. Ongoing debates in the United States around Mexican immigration mirror discourses of xenophobia and whiteness in the Dominican
Republic. The geopolitical borders between the Dominican Republic
and Haiti belie the flexibility and simultaneous rigidity of the boundaries between the two nations. Haitian immigrants coerced by physical
force, circumstance, and poor economic conditions into servitude in the
cane fields of the Dominican Republic are rendered nationless by the

Dominican Republic's unwillingness to acknowledge its African heritage. By segregating and subjugating the race "problem" within the intra-national boundaries of the *batey*, as well as creating hierarchies within the *batey*, the Dominican Republic performs routine national whitening. Abetted by a mythologized and whitewashed history, the Dominican Republic not only facilitates Haitian marginalization in the Dominican Republic, but also the marginalization of blackness more broadly in global national contexts.

The racial politics of the Dominican Republic can best be described as a palimpsest on which nationalist discourses on race, whitening, and anti-Haitianism have been etched historically. So deep-seated are these ideologies that a binary discourse in Black and White has come to contextualize one island nation in differentiation from the other. Aggravating the historical wound is the impending threat of Haitian migration to the Dominican Republic, as if Haitian migration were synonymous to carcinogens invading a *pure* body, ultimately leading to death. The fear of Haitian "invasion" is pandemic to the point of enacting segregationist appeals that forge separation of Haitians and Dominican within various economic sectors of the country: the *batey* being an example. By critically analyzing these racialized ideologies and discourses, we can prophetically predict the outcome for Haitians subjugated by Dominican oppression. For instance, one can only imagine the refueling of the fear of fleeing Haitians onto Dominican soil subsequent to the massive earthquake of January 10, 2010, and its aftermath. Certainly as the earth shook to catastrophic proportion in Haiti so did the anti-Haitian ethos in the Dominican Republic. Yet, in the radical and prophetic tradition of Black sociology, uncovering these discourses compels us to shake loose the mechanisms of these ideologies and improve the lives of marginalized Haitian groups.

Notes

1. To view these images and read Sagás's critical commentary, see "Appendix B: Anti-Haitian Political Cartoons from the Dominican Press" (pp. 134–35) in *Race and Politics in the Dominican Republic* (2000).

References

"A *Batey* in the Dominican Republic." 2010. YouTube Website. Retrieved May 28, 2011 (http://www.youtube.com/watch?v=jxsTuolGAV0).

150 ～ Antonio D. Tillis

Anderson, Benedict. 2006. *Imagines Communities.* London: Verso.
Andrews, George Reid. 2004. *Afro-Latin America, 1800–2000.* New York: Oxford University Press.
Fontus, Maryse. 1989. *Haitian Sugar Cane Cutters in the Dominican Republic.* New York: Americas Watch.
"Haitian Exploitation in the Dominican Republic." 2007. YouTube Website. Retrieved May 28, 2011 (http://www.youtube.com/watch?v=kz1FoON7ayg). Al Jazeera.
Haney, Bill. 2007. *The Price of Sugar.* DVD. Los Angeles, CA: Uncommon Productions.
Howard, David. 2001. *Coloring the Nation: Race and Ethnicity in the Dominican Republic.* Boulder, CO: Lynn Rienner Publishers.
Logan, Rayford. 1968. *Haiti and the Dominican Republic.* London: Oxford University Press.
Pons, Frank Moya. 1995. *The Dominican Republic: A National History.* New Rochelle, NY: Hispaniola Books.
Sagás, Ernesto. 2000. *Race and Politics in the Dominican Republic.* Gainesville: University of Florida Press.
Smith, Anthony D. 1999. *Myths and Memories of the Nation.* New York: Oxford University Press.
Wade, Peter. 1997. *Race and Ethnicity in Latin America.* London: Pluto Press.
West, Cornel. 1993. *Race Matters.* Boston: Beacon Press.

7

~

"U.S. Blacks are beautiful but Brazilian Blacks are not racist"

Brazilian Return Migrants' Perceptions of U.S. and Brazilian Blacks

TIFFANY D. JOSEPH

Stony Brook University

An influx of immigrants from Latin America and the Caribbean has significantly changed the ethnoracial composition of the United States in recent decades. As race remains a strong structuring factor in U.S. society, immigrants, especially non-Whites, must learn to navigate U.S. race relations (Landale and Oropesa 2002). Because Brazilians are some of the newest Latin American immigrants to the United States, less is known about them compared to other immigrants (e.g., Mexicans, Dominicans), especially how they negotiate the U.S. racial system. Furthermore, in recent years, comparative research on race relations in the United States and Brazil has increased as U.S. and Brazilian scholars have examined the specific nuances of racial inequality in both countries (Bailey 2009; Guimarães 2001; Marx 1998; Sansone 2003; Telles 2004).

Using data from interviews with 49 Brazilians who migrated to the United States and then returned to their homeland of Brazil, this chapter explores how these individuals retrospectively negotiated U.S. race relations while in that nation.[1] The research question driving this study is, "How do Brazilian returnees interpret U.S. racial stratification while living in the United States?" I argue that returnees relied on their premigration understandings of racial stratification in Brazil, particularly with regard to the marginalized social position and cordial interracial behavior among Brazilians to interpret the social position of U.S. Blacks. Although previous research has examined similarities between Brazilian and U.S. race relations and how Latino immigrants develop an understanding of the U.S. racial system, this study connects both groups of literature by exploring one aspect of Brazilian return migrants' racial conceptions of the United States. Furthermore, few studies have compared Brazil–U.S. racial frameworks by conducting research with individuals who lived and "experienced race" in three contexts: in Brazil before migrating, while living in the United States as migrants, and in Brazil after U.S. migration. Therefore, this analysis contributes to the literature on Brazilian immigrants and their perceptions of racial stratification and attitudes in Brazil and the United States. Furthermore, by using a novel three-context methodology, this research continues in the prophetic tradition of ensuring a panoramic, triangulated view of racialized experiences.

Theoretical Background

Race in Brazil and the United States

Significant comparative research on racial classification and inequality in Brazil and the United States indicates that the social construction of race developed differently in each society (Andrews 1992; Marx 1998; Telles 2004). The rule of hypodescent, also known as the one-drop rule, has historically been used to racially classify individuals with any Black ancestry as "Black" and greatly influenced U.S. race relations. Informal and formal (legal) enforcement of the one-drop rule over the years yielded the Black-White racial binary, which has been fundamental for establishing racial boundaries and implementing discriminatory policies in the United States (Davis 1991; Feagin 2000). However, in Brazil, the rule of hypodescent has not similarly influenced race relations.

Gilberto Freyre's *Masters and Slaves* (1933) introduced the concept of racial democracy, which encouraged Brazilians to embrace their African heritage and encouraged racial miscegenation. Using the concept of racial democracy, Freyre argued that because Brazilians were racially mixed there could be no distinct racial groups and thus no basis for racial discrimination in Brazil. However, scholars argue that instead of creating a society with no racial differentiation and discrimination, racial democracy simultaneously yielded a fluid racial classification system and the suppression of overt racial discrimination (Bailey 2009; Dzidzienyo 2005; Marx 1998; Telles 2004). Thus, racial classification has primarily been associated with an individual's actual skin tone, not indicative of ancestry, and has had little social relevance with regard to racial group formation for Brazilians (Bailey 2009; Feagin 2000; Telles 2004). Brazilians of all skin tones acknowledge having African ancestry and many self-identify as racially mixed, not solely White or Black (Bailey 2009; Telles 2004). Furthermore, having multiracial ancestry has historically not excluded Brazilians from solely self-classifying as White.

Due to the concept of racial democracy and being perceived as a place where people of different colors peacefully coexisted, Brazil was considered a twentieth-century racial utopia when compared to the United States, where overt and legally sanctioned racism oppressed non-Whites for centuries. However, as various studies have documented racial inequality and covert racism in Brazil, academics and laypersons have challenged the reality of racial democracy (Bailey 2009; Sansone 2003; Telles 2004). For example, Telles's (2004) examination of vertical (socioeconomic) and horizontal (social) interracial relations in Brazil finds extreme socioeconomic inequality between Brazilians who are phenotypically White as compared to non-Whites and concludes that "while Brazil's fluid horizontal relations may be interpreted as signs of a less racist system, they also facilitate vertical racial domination" (p. 232).

Despite perceived differences in race in Brazil and the United States, both countries share some demographic and historical similarities. Both nations were colonized by European powers, were large slave-holding societies, and currently have the most populous and strongest economies in the Americas. In terms of slavery, more Africans were brought to Brazil than to the United States. In fact, Brazil was the last country in the Americas to abolish slavery in 1888. Experts estimate that currently more African-descended individuals are in Brazil than in any other part of the world outside of Africa (Bailey 2009; Dzidzienyo 2005; Sansone 2003; Telles 2004). Whereas in the United States Blacks comprise 12% of the total population, Brazilian Blacks account for nearly half of Brazil's population (Telles 2004). Although Brazil has been perceived as a racial "utopia" compared to the United States in the absence of overtly racist legislation, Black and mixed-race Brazilians demonstrate markedly lower social outcomes relative to White Brazilians in education, income, and other social indicators. Compared to U.S.

Blacks, Brazilian Blacks have significantly lower levels of social mobility (Telles 2004). The global economic power of the United States and its higher wealth distribution, lower poverty and inequality levels, and larger middle class relative to Brazil have allowed U.S. Blacks to benefit from U.S. economic power in ways that Brazilian Blacks have not—despite Brazil's burgeoning economic growth.

Brazilian Immigration to the United States

While many studies have documented the immigration experiences of Latin American and Caribbean immigrants in the United States, considerably less is known about Brazilian immigrants (Margolis 1994). Studies focusing on Brazilian immigrants in the United States have increased as their numbers have grown (Jouet-Pastre and Braga 2008; Margolis 1994; Reis and Sales 1999; Siquiera 2006). Although Brazilians have been migrating to the United States since the 1960s, their numbers increased significantly during Brazil's economic crisis in the 1980s and continue to grow in the twenty-first century (Marcus 2009). Studies on Brazil–U.S. migration reveal that this process began in Governador Valadares, a small city in the state of Minas Gerais, where U.S. mining executives arrived in the 1940s (Levitt 2007; Marcus 2009; Margolis 1994). When the industry declined in the 1960s, some executives returned to the United States with their Brazilian housekeepers and nannies. These social ties between the United States and Governador Valadares during Brazil's economic crisis created social networks that shaped Brazilian migration to the United States (Goza 1999).

The 2000 U.S. Census estimates that 247,020 foreign-born Brazilians are living in the United States, mostly in Massachusetts, New York, and Connecticut (Martes 2008; Siqueira and Jansen 2008). However, due to their predominantly undocumented status and difficulty with U.S. racial categories, researchers maintain that the Brazilian immigrant population is severely undercounted (Margolis 1994, 1998; Siqueira and Jansen 2008). Historically, Brazilian immigrants have been better educated than the general Brazilian population. These immigrants generally come from working- and middle-class backgrounds and are predominantly men (Goza 1999; Margolis 1994). They also tend to be younger than 40 years old and are lighter in skin tone than most Brazilians, most self-classifying as White (Goza 1999; Margolis 1994). However, Jouet-Pastre and Braga (2008) argue that these trends may change as women and those who are poorer, darker, and less educated migrate to the United States.

Like other immigrant groups, Brazilian immigrants come to the United States seeking better economic opportunities. Among Brazilian immigrants, those from Governador Valadares have a documented history of return migration to their native city (Martes 2008; Siqueira 2006). Experts estimate that 30% to 50% of migrants from Governador Valadares return home after their U.S. sojourn (CIAAT 2007; Siqueira 2006). This process is referred to as *Fazer à América* in Brazilian Portuguese, which translates to "making America" and is a process that consists of working two to five years, saving the money earned in the United States, and sending it back to Brazil to buy a car, or house, or to start a business upon returning (Martes 2008; Siqueira 2006). Therefore, Brazilians, especially those from Governador Valadares, view migration as a means of social mobility since Governador Valadares has few employment opportunities and wages in Brazil are very low. The Brazilian migrants' goal is to "make America" or realize the American Dream in Brazil after returning from the United States.

U.S. Racial Conceptions among Brazilian Immigrants

Despite an increase in research on Brazilian immigrants and comparative race studies in Brazil and the United States, few studies have examined how Brazilians negotiate race relations in the United States, a country with strictly defined racial patterns and a history of legal discrimination against non-Whites, none of which characterize Brazilian society. The racial structure of U.S. society is challenging for many Brazilian immigrants because they come to the United States with a Brazilian understanding of race that is more flexible than that of most U.S. citizens. Evidence of this is found in the limited existing literature on the topic. Margolis's (1994, 1998) foundational studies of Brazilian immigrants in New York City do not explicitly explore racial conceptions. However, she does find that the Brazilian immigrants in her study had more difficulty negotiating their ethnoracial classifications than other Latin American immigrants. They also perceived U.S. society as much more race-conscious and overtly racist than Brazil. Other studies on Brazilian immigrants document similar perceptions (Beserra 2003; Martes 2000; Sales 1999). The negotiation of Latino and Hispanic ethnoracial categories also presents challenges for Brazilian immigrants who are not Hispanic but who are classified in the United States as such even though Brazil is a Portuguese-speaking country (Joseph forthcoming; Marrow 2003; Martes 2007; Zubaran 2008). Recent studies by McDonnell and

Lourenço (2008, 2009) argue that Brazilian immigrants "transnationally" negotiate their ethnoracial classifications in the United States and U.S. race relations by making comparisons to the Brazilian racial system. As migrants who have a history of back-and-forth movement (literally and figuratively) between Brazil and the United States, Brazilian immigrants have a liminal positionality in the United States and experience race "here and there." This chapter contributes to the existing literature by focusing on how Brazilian immigrants negotiate one aspect of the U.S. racial system in relation to the Brazilian racial system: the social position of U.S. Blacks vis-à-vis Brazilian Blacks.

Data and Methods

Data for this chapter come from semistructured in-depth interviews conducted between October 2007 and October 2008 with 49 return migrants in Governador Valadares, Brazil, that country's largest immigrant-sending city to the United States. With a population of 246,000 persons, about 15% of Governador Valadares residents are living in the United States (CIAAT 2007; Margolis 1998). Eighty percent of Governador Valadares residents have at least one relative or friend in the United States (CIAAT 2007). The stability of the area's economy is dependent on remittances sent from the United States, an estimated $2.4 billion in 2004 (CIAAT 2007; Martes 2008; Siqueira 2006). Due to the flow of U.S. dollars and the cultural impact of U.S. migration in the city, the area has been nicknamed Governador Vala*dolares* (as in American dollars) and is well known throughout Brazil for its social, cultural, and economic ties to the United States (CIAAT 2007). Because I explored returnees' racial conceptions before, during, and after migration and thus data could not be gathered longitudinally, the interviews were divided into five sections that provided a retrospective account of each returnee's perceptions throughout the migration process.[2] The first section collected immigration-related data to jog returnees' memories about their United States migration. The remaining four sections examined: (1) self-ascribed racial classification before, during, and after immigration; (2) perceptions of race in Brazil and the United States; (3) experiences of racism in Brazil and the United States; and (4) influence of race on social interactions in Brazil and the United States. Interviews were conducted in Brazilian Portuguese and ranged from 30 to 90 minutes in length.

Interviews were audio-recorded and transcribed for extensive qualitative data analysis.[3] I used a grounded theory approach to derive the findings presented in this chapter, which means that I did not have preconceived notions about what results would emerge from the data before conducting analyses (Glaser and Strauss 1967). Using NVivo8 qualitative software, I relied on open and focused coding to analyze the data (Emerson, Fretz, and Shaw 1995; Strauss and Corbin 1998). This coding process consisted of closely reading each interview transcript and developing a list of recurring themes related to returnees' U.S. racial conceptions that emerged. I then reread each interview and coded each transcript line by line, placing all words, phrases, and sentences under the specific theme that matched the particular U.S. racial conception mentioned in that part of the interview (Emerson et al. 1995). After completing the coding process, I reviewed the findings on returnees' perceptions of U.S. racial stratification and noticed that they included comparisons of the socioeconomic positions and racial attitudes of United States and Brazilian Blacks. Finally, I used NVivo's counting application to calculate the number of returnees whose qualitative anecdotes specifically mentioned comparisons of U.S. and Brazilian Blacks versus the number of returnees who did not. This application allowed me to determine the representativeness of these findings among the sample.

The sample consisted of 26 women and 23 men (49 total) between ages 20 and 57 whose average length of stay in the United States was 7.7 years. The majority lived on the East Coast and returned to Governador Valadares between 1989 and early 2008. In terms of education, 84% of the sample had at least a high school diploma.[4] Furthermore, most of these individuals were working- or middle-class before migrating to the United States. Most respondents worked as housecleaners, babysitters, dishwashers, busboys and busgirls, in construction, or a combination of these jobs while living in the United States. Of the return migrants interviewed, 61% spoke little or no English. With regard to reasons for immigrating, 45% immigrated primarily to work, 18% because of family in the United States, and 37% immigrated for other reasons.[5] Before immigrating, 80% intended to return to Brazil; 59% immigrated once, whereas 41% migrated more than once, supporting Margolis's (1994) notion of back-and-forth migration. Although 63% of returnees obtained tourist or work visas before immigrating, only 25% acquired a green card or U.S. citizenship.[6]

I had access both to returnees' premigration classifications using Brazilian census-derived categories and to their retrospective racial self-classifications while living in the United States using U.S. Census-derived categories.[7] Results show that participants' retrospective racial classifications in Brazil premigration are very different from their racial classifications in the United States. For example, before immigrating, half of the sample self-classified as White in Brazil, whereas 30% of the sample self-classified as White in the United States. Participants were recruited through snowball sampling, which was effective for this project due to extensive U.S. migration history from Governador Valadares. This, in addition to using local contacts such as Brazilian immigration researchers and immigration organizations, yielded the sample. I also recruited a phenotypically diverse sample to account for the different racial percep- tions and experiences returnees might have had in the United States and Brazil based on their physical appearances. Given that these data were collected among a small sample of return migrants in Governador Valadares, I acknowledge the selectivity of this group. Immigration in general is a highly selective process, which differentiates migrants from individuals who decide not to migrate. Likewise, among Brazilian immi- grants in the United States, there are those who do and do not com- plete the return migration to Brazil for several reasons. Among return migrants in Governador Valadares, the sample was also selective based on whom I was able to recruit to participate in the project. Therefore, the findings reported are unique to these individuals and are not intended to be generalizable to all Brazilian immigrants in the United States or Brazilian migrants who have returned to Governador Valadares.

Results: Brazilian Immigrant Experiences and Views

The data reveal two findings regarding how returnees perceived and compared U.S. and Brazilian racial stratification vis-à-vis U.S. and Brazil- ian Blacks. The first indicates that Brazilian return migrants recognized a difference between the societal position of U.S. and Brazilian Blacks. Specifically, they believe that U.S. Blacks have more opportunities for social mobility in their homeland than do Brazilian Blacks in theirs. The second finding signifies returnees' perception of a difference in the racial attitudes of U.S. and Brazilian Blacks, specifically that U.S. Blacks are more "racist" and self-segregating than Brazilian Blacks. Return migrants who made specific comments comparing U.S. and Brazilian Blacks: (1) were generally younger than age 30 when they migrated to the United States; (2) resided in the United States for five years or less; (3) arrived in the United States between 1990 and 2006, or a combination thereof. The returnees in these demographic categories comprise nearly 80%, 47%, and 61% of the sample, respectively. Additional qualitative analyses of these findings showed similarities across gender, various racial classifi- cations, and all education levels among returnees. Finally, it is important to note that these findings reflect a relative comparison solely between a group of U.S. and Brazilian Blacks and not between U.S.–Brazilian Blacks and the broader U.S. and Brazilian populations.

'U.S. Blacks are beautiful': Comparing U.S. and
Brazilian Blacks' Socioeconomic Positions

Interview questions asking returnees about their perceptions of racism in the United States and Brazil elicited responses in which they compared the socioeconomic position of U.S. and Brazilian Blacks. At times returnees voiced their surprise at seeing highly educated and well-dressed U.S. Blacks living in nice homes and driving expensive cars, especially when compared with Brazilian Blacks who are generally poor and have low education levels.[8] Some returnees also believed U.S. Blacks had more power and wealth than U.S. Whites based on their encounters living with or working for U.S. Blacks. For example, Luiz, a Black Brazilian who lived in New Jersey for about three years, expressed a perception that U.S. Blacks are more highly respected and have access to more opportunities than Brazilian Blacks:

> The Black American is very important in the United States and in Brazil, [the Brazilian Black] is inferior. [With regard to] social class, at work, in life, in films, [U.S. Blacks] have more of a chance. Here [in Brazil], the poor population is more Black. Here the Black Brazilian is inferior. The Black American valorizes himself. And in Brazil, [Brazilian Blacks] don't have the value that exists [in the United States for Blacks]. He has more opportunities than the Brazilian, to rise up and be something.
>
> —Luiz, Black, age 43, New Jersey[9]

The following additional quotes from returnees Mateus, Jéssica, and Gustavo demonstrate similar perceptions about the elevated status of Blacks in the United States:

> We [Brazilians] would say that Americans don't like Black people, but after I was there living in the country, I came to see that this wasn't the case because I knew a lot of Blacks there. The majority of them have better lives than Whites. I lived in an apartment complex, [and] every Black person had a nice car and every White person had an ugly car. . . . There in the United States, the White sometimes fights with

the Black because the Black has more power. I don't know if you noticed this there, the Black is well-dressed, has nice cars, lives in nice places. I was sometimes perplexed by this.

—Mateus, Moreno/mixed, age 42, Rhode Island

Here [in Brazil] people of color, [non-Whites] do not have a good financial condition. . . . There [in the United States], it is different. . . . There are many Blacks with a financial situation much better than Whites. . . . They take care of their hair; I think the Black person there is marvelous. Here [in Brazil it] . . . is completely different. There, Blacks dye their hair, they take care of themselves. Maybe it's because of their financial situation or something, but [Brazilian] Blacks don't worry about their physical appearance. . . . [U.S. Blacks] are different, [the United States] is different. Blacks there are much prettier than Blacks here, they make many efforts to make themselves physically beautiful.

—Jéssica, White, age 32, Massachusetts

Even though there's [racial] prejudice, I think that the [U.S.] Black has more opportunity, even with prejudice. But it's because [U.S. Blacks] struggled and fought for this. I think the Black is more present in institutions, in jobs. I think they benefit more than [Blacks] in Brazil. . . . I think that the [U.S.] Black, he fights a lot for his dignity. If he senses prejudice in any situation, he tells it and fights. In Brazil, [marginalized] people lower their heads and stay quiet. It's the type of thing that I got scared when I saw [U.S.] Blacks in nice cars. . . . I saw that and it scared me because I was thinking this isn't common in Brazil: "Look, the Black here can drive a nice car and the Black in Brazil can't," I was thinking, . . . "those Blacks [are] extremely chic (laughs) and beautiful."

—Gustavo, White, age 37, Massachusetts

These quotes demonstrate that returnees of various skin tones noticed the different social positions and political activities of U.S. and Brazilian Blacks.[10] Roughly 30% of returnees also commented on the physical attractiveness of U.S. Blacks relative to Brazilian Blacks. However, return migrants clearly made generalizations about all U.S. and Brazilian Blacks based on their interpersonal encounters with and observations of them in each country. The previous quotes also demonstrate return migrants' limited understanding of the history of U.S. race relations or the institutional and societal manifestations of U.S. racism. This is particularly noticeable in Mateus's quote: "Blacks have more power than Whites." Returnees had no knowledge or awareness of the social position of U.S. Blacks as a whole when compared to the entire U.S. population and assumed that U.S. Blacks' participation in mainstream U.S. consumption patterns was an indicator of stability and a high social class.

Although the U.S. Black middle class has increased in the last few decades, studies show that their class status is tenuous and their wealth is significantly less than their White counterparts (Conley 1999; Lacy 2007; Oliver and Shapiro 1995; Pattillo McCoy 1999; Shapiro 2004). However, because U.S. Blacks can financially participate in U.S. society more than most Brazilians of all colors, returnees consider such purchasing power unusual when compared to their memories of Brazilian Blacks. Because of more unequal distribution of wealth, low wages, and the high prices of imported goods in Brazil, the majority of Brazilians, especially darker ones, have very little money and little purchasing power. Thus return migrants' U.S. perceptions were based on personal observations of what they considered to be indicators of high social status in Brazil (i.e., having a nice car, clothes, or both).

Additionally, due to the importance of social class in Brazilian society, returnees most likely ascribed more positive attributes to U.S. Blacks than Brazilian Blacks because higher social class or the appearance of it (e.g., expensive clothes, houses, cars, grooming services) enhances one's social prestige in Brazil and may socially "Whiten" individuals (Schwartzman 2007; Telles 2004).[11] Jéssica and Gustavo's earlier quotes specifically mention a perception that U.S. Blacks are more beautiful and invest in their physical appearance in a way that Brazilian Blacks do not. Jéssica also makes the direct link between how one's financial position can influence his or her ability to beautify themselves. Furthermore, many returnees used the word *chique*, which means chic in English, to describe U.S. Blacks. Returnees' emphasis on the beauty of U.S. Blacks implies that Brazilian Blacks are not beautiful. Other studies of Brazilians in the United States and in Brazil also note how physical attractiveness and positive characteristics are attributed to U.S. Blacks compared to Brazilian Blacks (Margolis 1994; Marrow 2003; Twine 1998).

These perceptions indicate that the sample Brazilian returnees used a Brazilian lens of social stratification to negotiate U.S. race relations, more specifically the socioeconomic position and physical appearance of U.S. Blacks. Brazilians come from a country where most Blacks live in extreme poverty, have limited social opportunities, and are perceived to accept their marginalized social position. Despite living in a country that valorizes racial democracy and racial mixing, Telles (2004) and Twine (1998) argue that social cordiality can exist among all Brazilians if non-Whites accept their marginalization in Brazil. This relates to Luiz's and Gustavo's quotes where they noticed distinct differences in the political activity of U.S. and Brazilian Blacks and acknowledged that such activity might have played a role in U.S. Blacks' success. Inversely, Gustavo's quote also mentions how Brazilian Blacks "lower their heads and keep quiet" as victims of racial oppression.

The higher socioeconomic position of U.S. Blacks also surprised and confused returnees because they expected U.S. Blacks to be as or more marginalized and socially disadvantaged as Brazilian Blacks given the amount of overt racism to which U.S. Blacks were historically and legally subjugated. Seeing well-educated Blacks in expensive homes and cars did not align with returnees' preconceived notions of U.S. race relations. Their premigration perceptions of Brazilian Blacks as poor and disenfranchised in combination with their observations of U.S. Blacks as middle class and beautiful created a dissonance for returnees in their attempt to understand U.S. race relations. As temporary migrants who maintained transnational ties to Brazil while living in the United States, such a stark contrast in U.S. Blacks' social status reminded returnees of Brazilian Blacks' lower and more marginalized position in addition to broader social inequality in Brazil.

Living in the United States gave these participants a new lens which allowed them to recollect and reflect on the social position of Blacks in both countries. In terms of socioeconomic indicators such as income, education, and occupation, U.S. Blacks are higher on the social hierarchy scale in the United States than their Brazilian counterparts (Bailey 2009; Sansone 2003; Telles 2004). Such a transnational comparison may not have been possible had these returnees remained in Brazil and not migrated to the United States. Thus, temporarily migrating to the United States and encountering middle-class U.S. Blacks influenced returnees' perception of racial inequality among Blacks in Brazil and the United States.

'. . . But Brazilian Blacks aren't racist': Comparing Brazilian and U.S. Blacks' Racial Attitudes

Despite acknowledging the elevated socioeconomic positions of U.S. Blacks relative to Brazilian Blacks, 40% of returnees of various racial classifications also reported a perception that U.S. Blacks were more racist than their Brazilian counterparts. Specifically, these returnees noted that U.S. Blacks, especially those who were middle and upper class, tended to live in separate residential neighborhoods and attended all or predominantly Black churches and schools. Returnees identified such behavior as self-segregating and racist. *Racista* (racist) and *preconceito* (prejudiced) were the specific Portuguese words return migrants used to describe their perception of U.S. Blacks' racial attitudes. Compared to this, return migrants felt Brazilian Blacks, despite being poor, had much more cordial interactions with non-Black Brazilians than did U.S. Blacks with Americans of other ethnoracial backgrounds. Almost half of the returnees interviewed mentioned this perception:

> The Blacks in the United States, I see that they themselves separate themselves from Whites; I found that strange there. I don't know if that's because here in Brazil we are mixed. It could have to do with discrimination, but it's more personal. No one talks to you or leaves their neighborhood. For instance, there are some parts in some states that only have Black places or White places—isn't that true? And I find this very strange, one thing that doesn't exist here [in Brazil], thank God.
>
> —Juliana, Morena/mixed, age 41, Massachusetts

> There is racism everywhere. There is racism with the Black in Brazil, here it exists, but not to the degree as it does in the U.S. I don't see it; that is my opinion. The Black in the U.S. likes his own place; he doesn't mix much either. You see Blacks in all social classes, but in general, the Black, at least in New York where I live[d], he has his own neighborhood, his own club, his own music. This is what I saw; they claim they are not racist, but I see that they stick together to a certain degree. They are people with much culture, tremendous artists, the [Black] middle class associates together in one place.
>
> —Ricardo, White, age 50, New York

> Look, I think, it's like I told you before, from what I saw, it seems that the Black [in the United States] is more racist than the White. And like I said at times, I don't know if it is

different now because it's been years [since I was in United
States]. I cleaned, I worked cleaning a house and [the own-
ers] were Black, they didn't have any type of relationships
with Whites. They lived, I don't remember the name of the
place, but there were only Blacks in that area, all the houses
were mansions. . . . And one day, I heard a conversation
and they said they were Black and didn't want to mix with
anybody. . . . I noticed this there, I don't know what you
think, but I noticed that the Black seems to want to be better than the White. . . .

—Letícia, Black woman, age 45, New York,
New Jersey, and Massachusetts

These quotes provide specific examples of returnees' perceptions
that U.S. Blacks perpetuate racist and self-segregating behavior. While
return migrants specifically identified this behavior among U.S. Blacks,
returnees did not report observing similar behavior among Whites and
other ethnoracial groups in the United States. Nearly all returnees told
me that they lived in Brazilian communities and worked and socialized
predominantly with other Brazilians while living in the United States.
Yet, these individuals did not perceive this behavior, the same behavior
they observed among U.S. Blacks, as racist or self-segregating. Additionally, due to residential segregation and personal preference in the
United States, various ethnoracial groups, not only U.S. Blacks, live
in ethnically and racially homogenous neighborhoods. However, U.S.
Blacks were specifically labeled as racist and self-segregating for residing
in predominantly Black neighborhoods and frequenting predominantly
Black institutions. U.S. Blacks were most likely singled out relative to
other groups in the United States as a consequence of their higher
visibility in mainstream U.S. society vis-à-vis Blacks in Brazil. Lower
levels of residential segregation in Brazil also meant that returnees were
accustomed to seeing Brazilians of different skin colors living in proxim-
ity to each other despite dramatically different class positions correlated
with skin tone. Since Brazil has a larger African-descended population
and less residential segregation than the United States, large numbers of
U.S. Blacks living in separate neighborhoods seemed like racist behavior
to returnees.

Brazilian returnees' perceptions of U.S. Blacks as racist once again
revealed their lack of awareness about the history of racial inequality
in the United States. Due to racist legislation, Blacks were prohibited
from residing in certain communities or attending "White" schools. In

response to such policies and because they wished to organize institutions they controlled, U.S. Blacks and other ethnoracial minorities had to develop their own community, educational, and religious institutions (Almaguer 1994; Feagin 2000; Tuan 1999). Thus, among racially and ethnically segregated neighborhoods are a legacy of discriminatory housing policies that, while officially illegal, persist in contemporary U.S. society (Charles 2003; Emerson, Chai, and Yancey 2001; Harris 1999; Massey and Denton 1993). Furthermore, research on U.S. residential segregation suggests that, for the most part, many Whites do not want to live in the same neighborhoods as Blacks (Charles 2003; Emerson et al. 2001; Harris 1999; Massey and Denton 1993). Thus, returnees' perceptions that U.S. Blacks live in separate communities by choice are not completely accurate.

Overall, return migrants used a Brazilian lens to compare the social behavior of U.S. and Brazilian Blacks. Returnees perceived Blacks in Brazil as more cordial and willing to live and interact with Brazilians of all colors. The previous quotes also support their beliefs that Brazilian Blacks live in harmony with fellow Brazilians in the same communities. Most returnees often suggested that Brazil overall and Governador Valadares specifically were more racially mixed spatially relative to the United States and that Black neighborhoods and White neighborhoods or Black cities and White cities did not exist. While limited previous research on residential segregation in Brazil indicates that levels are significantly lower than in the United States, non-White Brazilians are much more likely than White Brazilians to have fewer life opportunities, be more physically distant from the (White) middle class, and live in poverty (Telles 1992, 2004). Such quality-of-life differences suggest that many respondents are romanticizing certain aspects of the racial and social climates of their native locales.

Discussion and Conclusion:
The Future of Studies on Brazilian Immigrants

This chapter demonstrates two ways that Brazilian return migrants used a Brazilian lens of racial stratification to negotiate U.S. race relations while they lived in the United States. The salience of Black Americans' higher socioeconomic status and their perceived racist behavior provides a broad contrast to returnees' perceptions of Brazilian Blacks. Returnees' observations of the elevated social position of U.S. Blacks relative to Brazilian Blacks are valid because U.S. Blacks do have higher levels of education, income, and opportunities for social mobility despite being a smaller percentage of the U.S. population. Conversely, in Brazil Afro-descended individuals are among the poorest and least educated Brazilians, yet represent nearly half of the population. Because social class enhances an individual's social prestige in Brazil, returnees had more favorable opinions of the beauty of U.S. Blacks relative to Brazilian Blacks. Returnees also discussed the political activism and visible presence of U.S. Blacks in mainstream society. Although this research was conducted before the election of President Barack Obama, returnees mentioned that the political activism of U.S. Blacks played a role in their collective social advancement, which returnees noted was lacking among Brazilian Blacks. However, some returnees were critical of what they perceived as racist and self-segregating behavior among U.S. Blacks, which they felt was not as present among Brazilian Blacks. Their lack of knowledge about U.S. race relations led returnees to ascribe racist behavior to U.S. Blacks whom they perceived as living in segregated neighborhoods by choice and discriminating against non-Blacks.

These findings are relevant because they provide additional evidence of qualitative differences in U.S. and Brazilian race relations with regard to the racial stratification of Blacks in both countries. Previous quantitative studies of racial inequality in Brazil and the United States highlight similar differences between the social outcomes for U.S. and Brazilian Blacks and confirm that U.S. Blacks are much "better off" than Brazilian Blacks. However, the qualitative data in this study provides more in-depth information on such perceptions among a small group of Brazilians who lived and experienced race in the United States. Their unique experience as return migrants allowed them to make observations and compare the U.S. and Brazilian racial systems on an individual level. Thus, this chapter demonstrates how everyday people make sense of one aspect (i.e., stratification) of the racial structure of the United States and Brazil.

These findings also demonstrate that Brazilians are aware of anti-Black racial inequality in Brazil. Previous studies on the Brazilian racial system maintain that Brazilians were in denial about the extent of racial inequality in their society, particularly with regard to Brazilian Blacks (Dulitzky 2005; Dzidzienyo 2005; Fry 2000; Twine 1998). Furthermore, the emphasis on the racial democracy ideology in early twentieth-century Brazil, which argued that racism could not exist because Brazilians were racially mixed, also influenced Brazilians' perceptions of racism (Bailey 2009; Freyre 1933; Guimarães 2001). However, Brazilian return migrants of all skin tones in this study were conscious of racism in Brazil and its impact on Brazilian Blacks. These individuals were most likely aware of such racial stratification before migrating to the

United States. However, living in the United States and encountering upwardly mobile Blacks provided another perspective of racial stratification that coincided with and enhanced their premigration perceptions of Brazilian Blacks.

Even though this study focuses on a small sample of Brazilian return migrants, it has broader implications for exploring how immigrants in the United States develop an understanding of historical and contemporary U.S. racial relations. Immigrants come to the United States with preconceived notions about race and conceptions of race from their countries of origin. Such preconceived ideas influence these individuals' observations of and interactions with different ethnoracial groups. However, how immigrants negotiate and apply these preconceived ideas to their experience and observations of race in the United States do not align with the historical reality of U.S. race relations. In this study, Brazilian returnees' awareness of racial stratification in Brazil, more specifically the marginalized position and interracial cordiality of Brazilian Blacks collided with their observations of "racist," socially mobile U.S. Blacks who were perceived as highly educated, well-dressed, and beautiful. Yet, their perceptions were clearly uninformed by the complete and tumultuous history of Black-White race relations, which continues to shape and inform the U.S. racial system. Additional research is needed to assess how the findings here might differ based on U.S. region, Brazilian region, or both; the level of U.S. Black–Brazilian interactions for Brazilian immigrants; and the effects of Barack Obama's two-term presidency. Other work is needed that nuances the role of skin tone of both U.S. Blacks and Brazilians on the latter group's views as well as media representations of U.S. blackness. In highlighting immigrants' negotiations of the U.S. racial hierarchy and pointing toward new areas of necessary research, this study offers a prophetic examination of the rigidity and fluidity of racial perceptions, racial hierarchies, and racial structures in and beyond the United States.

Other immigrants from Latin America and beyond learn how to navigate the U.S. racial system by making observations of and interacting with various groups. Such navigation not only influences these migrants' perceptions of other ethnoracial groups, but also may shape assimilation and incorporation processes—from their choice of neighborhoods in which to live and marriage partners to what they "teach" their U.S.-born children about U.S. Blacks and other ethnoracial groups in the United States. Thus, migrants' perceptions of certain "racial" groups and inequality in their countries of origin may shift on migrating to the United States and encountering a different society that has more or less (racial) stratification relative to their native countries.

Notes

1. I interchangeably use the terms "returnees" and "return migrants" to refer to Brazilian return migrants.

2. Most social science studies gather data retrospectively, and it is understood that participants' memories of social events may degrade over time (Trivellato 1999; Wellman 2007).

3. Because I am not a native Brazilian Portuguese speaker, I hired three Brazilian college students to transcribe the interviews. Transcripts remained in Portuguese for data analysis to ensure the authenticity of participants' words and minimize any nuances that could be lost in translation. Only the responses included in this chapter are translated (as accurately and sensibly as possible) for an English-speaking audience. Additionally, knowledge gained about Brazilian race relations while living and conducting research in Governador Valadares has also been essential for "translating" semantic differences regarding Brazilian discussions of race for a U.S. audience.

4. The complete breakdown is: 16%, less than high school; 53%, high school diploma; 22%, college degree; and 8%, post baccalaureate degree.

5. These included studying, visiting family, and a desire to spend time in the United States.

6. These demographics align with those of other qualitative studies conducted among Brazilian immigrants in the United States.

7. The U.S. Census asks Hispanic-origin individuals to classify both ethnically as Hispanic and racially (i.e., Black, White). However, I combined the "Hispanic/Latino" categories in my interviews because previous studies suggest that Brazilian immigrants are exposed to both terms in the United States and some returnees used the terms interchangeably during pretest interviews in the summer of 2007 (Martes 2007). "Yellow" refers to individuals of Asian ancestry in the Brazilian Census. Some returnees felt "yellow" best described their skin tones despite having no Asian ancestry.

8. Sixteen of forty-nine (30%) returnees specifically mentioned this surprise in their interviews. Thirty-one of forty-nine (63%) returnees mentioned a common societal perception that Brazilian Blacks are poor, uneducated, and have limited opportunities. Nearly all (90%) returnees believed that racism exists in Brazil and is directed toward Brazilian Blacks.

9. Each quote was translated from Portuguese and includes the participant's pseudonym, open-ended racial classification as reported at the time of the interview, age, and U.S. state of residence. I include lengthy quotes to demonstrate the depth and representativeness of returnees' racial conceptions across differences in race, age, and U.S. location

10. About 20% (n=9) of returnees specifically mentioned the political activism of U.S. Blacks compared to their Brazilian counterparts.

11. "Social whitening" refers to a phenotypically non-White person's ability to receive privilege comparable to those of Whites' social treatment due to socioeconomic status (Schwartzman 2007; Telles 2004).

References

Almaguer, Tomas. 1994. *Racial Fault Lines: The Historical Origins of White Supremacy in California.* Berkeley: University of California Press.

Andrews, George Reid. 1992. "Racial Inequality in Brazil and the United States: A Statistical Comparison." *Journal of Social History* 26 (2):229–63.

———. 2009. *Legacies of Race: Identities, Attitudes, and Politics in Brazil.* Palo Alto, CA: Stanford University Press.

Beserra, Bernadete. 2003. *Brazilian Immigrants in the United States: Cultural Imperialism and Social Class.* New York: LFB Scholarly Press.

Centro de Informação, Apoio e Amparo à Familiar e au Trabalhador no Exterior (CIATT). 2007. "Um Estudo sobre a Imigração em Governador Valadares." Governador Valadares, BR.

Charles, Camille Zubrinsky. 2003. "The Dynamics of Racial Residential Segregation." *Annual Review of Sociology* 29:167–207.

Conley, Dalton. 1999. *Being Black, Living in the Red.* Berkeley: University of California Press.

Davis, James. 1991. *Who Is Black? One Nation's Definition.* University Park: Pennsylvania State University Press.

Dulitzky, Ariel. 2005. "A Region in Denial: Racial Discrimination and Racism in Latin America." Pp. 39–60 in *Neither Enemies Nor Friends: Latinos, Blacks, Afro-Latinos,* edited by A. Dzidzienyo and S. Oboler. New York: Palgrave.

Dzidzienyo, Anani. 2005. "The Changing World of Brazilian Race Relations?" Pp. 137–56 in *Neither Enemies nor Friends: Latinos, Blacks, Afro-Latinos,* edited by A. Dzidzienyo and S. Oboler. New York: Palgrave.

Emerson, Michael O., Karen J. Chai and George Yancey. 2001. "Does Race Matter in Residential Segregation? Exploring the Preferences of White Americans." *American Sociological Review* 66 (6):922–35.

Emerson, R. M., Rachel I. Fretz, and Linda L. Shaw. 1995. *Writing Ethnographic Fieldnotes.* Chicago: University of Chicago Press.

Feagin, Joe. 2000. *Racist America: Roots, Current Realities, and Future Reparations.* New York: Routledge.

Freyre, Gilberto. 1933. *Casa Grande e Senzala.* Rio de Janeiro: Editora Record.

Fry, Peter. 2000. "Politics, Nationality, and the Meanings of Race in Brazil." *Daedalus* 129 (2):83–118.

Glaser, Barney G. and Anselm Strauss. 1967. *The Discovery of Grounded Theory: Strategies for Qualitative Research.* Edison, NJ: Aldine Transaction.

Goza, Franklin. 1999. "Immigrant Social Networks: The Brazilian Case." Retrieved July 10, 2012 (http://iussp2005.princeton.edu/download. aspx?submissionId=50570).

Guimarães, Antonio Sérgio. 2001. "Race, Class, and Color: Behind Brazil's Racial Democracy." *NACLA Report on the Americas* 34 (6):38–39.

Harris, David R. 1999. "Property Values Drop When Blacks Move In, Because . . .": Racial and Socioeconomic Determinants of Neighborhood Desirability." *American Sociological Review* 64 (3):461–79.

Joseph, Tiffany D. Forthcoming. "Latino, Hispanic, or Brazilian: Considerations for Brazilian Immigrants' Racial Classification in the U.S." In *The Discourse and Politics of Immigration in the Global North*, edited by J. Capetillo, G. Jacobs, and P. Kretsedemas. New York: Routledge.

Jouet-Pastre, Clemence and Leticia J. Braga. 2008. *Becoming Brazuca: Brazilian Immigration to the United States.* Cambridge, MA: Harvard University Press.

Lacy, Karyn R. 2007. *Blue-Chip Black: Race, Class, and Status in the New Black Middle Class.* Berkeley: University of California.

Landale, Nancy and R. S. Oropesa. 2002. "White, Black, or Puerto Rican? Racial Self-Identification among Mainland and Island Puerto Ricans." *Social Forces* 81(1):231–54.

Levitt, Peggy. 2007. *God Needs No Passport: How Migrants Are Transforming the American Religious Landscape.* New York: New Press.

Marcus, Alan P. 2009. "Brazilian Immigration to the United States and the Geographical Imagination." *Geographical Review* 99 (4):481–98.

Margolis, Maxine. 1994. *Little Brazil: An Ethnography of Brazilian Immigrants in New York City.* Princeton, NJ: Princeton University Press.

———. 1998. *An Invisible Minority: Brazilians in New York City.* Boston: Allyn and Bacon.

Marrow, Helen. 2003. "To Be or Not to Be (Hispanic or Latino): Brazilian Racial and Ethnic Identity in the United States." *Ethnicities* 3(4):427–64.

Martes, Ana Cristina Braga. 2000. *Brasileiros nos Estados Unidos: Um Estudo Sobre Imigrantes em Massachusetts.* São Paulo, Brazil: Paz e Terra.

———. 2007. "Neither Hispanic, nor Black: 'We're Brazilian.'" Pp. 231–56 in *The Other Latinos: Central and South Americans in the United States*, edited by J. L. Falconi and J. A. Mazzotti. Cambridge, MA: Harvard University Press.

———. 2008. "The Commitment of Return: Remittances of Brazilian Emigrés." Pp. 125–50 in *Becoming Brazuca: Brazilian Immigration to the United States*, edited by C. Jouet-Pastre and L. J. Braga. Cambridge, MA: Harvard University Press.

Massey, Douglas and Nancy Denton. 1993. *American Apartheid.* Cambridge, MA: Harvard University Press.

Marx, Anthony. 1998. *Making Race and Nation: A Comparison of the United States, South Africa, and Brazil.* New York: Cambridge University Press.

McDonnell, Judith and Cileine de Lourenço. 2008. "Brazilian Immigrant Women: Race, Ethnicity, Gender, and Transnationalism." Pp. 151–73 in *Becoming Brazuca: Brazilian Immigration to the United States*, edited by C. Jouet-Pastre and L. J. Braga. Cambridge, MA: Harvard University Press.

———. 2009. "You're Brazilian, Right? What Kind of Brazilian Are You? The Racialization of Brazilian Immigrant Women." *Ethnic and Racial Studies* 32(2):239–56.

Oliver, Melvin and Thomas Shapiro. 1995. *Black Wealth White Wealth: A New Perspective on Racial Inequality.* New York: Routledge.

Pattillo-McCoy, Mary. 1999. *Black Picket Fences. Privilege and Peril among the Black Middle Class.* Chicago: University of Chicago Press.

Reis, Rossana and Teresa Sales. 1999. "Cenas do Brasil Migrante." São Paulo, BrazilSao Paulo: Boitempo.

Sales, Teresa. 1999. *Brasileiros Longe De Casa.* Sao Paulo, Brazil: Cortez Editora Ltda.

Sansone, Livio. 2003. *Negritude sem Ethnicidade: O Local e O Global Nas Relações Raciais e Na Produção Cultural Negra do Brasil.* Salvador: Edufba/ Pallas.

Schwartzman, Luisa Farah. 2007. "Does Money Whiten? Intergenerational Changes in Racial Classification in Brazil." *American Sociological Review* 72(6):940–63.

Shapiro, Thomas. 2004. *The Hidden Cost of Being African American: How Wealth Perpetuates Inequality.* Oxford: Oxford University Press.

Siqueira, Carlos Eduardo and Tiago Jansen. 2008. "Updating Demographic, Geographic, and Occupational Data on Brazilian in Massachusetts." Pp. 105–24 in *Becoming Brazuca: Brazilian Immigration to the United States,* edited by C. Jouet-Pastre and L. J. Braga. Cambridge: Harvard University Press.

Siqueira, Sueli. 2006. "Migrantes e Empreendedorismo na Microregião de Governador Valadares: Sonhos e Frustrações no Retorno." PhD dissertation, Department of Sociology, Federal University of Minas Gerais, Belo Horizonte, BR.

Strauss, Anselm and Juliet Corbin. 1998. *Basics of Qualitative Research.* Thousand Oaks, CA: Sage Publications.

Telles, Edward E. 1992. "Residential Segregation by Skin Color in Brazil." *American Sociological Review* 57 (2):186–97.

———. 2004. *Race in Another America: The Significance of Skin Color in Brazil.* Princeton: Princeton University Press.

Trivellato, Ugo. 1999. "Issues in the Design and Analysis of Panel Studies: A Cursory Review." *Quality and Quantity* 33(3):339–52.

Tuan, Mia. 1999. *Forever Foreigners or Honorary Whites? The Asian Ethnic Experience Today.* New Brunswick: Rutgers University Press.

Twine, France Winddance. 1998. *Racism in a Racial Democracy: The Maintenance of White Supremacy in Brazil.* New Brunswick: Rutgers University Press.

Wellman, Barry. 2007. "Challenges in Collecting Personal Network Data: The Nature of Personal Network Analysis." *Field Methods* 19(2):111–15.

Zubaran, Carlos. 2008. "The Quest for Recognition: Brazilian Immigrants in the United States." *Transcultural Psychiatry* 45(4):590–610.

8

~

Africa Speaks

The *"Place" of Africa in Constructing*
African American Identity in Museum Exhibits

DERRICK R. BROOMS

University of Louisville

Africa has figured prominently in African American identity, particularly since the 1960s. During the Civil Rights era of the 1960s and 1970s, African Americans experienced a renewed interest in African culture and history, and developed a culture of Black pride—"Black is Beautiful"— to accompany African American protest activities. The creation of new symbolic forms and the abandonment of old, discredited symbols and rhetoric reflected prophetic efforts to foster internal solidarity and challenge the prevailing definitions of Black American ethnicity (Coombes 1988; Karp and Lavine 1991). As a geographical location of genealogy and culture, as an idea, and as a cultural ideology, Africa was central to these efforts. Many African Americans incorporated aspects of African fashion, African-inspired names, and African cultural heritage into their everyday lives. Yet it is within institutions, such as museums, where messages about the relationship between Africa and African American identity were reified (Ruffins 1998). This chapter focuses on representational strategies used in Black-centered museums to define and display African American cultural identity.

There is scant literature in sociology regarding African Americans and museums and, more specifically, there is little discussion about the influence of museums on African American identity formation (Eichstedt and Small 2002; Ruffins 1992; Stewart and Ruffins 1986). As institutions of interpretation, museums both reify and examine (through tools of interpretation) the ideas and objects they select and present (Greenberg, Ferguson, and Nairne 1996; Hall 1997; Sherman and Rogoff 1994; Weil 2002). This study considers how museums consciously and unconsciously create an interpretative framework for Diasporic identity. In so doing, it draws on an understudied site to offer a prophetic exploration of identity that outlines how Blackness in America is connected to Black American constructions of an African past.

Davis and Gandy (1999) contend that media representations play an important role in informing the ways that we understand social, cultural, ethnic, and racial differences (p. 367). Furthermore, the tension between one's chosen identities and given identities appears in stark form in African American history. For example, Du Bois's ([1903] 1994) "double consciousness" expresses how Blacks embrace their national identity in hopes of future returns of equal status American citizenship for their racial group. However, we have little empirical evidence about how this concept works via visual representations. Since most African Americans choose a dual "Black and American" identity over a "Black only" or "American only" identity (Smith 1992), it is important to know more about how they manage their dual identity within cultural institutions. In addition to the experience of dual or integrated Black and American identities, Blacks frequently grapple with how African American identity is socially constructed by internal and external forces. Evidenced by the changing nomenclature of African Americans, race and ethnicity are two key building blocks of identity. For example, the change from Black Americans to African Americans was a rational choice to supplant previous notions of a purely race-based identity that had been derived by non-African Americans (Fortes 1987). This change is coupled with museum exhibition practices in Black-centered museums in projecting African American identity. These projections span from the naming of Black-centered museums to museum collections to museum exhibits, which are the focus of this analysis.

Drawing on data from exhibition analysis and participation observation at two Black-centered museums, this study situates museums as sites where racialized ideologies are created, organized, and maintained for those identified as African American. While the use of Africa in Black-centered museums relies heavily on cultural construction, its mere

presence in the museum is part of the larger African American coun-
ternarrative and serves as an essential "racial project" (Omi and Winant
1994) in rearticulating and reimagining African American identity. The
museums selected for this study are those organized by and for African
Americans and are specifically designed as historical museums, cultural
museums, or both. These museums provide key sites to explore the
use of Africa as a representative tool for African American identity and
thus a symbol for collective memory. I use these museums as sites for
projecting images of identity and as a prism through which to investigate how Black-centered museums engage in identity work to reaffirm
African American identity through exhibition practices.

   This research focuses on three key questions. First, how is Africa
presented in these museums? Second, how do the sample museums
consciously and unconsciously create an interpretative framework that
informs the African American experience? Third, how does the presentation of Africa inform us about how African American identity is
articulated? Using Africa as a representational tool and as a cultural
link has been both subjectively and selectively defined in Black-centered
museums. This analysis lends insight into the structures, institutional
practices, and ideological articulations of race; it also describes connections between past and current racialization processes in the United
States. As a result, this research contributes to the understanding of
the construction and social reproduction of race and culture (Bourdieu
1993; Nagel 1994). Furthermore, this research elucidates the ways that
racial categories and the meanings of racial identity are negotiated, created, and maintained by individuals and groups, as well as outside agents
and organizations, in and through museums.

Africa, African Americans, and Museums

Drawing on research in the field of museum studies, I examine the
negotiation of African American identity within and across museums by
studying work that demonstrates the "poetics and politics" of museum
displays (Greenberg et al. 1996; Karp and Lavine 1991; Weil 2002),
issues of identity (Coombes 1988), and expressions of African American
interests (Eichstedt and Small 2002; Horton and Crew 1989; Ruffins
1992; Stewart and Ruffins 1986). Museums are important sites where
knowledge and power are created. According to Macdonald and Fyfe
(1996):

> Museums are never just spaces for the playing out of wider
> social relations. A museum is a process as well as a structure;

it is a creative agency as well as a "contested terrain." It is because museums have a formative as well as a reflective role in social relations that they are potentially of such influence. (P. 4)

The past 20 years have seen an explosion of museums dedicated to preserving and interpreting the African American experience in America. This work has benefitted from significant contributions from both the public and private sectors. While ethnic museums can provide an important space for negotiating and managing identities, their representations are simultaneously situated alongside—and often against—those images projected by mainstream media (Eichstedt and Small 2002; Stewart and Ruffins 1986). Collective identity in Black-centered museums creates a space for interrogating generational influences and the tensions arising from the relationship between the past and the present.

Within museums and across other social, cultural, and educational institutions, complex debates are currently taking place about the way that African American history should be told, the selection of cultural images, and how African Americans should be represented. For example, Ruffins (1998) questions whether the story of Black separation, isolation, and achievement despite adversity should be the primary narrative and context for discussions about African Americans. She asserts that in most African American museums, some version of this narrative is absolutely central because it fulfills African Americans' need for a validating and distinctive history. However, for other Americans troubled by the history of segregation, the great narrative of African American life has much more to do with integration into and acceptance by mainstream American life. This ideology has been instrumental in the selecting of images and stories presented about African American life in non-Black museums (Ruffins 1998).

Museums, Identity Construction, and the Racialization Process

Identities are not easily known or clearly experienced phenomena. Personhood, Fortes (1987) observes, poses problems that individuals have to solve. These include formulating answers to the questions about how we know ourselves, the person we are supposed to be, and how we display our personhood. These questions arise out of the distinction that is commonly made between the person (i.e., the socially defined aspect of the self) and the individual (i.e., the uniquely experienced side of the self). Identities are constructed in performance (Goffman 1959) and interaction with others (Becker 1986; Cooley 1902; Mead 1934). Some identities, such as race, gender, and ethnicity, seem to be more permanent than others. Saussure (1974) argues that identity is a function of differences within a system. Therefore, any identity is relational and depends on other concepts for its distinctiveness (Hall and du Gay 1996). Applying this dynamic means that cultural and ethnic identities are understood based on their distinctions from and opposition to other cultures and ethnicities (Morley and Robins 1995). Therefore, the critical factor for identifying an ethnic group becomes the "social boundaries, which define the group with respect to other groups, not the cultural reality within the borders" (Schlesinger 1987:235). Some scholars argue that our own internal claim to ethnicity makes us an ethnic group (Cornell and Hartman 1998; Jenkins 1994) in addition to recognition and validation by others.

The notion of racialization emerges from research that calls attention to the way objects (Small 1997), people (Davis 1991), and processes (Miles 1989; Omi and Winant 1994) become identified as "racial." Such terms highlight the fact that objects, people, and relations are never inherently about race, but rather become racialized through a social process of meaning-making and resource allocation. Racial categories and labels play an important role in defining groups and individuals who belong to those groups. This has been especially true for racial and ethnic groups in general and for Blacks in particular. For example, over the past century the standard term for Blacks has shifted from "Nigger," to "Darkie," to "Colored" to "Negro" to "Black" and, more recently to "African American." The more recent changes can be considered attempts by Blacks to define themselves and to gain respect and standing in a society that has historically considered them subordinate and inferior (Martin 1991; Thompson and Akbar 2003; Smith 1992). The variation of names both reflects and in turn shapes racial understanding and dynamics. It establishes often-contradictory parameters of racial identity into which both individuals and groups must fit (Martin 1991; Waters 1990). When viewed broadly, U.S. racial classifications reflect prevailing conceptions of race, establish boundaries to understand racial identity, influence the allocation of resources, and frame diverse political issues and conflicts (Feagin 2000; Omi and Winant 1994).

Anderson (2002) notes that the issues that concern African American museums are not unrelated to larger, more general themes that draw attention in the international world of ideas, such as modernism, deconstructionism, and other topics in the arena of contemporary criticism. As a result, the critical, sociohistorical, and art historical contributions of African American museums are urgently needed in mainstream discussions of such themes. Additionally, African cultures are perceived as part of the symbolic and actual legacy of Black people in America (Anderson 2002). This point was especially made with the proposition to rename/relabel Blacks as "African Americans." The ideology behind this movement was to connect to a homeland and to establish a cultural heritage (Martin 1991). Kaeppler (1992) discusses the representation of ethnic groups within and outside of their respective communities. The capacity for museums to influence public perceptions—and, hence, representations of cultures—rests in part on the fact that museums are regarded as "historical treasure houses" in which material culture and links with history are enshrined. This is an important concept in this research because each exhibit is ensconced within multiple narratives and can be viewed from a variety of perspectives to potentially influence identity development. The exhibitions examined in this study help illuminate some of the ways that museums produce communal ties based on the presentation of a shared racial and cultural heritage produced in the museum. By examining the museum as a mechanism by which groups organize, maintain, and recreate themselves—who they are and what their identity means—this research seeks to clarify and organize the growing literature documenting the shifting, volitional, situational nature of racial identity.

Collective Memory and Museums

"Memory" is an ongoing process of negotiation through time (Olick and Levy 1997). Examining the influence of local collective memory, formed in mnemonic communities (Zerubavel 1996) or micro "communities of memory" (Irwin-Zarecka 1994), enables one to investigate how museums activate cultural constraints, reinterpret past historical events and figures, and act as a symbolic basis for group identity. Black-centered museums construct and institutionalize collective memory through representational practices. Black-centered museums, through their narratives of a mythologized African past and a consistent positing of colonial Africa as subject, institutionalize a collective memory of culture and history that rearticulates Black local identity to a broader global identity. This collective memory is embedded in ethnic nationalism and intensifies individuals' awareness of historical identity. The assertion here is not that all African Americans subscribe to a global identity (i.e., identify with Africans and those throughout the Diaspora), but rather that representations of Africa in African American museums bring issues such as global identity to the fore of consciousness. Thus, by rearticulating collective images of the Black past, African American museums are key sites for displaying the role of human agency in shaping culture—and identity.[1]

Studying Black-Centered Museums:
Methodologies, Data, and Analysis

In order to investigate Black-centered museums in the United States, I initially created a list of more than 100 sites and then subsequently narrowed the list to museums of history and culture. The study was then proscribed by geographic spaces accessible to the researcher, which included Washington, D.C., and the Chicago metro area. Because there are multiple windows into the world of museum exhibiting, several methodologies are employed in conducting this research including participant observation, interpretative methodology, and content analysis. Data were collected based on the museum as an overall "space" as well as via museum collections in temporary as well as permanent displays, exhibits, texts, and tours. A mixed methodology allowed for the study of issues such as signifying practices, negotiating standards of balance and objectivity, informational content, and representations of the "Other." Moreover, these approaches enabled me to identify and uncover patterns and themes related to race, ethnicity, identity, culture, and memory (Hall 1992, 1994).

Black-centered sites were selected to examine museums whose main purpose is to preserve and interpret the historical experiences and achievements of African Americans. Two sites were selected, the DuSable Museum of African American History and the Black Holocaust Museum. The DuSable Museum was founded in 1961 in the front room of Margaret and Charles Burroughs's Chicago home. The Burroughs started this museum because they believed the public should have a better understanding of Black history, art, culture, and the contributions Blacks made to the nation and world. The museum's namesake, Jean Baptiste Pointe DuSable, was a Black Haitian trader and the first settler of Chicago. The DuSable Museum is the oldest museum of its type in the country and the only major independent institution in Chicago established to preserve and interpret the historical experiences and achievements of African Americans. The second site, the Black Holocaust Museum, was founded in 1988 in Milwaukee, Wisconsin, by James Cameron to share the history, tragedy, suffering, and torment of those who experienced the "peculiar institution" of slavery. It also chronicles Reconstruction and the history of Blacks during the Civil Rights movement. According to Cameron, the museum is devoted to preserving the history of lynching in the United States and the struggle of Black people for equality.[2]

Findings: Placing Africa in Black-Centered Museums

Africa is used as both a segue and a connecting point for Africa and America at the museums examined in this study. Furthermore, Africa is positioned as the foundation of African American life. About 50% of the space in the DuSable Museum focuses on the African American experience using an historic narrative that covers the seventeenth through nineteenth centuries. The fourth collection on this historical tour, "Africa Speaks," is a central museum exhibit. The written description at its entrance informs visitors that the primary objective of the exhibit is to showcase the diverse peoples, cultures, and countries in Africa, but more importantly to illustrate the link that African Americans have to their ancestral legacy beyond the institution of slavery. To emphasize this point, the museum relies on objects (i.e., masks, drums, and other totems) and the pathways from Africa (i.e., middle passage, slavery, and the slave trade) to explain African American connections to the continent. Traditional handcrafted artifacts are displayed in this large, open space and establish a distinct visual relationship between Africa and the African experience in America.

In the "Africa Speaks" exhibit, African artifacts are displayed in eight glass cases along the walls and in four additional cases located in the center of the room. Six objects are exhibited in the first glass case with descriptors identifying the object, the tribe of origination, and the African country of origin. The materials of which the objects are comprised as well as each object's probable function are included in captions. A variety of artifacts are located in other glass cases; they are illuminated sequentially with miniature labels to describe their place of origin and creator. Although this type of labeling is typical, detailed *interpretative information* is lacking. As displayed, the cultural artifacts are presented just as they would be in any art museum or exhibit and provide minimal contributions to an understanding of Black identity and African/African American connectedness for the casual observer. Yet a detailed label accompanies each of the objects on display that reminds viewers of the importance of African culture and its connection to descendants in the Diaspora. Moreover, according to the "Africa Speaks" exhibit, African American history and connections to Africa date back to and are connected to dynasties as early as 2500 B.C. and span the entire continent. As Baxandall (1991) asserts, labels are not, properly speaking, descriptions of the objects to which they refer. Rather, they are *interpretations* that serve to open a meaningful space between the object's maker, its exhibitor, and its viewer. The maker is given the task of intentionally and actively building cultural translations and critical meanings. From the labels provided here the visitor is clearly not afforded great insight about the object but rather is provided information to simply connect the object to Africa.

At America's Black Holocaust Museum, the main hallway walls are home to the mural "An African Village," which depicts life in a West African village. Images of civilization, family, and common customs are highlighted to give visitors a glimpse into the rarely shown images of a great culture and people. As an experiential space, visitors can feel Africa "speaking" to and through African Americans via the visual use of large images, color, and broad phenotypic commonalities. The mural depicts an African mother, father, and two children engaged in family work. There are no prominent physical features other than brown faces and bodies. This depiction suggests an indelible connection between this "universal" African family and any African American family or African American individual that might visit the exhibit. Furthermore, the mural intentionally attempts to bind together Africans in the Diaspora across common communal activities. As an intentional aspect of museum design, visitors must initially walk through the "African Village" in order to experience the remaining exhibits. Similar to the DuSable Museum, this is an important design approach to establish two key points. First, the mural reinforces the reality that African American history did not begin with slavery. Second, it affirms that African Americans are connected to Africa in foundational ways such as through family ties, cultural practices, and family orientations. Thus this exhibit provides the crucial starting point for a museum experience designed to cultivate a broad common racial and cultural identity among the people of African descent who visit it.

It is also important to note where Africa is literally "placed" in the museum. At both museums, Africa is intentionally positioned to be a central feature and a key component of the experience for visitors to better comprehend the connection between the diasporic legacy and the African American experience. Furthermore, the name of the DuSable exhibit itself, "Africa Speaks," has both an explicit and implicit meaning. It suggests that after being colonized, misappropriated, stereotyped, and denigrated, Africa will no longer be silent or perhaps silenced. The utility of Africa as an overarching cultural image and message is manifold. First, Africa is used as a racial project to (re)affirm African American cultural identity (Omi and Winant 1994). Second, the use of Africa is an example of symbolic practices where meanings are carried through African signs and images (Eichstedt and Small 2002; Ruffins 1992; Stewart and Ruffins 1986). These results suggest that a hyphenated pluralist identity is presented and an African/African American identity of empowerment is reaffirmed by valorizing Africa through the intentional display of artifacts and a common historical memory (Ducharme and Fine 1995; Ruffins 1992, 1998).

Space Usage and Identity Formation

In the DuSable Museum and the Black Holocaust Museum, the role of Africa is a central feature of the museum's focus on history, culture, and its construction of African American identity. Africa does not have the same meaning for everyone. However, at the two museums studied here, collective memory is intentionally and specifically constructed by using Africa as a cornerstone for African American identity (Baxandall 1991; Ruffins 1992, 1998). The choice of Africa is not arbitrary. Africa, or rather the representations that produce shared memories, is a paradigmatic case for the relation of memory and modernity. Key in this regard is Waters's (1990) notion of ethnic options in which she maintains that African Americans have limited available ethnic options. In museums, however, these limitations are counterbalanced by carefully constructed Africa-centered images and racial and ethnic projections (Ruffins 1992, 1998).

Most ethnic groups in the United States have recognized their tie to the motherland. However, social, cultural, and educational institutions are key sites in which historical memory is contested. Many African Americans use Africa and other racial projects in the process of remembering and historical memory. Halbwachs ([1925] 1992) makes a distinction between social memory and historical memory. Social memory is the memory of things one has experienced personally and that the group of which one is a part has experienced. Historical memory, on the other hand, and the recall process most useful here, is memory that has been mediated. Thus for African Americans, Africa becomes an experience mediated by representations. Transforming old identities from Black American to African American, as well as the consumption of African cultural heritage, produces a rearticulation of identity (Martin 1991; Thompson and Akbar 2003; Smith 1992). Cultural memory as a representational strategy is important in the use of Africa in Black-centered museums. Assman and Czaplicka (1995) assert that cultural memory is maintained through cultural formation (i.e., texts, rites, monuments) and institutional communication (i.e., recitation, practice, observance). Cultural memory preserves the store of its unity and peculiarity.

In the DuSable Museum and the Black Holocaust Museum, the connections to Africa are clearly stated by both the presence of African cultural artifacts and constructed spaces that enable visitors to "pass through" the respective African villages. In the DuSable Museum, the handmade and traditional African artifacts exhibited in "Africa Speaks" lend cultural authenticity to the museum and their "place" in the museum plays an important role in establishing an African cultural connection to (and with) African Americans. Similarly, the "African Village" of the Black Holocaust Museum shows the routes—and roots—of Africans in America. Both museums use a linear approach through these permanent exhibits to establish a foundation for understanding the African American experience in an historical perspective. The museums show, contrary to what has been propagated in the past, that African American history did not *begin* with slavery. The "African Village" in particular allows for a discussion of life in Africa *prior to* the deportation of Africans. This is a significant educational initiative, especially for children and young adults who might have been taught otherwise (Loewen 1995; Zinn 2003). These two institutions are clearly engaged in a racial venture of projecting African American identity and using Africa in this endeavor (Omi and Winant 1994).

The use of Africa in Black-centered museums is an important representational strategy to purposely imagine and project identity and its related images. To a large degree, the construction of a collective identity is essentially an act of constructing and reconstructing the past. Moreover, the essence of inclusion is the act of official recognition and is influenced by varied actors. Recognition of group identity, individual identity, or both, or misrecognition of identity shapes the development of collective identity. Taylor (1995) explains this process:

> Our identity is partly shaped by recognition or its absence, often by the misrecognition of others, and so a person or group of people can suffer real damage, real distortion, if the people or society around them mirror back to them a confining or demeaning or contemptible picture of themselves. (P. 249)

The primary arenas in which the act of memory construction takes place are symbolic. The images triggered by the symbols cumulatively create memories of the collective past. Commonly, one encounters monuments, museums, and holidays that symbolize some event of heroism or disaster believed to be central to the collective's history. Yet as one analyzes these images and events, what is embraced as significant is as important as what is excluded or ignored (Olick and Levy 1997; Ruffins 1992, 1998; Schwartz 1996, 1997).

Conclusion

This investigation highlights the socially constructed aspects of ethnicity, culture, and identity as well as ways ethnic boundaries, identities, and cultures are negotiated, defined, and produced through social interaction inside and outside ethnic communities (Nagel 1994). The exhibits and artifacts displayed at the DuSable Museum and the Black Holocaust Museum illustrate an important facet of the racial and cultural transformation that began in the 1960s and 1970s with Black identity movements. My results show that, in rearticulating African American identity via institutions such as Black-centered museums, Africa is used as a symbolic identifier for ethnicity, culture, and identity. At the DuSable Museum, Africa is used as a prism to consciously and unconsciously communicate an African American cultural and historical legacy. First, physically placing "Africa" before slavery in museum exhibitions reminds viewers that African American history did not begin with slavery. This fact is provided via written information at the "Africa Speaks" exhibit and as a life-sized mural at the Black Holocaust Museum. And in doing so, these Black-centered museums position Africa as a cultural link to the African American experience, broadly defined, and constitute a racial project to rearticulate and reimagine African American identity (Hall 1997; Omi and Winant 1994). Further questions for consideration in investigations of Black-centered museums' articulation of African American identity include: What factors undermine this racial project for certain groups of African Americans? Are similar messages evident for poor and nonpoor African Americans? Immigrants of color? What confounding factors exist? Would similar findings emerge in a larger sample of Black-centered museums?

The use of Africa in projecting African American identity is an example of the dynamic, creative nature of ethnic culture and reveals the role scholars and institutions play in cultural construction (Ruffins 1998; Stewart and Ruffins 1986). The African nexus is articulated through cultural practices, organizations, and institutions. Furthermore, this connection serves as a symbolic basis for group identity through collective memory (Koonz 1994; Schuman and Scott 1987). These results illustrate how Black-centered museums provide a prophetic lens to foster individual and collective racial identity development. They reflect a creative, safe space for contestation of symbols that devalue African and African American culture as well as an environment in which persons can expand their understanding of the legacy of Blacks in the Diaspora. Furthermore, Black-centered museums resist hegemonic interpretations of history that posited African Americans as peripheral onlookers as opposed to active participants. Moreover, the use of such museums has been a key vehicle in reinterpreting African American cultural history, renewing cultural symbols, and reconstructing ethnic and racial identity.

Notes

1. The notion of a mythological Black past is taken from Herskovits's classic, *The Myth of the Negro Past* (1941), in which he delineates African cultural influences on American Blacks and showcases the vibrancy of African American culture.

2. The Black Holocaust Museum closed its doors in 2008 due to financial difficulties. This speaks to the fragility of Black museums and their dependency on both private and public funding.

References

Anderson, Benedict. 2002. *Imagined Communities: Reflections on the Origin and Spread of Nationalism.* Rev. ed. New York: Verso.

Assman, Jan and John Czaplicka. 1995. "Collective Memory and Cultural Identity." *New German Critique* 65:125–33.

Baxandall, Michael. 1991. "Exhibiting Intention: Some Preconditions of the Visual Display of Culturally Purposeful Objects." Pp. 33–41 in *Exhibiting Cultures: The Poetics and Politics of Museum Display*, edited by I. Karp and S. D. Lavine, Washington, DC: Smithsonian Institutional Press.

Becker, Howard. 1986. *Doing Things Together: Selected Papers.* Evanston, IL: Northwestern University Press.

Bourdieu, Pierre. 1993. *The Field of Cultural Production.* Oxford: Polity.

Cooley, Charles Horton. 1902. *Human Nature and the Social Order.* New York: Scribner's.

Coombes, Annie E. 1988. "Museums and the Formation of National and Cultural Identities." *Oxford Art Journal* 11(2):57–68.

Cornell, Stephen E. and Douglas Hartmann. 1998. *Ethnicity and Race: Making Identities in a Changing World.* Thousand Oaks, CA: Pine Forge Press.

Davis, F. James. 1991. *Who Is Black? One Nation's Definition.* University Park: Pennsylvania State University Press.

Davis, Jessica L. and Oscar H. Gandy, Jr. 1999. "Racial Identity and Media Orientation: Exploring the Nature of Constraint." *Journal of Black Studies* 29(3):367–97.

Du Bois, W. E. B. [1903] 1994. *The Souls of Black Folk.* Rev. ed. New York: Dover.

Ducharme, Lori J. and Gary Alan Fine. 1995. "The Construction of Demoni-
zation of Nonpersonhood: Constructing the Traitorous Reputation of
Benedict Arnold." *Social Forces* 73(4):1309–31.

Eichstedt, Jennifer L. and Stephen Small. 2002. *Representations of Slavery: Race
and Ideology in Southern Plantation Museums.* Washington, DC: Smithsonian Institution Press.

Feagin, Joe R. 2000. *Racist America: Roots, Current Realities, and Future Reparations.* New York: Routledge.

Fortes, Meyer. 1987. *Religion, Morality, and the Person: Essays on Tallensi Religion,* edited by J. Goody. Cambridge, UK: Cambridge University Press.

Goffman, Erving. 1959. *The Presentation of Self in Everyday Life.* 2nd ed. Gar-
den City, NY: Anchor.

Greenberg, Bruce W., Reesa Ferguson, and Sandy Nairne, eds. 1996. *Thinking
about Exhibitions.* New York: Routledge.

Halbwachs, Maurice. [1925] 1992. *On Collective Memory,* translated by L. Cos-
er. Chicago: University of Chicago Press.

Hall, Stuart. 1992. What Is this 'Black' in Black Popular Culture? Pp. 21–33 in
Black Popular Culture: A Project by Michele Wallace, edited by G. Dent.
Seattle, WA: Bay Press.

———. 1994. "Cultural Identity and Diaspora." Pp. 222–37 in *Colonial Discourse and Post-Colonial Theory: A Reader,* edited by P. Williams and
L. Chrisman. New York: Columbia University Press.

———. 1997. "The Work of Representation" Pp. 13–74 in *Representation:
Cultural Representations and Signifying Practices,* edited by S. Hall. London: Sage.

Hall, Stuart and Paul du Gay, eds. 1996. *Question of Cultural Identity.* Thousand Oaks, CA: Sage.

Herskovits, Melville J. [1941] 1990. *The Myth of the Negro Past.* Boston: Beacon Press.

Horton, James Oliver and Spencer R. Crew. 1989. "Afro-American Museums:
Toward a Policy of Inclusion." Pp. 215–36 in *History Museums in the
United States: A Critical Assessment,* edited by W. Leon and R. Rosenz-
weig. Urbana: University of Illinois Press.

Irwin-Zarecka, Iwona. 1994. *Frames of Remembrance: The Dynamics of Collective
Memory.* New Brunswick, NJ: Transaction Publishers.

Jenkins, Richard. 1994. "Rethinking Ethnicity: Identity, Categorization and
Power." *Ethnic and Racial Studies* 17(2):197–223.

Kaeppler, Adrienne L. 1992. "Ali'i and Maka'ainana: The Representation of
Hawaiians in Museums at Home and Abroad." Pp. 458–75 in *Museums
and Communities: The Politics of Public Culture,* edited by I. Karp and
S. D. Lavine. Washington, DC: Smithsonian Institutional Press.

Karp, Ivan and Steven D. Lavine. 1991. *Exhibiting Cultures: The Poetics and Politics of Museum Display.* Washington, DC: Smithsonian Institutional Press.

Koonz, Claudia. 1994. "Between Memory and Oblivion: Concentration Camps
in German Memory." Pp. 258–80 in *Commemorations: The Politics of*

National Identity, edited by J. Gillis. Princeton, NJ: Princeton University Press.

Loewen, James W. 1995. *Lies My Teacher Told Me: Everything Your American History Book Got Wrong.* New York: New Press.

Martin, Ben. 1991. "From Negro to Black to African American: The Power of Names and Naming." *Political Science Quarterly* 106(1):83–107.

Macdonald, Sharon and Gordon Fyfe, eds. 1996. *Theorizing Museums: Representing Identity and Diversity in a Changing World.* Cambridge, MA: Blackwell Publishers.

Mead, George. 1934. *Mind, Self and Society.* Chicago: University of Chicago Press.

Miles, Robert 1989. *Racism.* London: Routledge.

Morley, David and Kevin Robins. 1995. *Spaces of Identity: Global Media, Electronic Landscapes and Cultural Boundaries.* New York: Routledge.

Nagel, Joane. 1994. "Constructing Ethnicity: Creating and Recreating Ethnic Identity and Culture." *Social Problems* 41(1):152–76.

Olick, Jeffrey and Daniel Levy. 1997. "Collective Memory and Cultural Constraint: Holocaust Myth and Rationality in German Politics." *American Sociological Review* 62(6):921–36.

Omi, Michael and Howard Winant. 1994. *Racial Formation in the United States.* New York: Routledge.

Ruffins, Fath Davis. 1998. "Culture Wars Won and Lost, Part II: The National African American Museum Project." *Radical History Review* 70:78–101.

———. 1992. "Mythos, Memory, and History: African American Preservation Efforts, 1820–1990." Pp. 506–611 in *Museums and Communities: The Politics of Public Culture*, edited by I. Karp and S. D. Lavine. Washington, DC: Smithsonian Institutional Press.

Thompson, Vetta L. Sanders and Maysa Akbar. 2003. "The Understanding of Race and the Construction of African American Identity." *Western Journal of Black Studies* 27(2):80–89.

Saussure, Ferdinand. 1974. *Course in General Linguistics.* London: Fontana.

Schlesinger, Philip. 1987. "On National Identity: Some Conceptions and Misconceptions Criticized." *Social Science Information* 26(2):219–64.

Schuman, H. and J. Scott. 1987. "Generations and Collective Memories." *American Sociological view*, 54:359–81.

Schwartz, Barry. 1996. "Memory as a Cultural System: Abraham Lincoln in World War II." *American Sociological Review* 61(5):908–27.

———. 1997. "Collective Memory and History: How Abraham Lincoln became a Symbol of Racial Equality." *Sociological Quarterly* 38(3):469–96.

Sherman, Daniel and Irit Rogoff, eds. 1994. *Museum Culture: Histories, Discourses, Spectacles.* Minneapolis: University of Minnesota Press.

Small, Stephen. 1997. "Contextualizing the Black Presence in British Museums: Representations, Resources, and Response." Pp. 50–66 in *Cultural Diversity: Developing Museum Audiences in Britain*, edited by E. Hooper-Greenhill. London: Leicester University Press.

Smith, Tom W. 1992. "Changing Racial Labels: From 'Colored' to 'Negro' to 'Black' to 'African American.'" *Public Opinion Quarterly* 56(4):496–514.

Stewart, Jeffrey C. and Fath Davis Ruffins. 1986. "A Faithful Witness: Afro-American Public History in Historical Perspective, 1828–1984." Pp. 307–38 in *Presenting the Past: Essays on History and the Public*, edited by S. P. Benson, S. Brier, and R. Rosenzweig, Philadelphia, PA: Temple University Press.

Taylor, Charles. 1995. "The Politics of Recognition." Pp. 249–63 in *Campus Wars: Multi-Culturalism and the Politics of Difference*, edited by J. Arthur and A. Shapiro Boulder, CO: Westview Press.

Waters, Mary. 1990. *Ethnic Options: Choosing Identities in America*. Berkeley: University of California Press.

Weil, Stephen E. 2002. *Making Museums Matter*. Washington, DC: Smithsonian Institution Press.

Zerubavel, Eviatar. 1996. "Social Memories: Steps to a Sociology of the Past." *Qualitative Sociology* 19(3):283–99.

Zinn, Howard. 2003. *A People's History of the United States: 1492–Present*. New York: HarperCollins.

Epilogue

~

Back to the Future of Race Studies

A New Millennium Du Boisian Mode of Inquiry

Persistent inequities in the supposed postracial era highlight the enduring significance of race and race studies. These inequities, manifested
on structural and interpersonal levels, continue despite assertions that
we have reached the "end of blackness" (Dickerson 2004) and are now
in a definitively "post-Black" (Touré 2011) era. The papers in this collection illumine more subtle forms of racism and their implications for
contemporary society. Although more covert than their antecedents, they
are no less deleterious in their effects. Moreover, the works included
in this volume show how racial inequities today are often ensconced
in microlevel beliefs and behavior as well as macrolevel structures. And
"colorblind" beliefs make identifying and combating this social problem challenging. The scholars and activists here contend that prophetic research and community action are necessary to stem the tide of
postracial rhetoric and challenge "white-framed" racism that is integral
to this postracial moment. Thus they offer new and unique ways of
analyzing race and race matters through a prophetic mode of inquiry
that is inherently inquisitive, proactive, culturally sensitive, introspective,
collaborative, and creative.

   This repositioning of race based on a prophetic stance means recognizing that rigorous academic scholarship is impotent without applied

efforts and social policy that empower Black communities and other disenfranchised people worldwide. This volume, then, bridges the gap between the structural disadvantages disproportionately prevalent in Black communities across the Diaspora and the discursive articulations of Black identities, cultures, and experiences in the popular media. Through this volume, we recommit our sociological practice—and ourselves—to the legacy of cutting-edge race scholarship that coalesced in the founding of the Association of Black Sociologists (ABS).

Yet, we recognize that while we are organizationally and intellectually indebted to the work, spirit, and legacy of founding members, this volume is also theoretically and methodologically indebted to the early sociological work of W. E. B. Du Bois. In many respects, our attempt to reframe the direction of race studies signals a resuscitation of the Atlanta Sociological Laboratory, the moniker bestowed on scholars engaged in sociological research at Atlanta University between 1895 and 1924 and led by Du Bois between 1897 and 1914. For nearly three decades the Atlanta Sociological Laboratory reported on the disparities Blacks experienced in America and produced findings used to positively impact their lives. Because of the nearly complete physical and social separation between Blacks and Whites, including those in the profession of sociology, the Jim Crow era efforts of this segregated group of scholars resulted in the development of a *Black sociology* that concentrated on academic and applied research as well as social policies to eliminate Blacks from social oppression on all fronts (Wright and Calhoun 2006). This work was multidisciplinary, methodologically mixed, and multifaceted. We contend that this type of research is especially needed today—and it must be relevant to the Black experience broadly defined and to other historically oppressed groups. This *new millennium Du Boisian inquiry* will reflect both the spirit and rigor of his original efforts—applied to a contemporary global context that is characterized by heterogeneic understandings of race and race matters. To conduct such inquiry, we must be willing to take critical positions on Black sociology such that our research, as well as teaching and service, does not become directly or indirectly entrenched in matters not relevant to the plight of disenfranchised groups in general and Black communities in particular. We contend that this volume represents one such endeavor.

A new millennium Du Boisian inquiry moves the best of past academic practice into uncharted territory. It requires us to broaden our queries to consider international correlates, unexpected implications of our new racialized society, as well as subjects and sites that have been heretofore rarely investigated. For some people, this type of focus is exciting; for others it will bring trepidation. Yet the writers in this volume strove to expand and extend the Du Boisian legacy beyond Black-White dynamics with academically robust studies that can be applied across a plethora of domains and for a myriad of social groups. Their findings remind us afresh to ask the questions: What is race? What are the most common racial projects in society today? How are they linked to the past? What does racism *look like*? And how can we eradicate it? How are Blacks and other people of color adaptive and resilient in the face of such challenges? Answers to these and related questions are not always evident and clear. Like other socially constructed phenomena, such ideas and issues are constantly changing and challenge scholars, teachers, grassroots leaders, and students to be ever vigilant in their work.

The reports chronicled in this volume impress upon us a variety of issues. We are challenged to reject so-called postracial edicts that are prominent in the public discourse and to engage in inter- as well as intraracial and ethnic critiques. Part of this process will involve gaining a better understanding of long-held yet incomplete views about prominent persons and groups in Black society—past and present. Furthermore, Black and non-Black scholars alike must expand their abilities to develop new concepts, theories, and understandings about the nontraditional ways that racial dynamics now manifest and race continues to matter. To this end, in addition to revitalizing and reappropriating historical Black inquiry, it will be important to consider how more contemporary social structures such as the media, popular culture, and the Internet influence what the technologically savvy masses know about race and race matters as well as how the Digital Divide affects their counterparts during this same process. Akin to a Du Boisian model, broad-based, traditional research should continue in order to compare and contrast quality-of-life indices of majority and minority groups; only by continuing to do so will scholars keep the larger society abreast of changes in the life chances of the populace, particularly for groups disproportionately affected by social problems such as poverty, classism, sexism, and health inequities. And just as large-scale studies can inform us about lived experiences, ethnographic work, theoretical projects, and other qualitative endeavors provide the singular ability to give voice to those who are often voiceless. The enclosed chapters further remind readers that one cannot accurately and thoughtfully consider race matters by myopically centering the U.S. experience. The Diaspora is far, wide, and diverse; it requires comparable theoretical and empirical lenses to be best understood. The chapters here bode well for continued studies on race matters in Africa, Brazil, South America, the Dominican Republic, and other locales where people of color reside. Writers herein have provided foundational information, processes, findings, and points of departure for the next steps in order to do justice to the legacy Du Bois and other scholars established in the tradition of Black sociology.

Because repositioning race and prophetic research will help inform arenas outside of academia, we are challenged to also remember the implications of our research on the political, social, economic, and cultural fabric of society. The kinds of studies we perform and how we illumine contemporary events will affect their place in the history we are currently creating. A new millennium Du Boisian mode of inquiry involves predicting social phenomena as much as it entails describing and explaining it. For example, what are the implications of the capture and deaths of Bin Laden and Muammar Gaddafi for Pakistan, Libya, the United States, and the broader global society? What effect will the Occupy Wall Street and Tea Party movements have on our understanding of race, class, gender, space, conflict, and compromise? How does race loom large as we consider the Wall Street bailout, the economic downturn in Greece, and the Republican-Democratic economic stalemate here in our country? Minimally, each scenario reminds us of some of the varied, often troubled outcomes when White, Black, and brown people attempt to negotiate the same space in a society that now has a nebulous understanding of race, ethnicity, national identity, and community. The work of academics must proactively speak to these types of issues in real time.

A bevy of race scholars have called for the emergence of race transcendent intellectual and political leaders. Extending this challenge, race transcendent *research* is critical. This charge does not mean that scholars will ignore race or endeavor to become colorblind, but rather strive to acknowledge, appreciate, and critique race and race matters from a culturally relative perspective. And in doing so, our work will become more nuanced, our research questions more complex, our teaching more engaging, our personal views more self-reflective, and our community action more fearless. Ultimately, the outcomes of our efforts will become more relevant to people both inside and outside academic walls. Since 1968 many ABS members have embraced the tenets of prophetic research and Black sociology in their efforts to ameliorate the negative social conditions Blacks experience in America and worldwide. We contend that a new millennium Du Boisian inquiry will continue this tradition and innovatively expand it. Given the current financial and physical challenges Blacks, other people of color, and growing segments of the White population experience, it is imperative that we, social science scholars, "go back to the future" with a renewed passion to critically analyze the supposedly postracial world in which we now live. Not to do so provides space for inaccurate and potentially harmful assessments of race issues similar to those espoused during the discipline's early years in this nation. Yet, embracing this challenge provides opportunities to impact society both positively and prophetically as well as establish an indelible link to the goals and objectives of early Black sociologists.

References

Dickerson, Debra J. 2004. *The End of Blackness.* New York: Pantheon Books.

Touré. 2011. *Who's Afraid of Post-Blackness? What It Means to Be Black Now.* New York: Free Press.

Wright, Earl, II and Thomas C. Calhoun. 2006. "Jim Crow Sociology: Toward an Understanding of the Origin and Principles of Black Sociology via the Atlanta Sociological Laboratory." *Sociological Focus,* 39(1):1–18.

Contributors

Sandra L. Barnes is a professor in the Department of Human and Organizational Development (HOD) and the Divinity School at Vanderbilt University. Her resrach interests include the sociology of religion, urban sociology, and inequality.

Eduardo Bonilla-Silva is professor and chair of the Department of Sociology at Duke University. He is author of *Racism without Racists: Color-Blind Racism and the Persistence of Racial Inequality in the United States.*

Derrick R. Brooms is assistant professor of sociology at the University of Louisville and studies African American male achievement.

Trenita Brookshire Childers is a graduate student in the Department of Sociology at Duke University. Her research interests include social stratification, inequality, medical sociology, and race and ethnicity.

Louwanda Evans is an assistant professor of sociology at Millsaps College. Her work examines race, class, gender, and emotional labor among African American pilots.

Joe Feagin is professor of sociology at Texas A&M University and author of dozens of books and articles on race, including *Racist America: Roots, Current Realities, and Future Reparations.*

Loren Henderson is an adjunct faculty member in the Department of Sociology at Northeastern Illinois University. Her research focuses on stratification; health disparities; diversity issues; and race, class, gender, and sexuality.

Cedric D. Herring is professor of sociology and public affairs at the University of Illinois at Chicago and editor of *African Americans and the Public Agenda: The Paradoxes of Public Policy.*

Hayward Derrick Horton is professor of sociology and public affairs at the State University of New York at Albany and coeditor of *Skin Deep: How Race and Complexion Matter in the "Color-Blind" Era.*

Tiffany D. Joseph is an assistant professor in the Sociology Department at Stony Brook University and researches the U.S.–Brazilian Diaspora.

Robert L. Reece is a doctoral student in the Department of Sociology at Duke University and cofounder of the blog *Still Furious and Still Brave: Who's Afraid of Persistent Blackness?*

Zandria F. Robinson is an Assistant Professor in the Dept. of Sociology at the University of Memphis. Her research interests include race, class, gender, and sexuality; urban sociology; popular culture; and feminism, with a focus on black feminist theory.

Antonio D. Tillis is associate professor and chair of African and African American Studies at Dartmouth College and editor of *Critical Perspectives on Afro-Latin American Literature.*

Earl Wright II is professor of Africana studies at the University of Cincinnati and coeditor of this volume.

Index

abolitionists, 53
affirmative action, 25, 74; in college
   admissions, 125–26; in sociology
   departments, 34, 35
Afghanistan War, 26, 29
African American cultural identity,
   71–72, 134–35, 141, 173–85,
   191–92
aggression. *See* "microaggressions"
AIDS, 5
Al Jazeera, 144
Alexander, Michelle, 42n35
"alexithymia, social," 126–27
Alice's Adventures in Wonderland
   (Carroll), 24, 39
Allen, Walter R., 120–21
American Recovery and Reinvestment
   Act, 108
American Sociological Association
   (ASA): people of color in,
   33–34, 38; public sociology and,
   40n16
AmeriCorps, 106
"Amerikan sociology," 23, 28
Anderson, Benedict, 140, 177–78
antihaitianismo, 142–43
Asian Americans, 4, 6, 42n33, 73
Assman, Jan, 182
Association of Black Sociologists
   (ABS), 5, 9–10, 30–36, 190

Atlanta University, 54–55, 190

Baisden, Michael, 20
bankruptcies, 97–98
Barkley, Charles, 136
batey (sugar cane community), 12,
   140, 143–49
Battle, Juan, 56–57
Baxandall, Michael, 180
Beale, Francis, 8
Bennett, Bill, 28
Bernstein, Jared, 103
Berry, Halle, 82
bigotry. *See* prejudice
Bigsby, Clayton, 79–82
Bin Laden, Osama, 91, 192
Birt, Robert, 72–73
Black Holocaust Museum (Milwaukee),
   179, 181–85
Black identity, African heritage in,
   71–72, 174–85
Black leadership: Bonilla-Silva on,
   25–26, 38–39; Du Bois on, 11,
   19–20, 49–66; models of, 17–21;
   Morehouse on, 50–52. *See also*
   "talented tenth"
Black Power movement, 8
Black Pride movement, 173
blackface performers, 30; whiteface
   and, 77, 78, 83

www.ingramcontent.com/pod-product-compliance
Lightning Source LLC
Chambersburg PA
CBHW050707280326
41926CB00088B/2862